YOU ARE
THE CHRIST

Discovering the Man from Nazareth
Through His Conversations

VOLUME 1

Purchased
April 23, 2009
Berean Bookstore
Bloomington, Illinois

You Are The Christ

Cover design & page layout
by Andrew Ramos of A&E Media

ISBN 1 932307 60 5

Published by the Ambassador Group

Ambassador International
427 Wade Hampton Blvd.
Greenville, SC 29609
USA
www.emeraldhouse.com

and

Ambassador Publications Ltd.
Providence House
Ardenlee Street
Belfast BT6 8QJ
Northern Ireland
www.ambassador-productions.com

The colophon is a trademark of Ambassador

TABLE OF CONTENTS

AD 29

INTRODUCTION

Who was, or who is, Jesus Christ? The answers to this question are diverse. Some people are convinced that Jesus, the man from Nazareth, lived, died, and is no more. Others were so certain that Jesus from Nazareth was the promised Christ, the Messiah promised in the Old Testament, that they chose martyrdom over denying their conscience. Devout Christians still suffer persecution and death because they are so certain that the man Jesus lives today in heaven as their Savior from sin. Every religion appears to teach something about the man from Nazareth; They cannot ignore this imposing figure. One modern religion teaches that Jesus was an angel who became a man for several years. Another religion teaches that Jesus was a literal son born through an incestuous union between God the Father and Mary, a daughter of one of God's spiritual wives. Many modern religions agree that Jesus Christ was a real person who influenced the historical, world-wide, religious scene, but that He is nevertheless an unimportant piece in the overall puzzle of humanity's destiny. There are views that claim that Jesus was a good man who intended to do good, but whose plan failed so miserably that he was crucified as a criminal. Other views teach that Jesus was indeed a uniquely spiritual being during the time between his baptism and crucifixion. Still others believe that Jesus set a good example for people to follow. A recently promoted view allows Jesus to be supernatural in many ways, but altogether human as the husband of Mary Magdalene, and father of her child.

Against this backdrop of mixed opinions and conclusions, Peter's words ring out like a deafening trumpet blast. One day he and the other disciples were with Jesus in the northern part of Palestine, near

Caesarea Philippi. Probably while they were standing in a group near a large temple dedicated to a pagan god, Jesus asked the little band of followers who they thought He was. Without hesitation Peter blurted out, "You are the Christ, the Son of the living God." Imagine that rugged Jewish fisherman, looking right into the face of a man who was built like him, dressed like him, who in many ways was similar to him, and proclaiming that He was the Son of God, the Christ! What did Peter mean? Did Peter comprehend the Christ concept? What did he mean by the words, "the Son of the Living God?" Where can an inquirer look to find the answer to these questions about the man from Nazareth?

Most of the readers of this book know very little about the author. However, given the opportunity to talk to me for an extended period of time, you would learn much about me. Conversation is a great way to discover truth about a person. The more two people talk the more intimately they will know each other—especially if those people are transparent and truthful. No person ever born was more transparent and truthful than the man from Nazareth. Jesus declared that He came to earth from heaven in order to declare God's truth (John 8:40). Some people who heard His teaching agreed that He spoke the truth (Matthew 22:16; Mark 12:14,32; Luke 20:21).

Jesus, who spoke only the truth, engaged in numerous conversations with individuals and with groups. Well over sixty of those conversations have been recorded in the Gospels and the first chapter of Acts. Through these conversations, Jesus, the man from Nazareth, reveals who He really is. His conversations uncover some of the most important doctrines about the Christ. Indeed, the conversations of the Son of God reveal much about the nature of God. Through His own words, God the Son reveals that He is one with God the Father. The doubts and questions of the ages that have surrounded the mysterious man from Nazareth are answered through His own conversations. The study of these conversations is profitable for anyone who desires to know Christ.

THE NEW TESTAMENT CALENDAR

In this book the conversations of Christ have been arranged, as much as possible, in chronological order. The exact time of some of His conversations is not easily identifiable. However, the majority of the Lord's interactions with people occurred in connection with particular events. Such connections help pinpoint where in His lifetime Jesus was engaged in the conversation. That being true, it is important to have a brief understanding of the calendar used for New Testament dates.

Occasionally dates in the New Testament were based on a particular ruler's reign or ascension to the throne. For example, Luke recorded that John began the ministry of preaching and baptizing in the wilderness in the fifteenth year of Tiberius Caesar's reign, which coincided with Pilate being governor of Judea. It also coincided with Herod's reign as tetrarch of Galilee, and his brother Philip's reign as tetrarch of Iturea and the region of Trachonitis, and Lysanias ruling as tetrarch of Abilene (Luke 3:1). At the same time Luke mentioned that Annas and Caiaphas were the high priests in Jerusalem (Luke 3:2). The contemporaneous reigns of these rulers leaves little doubt about when John was preaching in the wilderness. Similar dating according to rulers is discovered in Matthew 2:1; Luke 1:5, 2:1,2, and Acts 11:28, 18:2.

Most of the New Testament dates are reckoned according to the Jewish lunar calendar of that day. Old Testament priests determined the beginning of the new year based on the appearance of the new moon in our month April. The celebration of the feast of Passover at that time marked the beginning of the new year in the Jewish month Nisan. Each subsequent month also began with the appearance of the new moon. Therefore, the various months of the year were easily identified according to feasts and Sabbaths. However, by the time of Christ there was some disagreement about the precise day when the feasts should begin. This was due to a disparity between the Pharisaic method of dating and the Sadducean method. Before AD 70 the people generally followed the Sadducees' date setting, but after that time, the nation, having been scattered, adhered to the Pharisees' reckoning. This difference helps explain why Jesus and the disciples might have observed the Passover meal earlier than the religious leaders did (John 13-17).

The conversations of Christ are arranged in this book by sections according to the most popular method of dating His ministry. It begins with section one, the conversations of Christ during the year AD 26 (vol.1) and ends with His last conversation with the disciples before He ascended into heaven in the spring of AD 30 (vol.2). The ordering of each year will begin with the winter months (approximately January through March), followed by spring (April through June), summer (July through September) and fall (October through December). This quarterly breakdown follows the Jewish calender quite accurately. Again, good scholars are not in complete agreement with all of the proposed dates for Christ's activities. Furthermore, it is impossible to pinpoint the exact time of some of Christ's activities and conversations. Nevertheless, conservative scholars generally accept the format followed in this book.

AD 26-27

CHAPTER 1

JOHN UNDERSTOOD WHO JESUS WAS

MATTHEW 3:13-17

At some point most Christians will end up judging other people in spite of the fact that Jesus taught, "Judge not, that you be not judged" (Matthew 7:1). Does that mean that no one should ever judge another person, under any circumstances, or for any reason? Such a conclusion creates a dilemma in the light of Jesus' teaching, "Do not judge according to appearance, but judge with righteous judgment." (John 7:24). The truth is Jesus taught that there is a right way to draw conclusions, and that His people are supposed to judge other people appropriately. It is natural for people to draw conclusions about other people based on various kinds of evidence. Therefore, Jesus taught that when Christians draw conclusions about other people, they must look beyond initial appearances and try to ascertain the truth, the real motivations, the real issues, to discover what the real person is like.

This principle is common in the Scriptures. Isaiah wrote, "For the foolish person will speak foolishness, and his heart will work iniquity" (Isaiah 32:6). On at least two occasions Jesus taught that it is natural to speak words that flow out of the fullness of the heart (Luke 6:45; Matthew 3:7). Whatever is in the heart of a person comes out in the words he or she speaks. Because this principle is true, careful observation of a person's conversation will often reveal the truth about that person's character. A man's words will often uncover the deeper truth about the man. It is possible and fair to conclude that a person is angry or bitter by listening to his or her conversation. Other people give the clear impression that they are happy and confident in life by the words they speak. Isn't it true that most people draw conclusions about others based on what they say? By listening to a conversation one can often determine a person's interests and motivations in life.

This same principle works in relation to the man from Nazareth. Jesus, who is called the Christ, spoke volumes of words. He was a teacher. Surely, the reader can assess His character by studying His conversations that have been recorded in the Bible. What can be learned about the man from Nazareth by studying His conversations? One of the most obvious truths is that this Man was far more than just a good fellow from the little town of Nazareth. His own words reveal that He was something greater than a carpenter. From the outset of His ministry, Jesus' words impressed the masses with the fact that He was even superior to the other religious teachers of their day (Matthew 7:21). The crowds were astonished at Jesus' words (Matthew 13:54).

Another important truth discovered in Jesus' conversations is that different circumstances require different responses. Sometimes Jesus' conversations were didactic (teaching), sometimes they were compassionate, sometimes they offered practical advice, sometimes they rebuked, and sometimes they condemned. His response in any given situation depended on the attitude of the person who was engaged in the conversation.

It is only fitting that when Jesus stepped into public ministry His first recorded conversation would reveal an astonishing truth about His nature. Probably there were many people in the area around Nazareth who knew about Jesus, the carpenter's son. His childhood was marked by submission and wisdom. Perhaps He had a reputation with His peers and neighbors for being a promising young man. But it is unlikely that very many people in Jerusalem or out in the wilderness beside the Jordan River knew much about this man from Nazareth. This conversation that marked the beginning of His public ministry introduced Him to John the Baptizer's audience with words that must have made their ears tingle. Even John, Jesus' second cousin, was a little surprised at Jesus' words. Though John knew that Jesus was unique, the very Son of God, he was surprised to learn that God in the flesh would be fully identified with mankind. It was necessary!

Jesus' Words Were Shocking

Matthew's story about Jesus' earthly ministry began with Jesus coming to John to be baptized. The other three evangelists (Mark, Luke, and John) described the event more specifically by saying that Jesus came from Nazareth to be baptized. It was a long trip from Nazareth to the place where John was preaching and baptizing in those days. According to John 1:28, John the Baptist was preaching in Bethabara. According to John 3:23 John was at Aenon. Though neither of these locations can be located precisely, it had to be at least a two-day trip from Nazareth to that general region in the vicinity of the Jordan River.

Luke recorded that Jesus came out to John at a particular time in history. Luke 3:1-3 reveals that John was preaching in the wilderness in the fifteenth year of Tiberius Caesar's reign. This time period coincided with the tenure of the High Priest Caiaphas, which he shared with the former High Priest Annas. That would have put John's ministry somewhere around late AD 28 or early AD 29. No doubt John had preached for several weeks (or even months) before Jesus came to be baptized. Matthew's account emphasizes that Jesus' arrival at the Jordan River was at the exact time God ordained for His public ministry to begin.

Jesus also came to John with a definite purpose. He did not just happen to walk through the area on that particular day and decide to join the crowd of people getting baptized. It is true that John was baptizing many people, but Jesus came to John with a purpose. On that day, at that time, He intended to publicly identify Himself with John's baptism. This act also introduced the beginning of His public ministry. The word Matthew chose to describe Jesus' action is full of meaning. He employed the Greek word (translated *came*) that often speaks of a special public appearance. Matthew used the same word earlier in his Gospel to describe John's seemingly sudden, and unexpected, appearance (Matthew 3:1). When John began his ministry (*came*), he shook the culture with his preaching and baptizing that was associated with

3

repentance. Jesus made the long trip from Nazareth, at this exact time, specifically to submit to John's baptizing.

The text indicates that John was confused to learn that Jesus, the Christ, desired to be baptized by him (v. 14). John understood that his baptism was associated with repentance of sins. He knew that he was the forerunner who prepared the way for Messiah (Matthew 3:3). In order for him to make the rough places smooth, (see Isaiah's prophecy in 40:3) John challenged the people to repent of their sins. He told the masses of people who came to hear him preach that they needed to repent because the Kingdom was at hand (Matthew 3:2). He even chided the religious leaders for being curious about the ministry while at the same time refusing to repent of their sins. According to Matthew, when John, "saw many of the Pharisees and Sadducees coming to his baptism, he said to them, 'Brood of vipers! Who warned you to flee from the wrath to come?'" (Matthew 3:7). That was not an effective way to win friends and influence people. Apparently John was neither impressed nor motivated by the opinions of the masses. He was concerned to do God's will.

John's baptism was a public statement regarding the confession and repentance of personal sin. The records of Matthew, Mark, and Luke clearly establish this connection. Matthew recorded that, "Jerusalem, all Judea, and all the region around the Jordan went out to him and were baptized by him in the Jordan, confessing their sins" (Matthew 3:5-6). Mark recorded a similar observation by writing that "John came baptizing in the wilderness and preaching a baptism of repentance for the remission of sins" (Mark 1:4). The evidence clearly proves that John baptized people who identified themselves with repentance. Identification is the essence of baptism. Therefore, it was just and proper for John to confront the hypocritical religious leaders by telling them to, "bear fruits worthy of repentance, and do not begin to say to yourselves, 'We have Abraham as *our* father.' For I say to you that God is able to raise up children to Abraham from these stones" (Luke 3:8). Those leaders loved to keep their own rules. They were not interested in admitting publicly that they had sinned.

John understood what the association between repentance and baptism required. Each time he baptized a penitent sinner, that person publicly acknowledged that he was a sinner. That fact created a problem for him when Jesus requested baptism at his hands. John realized that Messiah was sinless. However, if Jesus was sinless, why did He seek to be associated with this kind of baptism?

Maybe John was mistaken. How could he be sure that Jesus from Nazareth was Messiah and, therefore, sinless? First, John was Jesus' second cousin. It is true that John had been gone from home and living in the wilderness for some time (Luke 3:2). Surely, John became convinced earlier that the boy growing up in Nazareth was the promised Messiah. And so John understood that Messiah could not sin. Then was Jesus from Nazareth the Messiah? John's own mother had confessed that Mary's child was the promised Messiah (Luke 1:42-43). Surely she taught John the truth about Jesus while he was growing up. Furthermore, the Holy Spirit moved John's father to prophesy that John was the ordained forerunner of Messiah (Luke 1:68-79).

It is clear that John was convinced that Jesus was the promised Messiah because he taught that fact to the people, and assured them that He would arrive on the scene soon (Mark 1:7). One day when Jesus was walking along the river bank, John pointed Him out to the masses and identified Him as the Lamb of God who takes away the sins of the world (John 1:29). Surely John knew who Jesus was, and surely he was convinced that this Jesus was the promised Messiah. And yet John the Apostle wrote in verses thirty-one and thirty-three that John the Baptist confessed that he did not know Jesus. How could that be? John's record states that John said, "I did not know Him; but that He should be revealed to Israel, therefore I came baptizing with water. And John bore witness, saying, 'I saw the Spirit descending from heaven like a dove, and He remained upon Him. I did not know Him, but He who sent me to baptize with water said to me, "Upon whom you see the Spirit descending, and remaining on Him, this is He who baptizes with the Holy Spirit" (John 1:31-33). What did John mean by this?

John knew that Jesus was sinless, and therefore, that He did not need to be identified with his baptism. He was so convinced of the sinless nature of Jesus that he even admitted that he (John) needed to be identified with Jesus not that Jesus needed to be identified with the baptism for repentance. Even though John knew much about Jesus and was convinced that Jesus was Messiah, still he did not fully understand all the details of the Father's plan.

Therefore, John's confession that he did not know Jesus was simply an expression of his limited human comprehension. It was a confession of the same kinds of limitations that exist today. Many people have gained much information about Jesus. They learned about Him in Sunday School when they were children. They continue to learn about Him every week when they attend church services. But knowing some of the details about Jesus' ministry is not the same as knowing Jesus Christ intimately. There is a difference between the ability to quote Bible verses about Christ and the joy of an ongoing intimate relationship with Him. It is good to plead like the disciples, "Lord teach us . . ." He will. The Lord teaches the eager learner in those quiet times spent alone with Him, removed from the bustle of life. Christians still learn about Christ the same way the disciples learned, by sitting at His feet.

John balked at the idea of baptizing Jesus. But the Lord assured John that His baptism was necessary (v. 15). He told John that His baptism was part of righteousness. Righteousness is God the Father's predetermined standard of right. Righteousness is what God has revealed as right in His Word. Notice that Jesus acknowledged that both He and John (*us*) were concerned to do the Father's will. That should be the desire for everyone who lives in a right relationship with God. God's children must always be concerned to think and do that which measures up to God's standard of righteousness.

What was the right thing in this matter of baptism? What did Jesus mean when He said that He and John needed to fulfill all righteousness? First, Jesus might have alluded to the importance of Him setting an example of obedience. The phrase, "permit it to be so" indicates that this baptism was not technically necessary. Jesus did not need to repent of sin. However, the baptism was necessary to paint the larger picture of obedience. The Son was clearly obedient to the Father in all things. Jesus made this fact clear from the time he was a child. One day when He was supposed to be with His family on a trip back to Nazareth from Jerusalem, Jesus' parents found Him in the temple reasoning with the scholars of the day. When His earthly parents chided Him, Jesus responded, "Why did you seek Me? Did you not know that I must be about My Father's business?" (Luke 2:49). That same dedication to His Father's work and will was obvious throughout Jesus' life. Even when He came to the last days of His ministry Jesus prayed to the Father, "I have glorified You on the earth. I have finished the work which You have given Me to do" (John 17:4). Jesus left many examples of obedience. Baptism could be another one.

Baptism is a matter of obedience to God. Peter emphasized that truth when he preached to the pilgrims who were in Jerusalem on Pentecost. He warned them to, "Repent, and let every one of you be baptized in the name of Jesus Christ for the remission of sins; and you shall receive the gift of the Holy Spirit" (Acts. 2:38). Notice that he challenged the people to confess their sins and be born again through the work of the Holy Spirit. Then he challenged them to be baptized in order to make a public declaration that they were identified with Jesus Christ. Their baptism did not gain salvation, but it was a public confession of salvation.

Second, righteousness was fulfilled because, through John's baptism, Jesus was identified with the sins of all humanity. Jesus Christ came to earth to take away the sins of the world. In order to do that He would need to be a man who lived perfectly under God's law. Since He Himself was perfect, and guilty of no sins, He would need to be identified with the sins He would remit. Isaiah had promised this astonishing identification hundreds of years earlier when he wrote that God the Father would, "divide Him [Jesus the Messiah] a portion with the great, And He shall divide the spoil with the strong, Because He poured out His soul unto death, And He was numbered with the transgressors, And He bore the sin of many, And made intercession for the transgressors" (Isaiah 53:12).

Another reason for Christ's baptism might have been to illustrate His coming death, burial and resurrection. Christ's vicarious suffering and death gave Him the authority to forgive and cover over sins. Paul explained and applied that picture in Romans 6:3-6 where he pictured Christ being buried and then rising to new life.

John conceded to baptize Jesus, but that did not imply that he understood all the details about the event. He did not. It does teach that John submitted completely to his Savior. That is always the proper response to Jesus' words.

The Father Confirmed Jesus' Words

After John baptized Jesus, He walked out of the Jordan River, and immediately, God the Father sent the Holy Spirit to confirm His ministry (v. 16). Matthew said that the heavens were opened to Him. This might have served as a reminder that the Father was always near the Son. It might also have served as an encouragement for the eternal Son. Jesus was now embarking on a journey that would end with the horrendous trial of His suffering and crucifixion. The suffering would culminate with His Father turning His back against His Son because He carried the sins of the whole world. The Father's encouragement was necessary during the difficult days of ministry.

The Heavenly Father opened the heavens to His Son, and then He sent the Holy Spirit who descended upon Christ in the form of a dove. Why a dove? This is the first and only time that the Holy Spirit is represented in Scriptures as a dove. It is possible that the Father sent the Holy Spirit in the form of a dove in order to represent Him and His work as kind, gentle, or settled. However, it seems more likely that this picture was to represent a particular kind of sacrifice. Let's review the picture. Jesus came to John to be baptized at the very beginning of His public ministry. The purpose of Jesus' ministry was to take away the sins of the world. Jesus was aware of His calling, purpose, and ministry before He ever descended from heaven and took on the form of a man. It is clear from Philippians 2:5-10 that the Christ left heaven with sacrifice in view. His entire ministry pointed to His sacrifice. John's baptism was a harbinger of Christ being identified with the sins for which He would offer Himself as the sacrifice.

In the Old Testament Law God approved of the dove as an acceptable sacrifice for sin (Leviticus 12:6). Wealthy people offered bulls, less wealthy people offered lambs, but poor people could not afford either one. God allowed them to offer doves. It is fitting that the Holy Spirit would come in the form of that sacrifice associated with poor people. Indeed, Jesus would prove throughout His ministry that He was identified with the poor. Isaiah had promised that the Christ would be associated with poverty when he wrote, "The Spirit of the Lord GOD is upon Me, because the LORD has anointed Me to preach good tidings to the poor; he has sent Me to heal the brokenhearted, to proclaim liberty to the captives, and the opening of the prison to *those*

8

who are bound" (Isaiah 61:1). Those are the words Jesus explained to the people in His hometown synagogue. They rejected Him. But the poor in spirit are still made rich through Jesus' sacrifice.

The dove, the sign of the Holy Spirit, rested upon Christ. Christ was already God incarnate. Being God in the flesh He did not need more of God. On the contrary, this was a picture of God the Father encouraging the human part of the Christ. Because Jesus Christ was fully human, He needed encouraging and strengthening. The Father provided the strength through the third member of the Godhead, the Holy Spirit. The resting of the Holy Spirit dove coincided with the Father's verbal affirmation of the Son. The Father confirmed His love for the Son in words that He and all the people present could hear. God the Father reminded Jesus and informed everyone present that Jesus is the unique, eternal Son of God and that He pleases the Father in every way.

Now John understood. He saw the heavenly Dove, he heard the voice, now he knew Jesus better than ever. That is why John could say with confidence,

> *I saw the Spirit descending from heaven like a dove, and He remained upon Him. I did not know Him, but He who sent me to baptize with water said to me, 'Upon whom you see the Spirit descending, and remaining on Him, this is He who baptizes with the Holy Spirit.' And I have seen and testified that this is the Son of God. (John 1:32-34)*

John's faith would waver (Matthew 11:3), but ultimately he was convinced that the Christ must identify with the sins of humanity and suffer in our behalf. Redeemed sinners understand this wonderful truth and accept Jesus of Nazareth as the eternal Savior. Sinners who prefer their sins to salvation scoff at the prospect and demand that Jesus of Nazareth be eternally just another man.

CHAPTER 2

Satan Knows Who Jesus Is

Matthew 4:1-11

Try to imagine a person living without sin, a person who is always victorious over temptation. It's hard to imagine that such a person ever lived. The Bible presents Daniel as a man who seemed to be consistently victorious. The record of Daniel does not indicate in any way that he stumbled and faltered in his spiritual life. However, the record of Daniel is not an exhaustive record of the man's entire life. He was human, and therefore, one can be quite certain that Daniel fell to temptation on occasion. Sin is the common denominator for all people. Most people seem to have one particular besetting sin. For Moses, it might have been uncontrolled anger. Elijah struggled with depression. Peter had a problem with honesty. Samson would not control lust. Thomas was a cynical doubter. Jacob was a deceiver.

Yielding to temptation should not be an option for a child of God. To yield is to sin. The Christians' adversary knows that. Satan knows that sinning saints are not effective saints. He despises effective saints because they disrupt his work. He prefers to see saints trudge along in mediocrity instead of pressing on, striving for victory. Satan shutters at the thought of God's people successfully running the race. The Letter to Hebrews draws a picture of a race and challenges God's people that, "since we are surrounded by so great a cloud of witnesses, let us lay aside every weight, and the sin which so easily ensnares us, and let us run with endurance the race that is set before us" (Hebrews 12:1). Laying aside the besetting weights is difficult. However, there is One who has gone before all Christians and has already taught us how to lay aside the weights and distractions. That same author wrote in the next verse that Christians should be, "Looking unto Jesus, the author and finisher of our faith, who for the joy that was set before Him endured the cross, despising the shame, and has sat down at the right hand of the throne of God" (Hebrews 12:1-2). Jesus has shown His followers how to run victoriously against temptations that hinder the race.

Jesus of Nazareth is the only person in history who did not sin. He is the only person described in the Bible as sinless. Satan knew that Jesus, the man from Nazareth was also the Son of God. He knew that if he could cause Jesus, who was the Christ, to sin, that it would destroy God's entire plan of salvation. Therefore, he attacked Jesus with a level of temptation that most Christians will never know. God recorded Jesus' victory over those tests in Matthew 4:1-11, Mark 1:9-11, and Luke 3:21-23. Satan engaged Jesus in conversation and tempted Him to doubt the Father's provision. He tried to get Jesus to accomplish something good on His own. Jesus' response to Satan in this conversation, teaches a critical lesson for Christians. While it is unlikely that Satan himself will tempt the average Christian, it is true that Christians have regular conversations with their consciences. What Christian has not argued about temptation within his soul? Jesus' conversation with Satan revealed His authority over temptation to sin.

The Holy Spirit Led Jesus Into The Wilderness

Because Jesus of Nazareth was God the Son, it is almost shocking to discover that the temptation He endured from Satan was Gods' will (v. 1). Jesus did not haphazardly wander out into the desert where He was suddenly, and unexpectedly confronted by Satan. Nor did Jesus decide on His own to go into the wilderness where, much to His surprise, He discovered that Satan was waiting for Him. Jesus went into the wilderness because God the Holy Spirit led Him there. This was the same Holy Spirit who rested on Him and affirmed His divinity after He came up from the waters of baptism (3:16). The Holy Spirit was God the Father's presence with God the Son. He abided on the human Jesus in order to empower Him. This abiding was so certain that Luke pointed out that Jesus went into the wilderness "being filled with the Holy Spirit" (Luke 4:1). Matthew's choice of verbs indicate that the Holy Spirit led Jesus to the wilderness. This took place immediately after John baptized Him and God the Father affirmed His love for Him. John baptized Jesus in order to introduce His public ministry and, as Mark put it, "immediately" the Holy Spirit compelled Him into the wilderness. (Mark 1:12). Mark's verb choice means that God the Holy Spirit virtually drove the Son of God into the barren wasteland.

The Scripture teaches that Jesus from Nazareth went into the wilderness specifically to be tempted by Satan. He was alone in a desolate place just west of the Dead Sea somewhere in the general direction of Jerusalem. Jesus had met John where he was baptizing in the hot depression along the Jordan River near the Dead Sea. Therefore it is likely that Jesus left John and went out to the wilderness area near Qumran or somewhere between Jericho and Jerusalem. The precise location of the temptation cannot be identified, though most modern guides in Israel attempt to. Wherever it was, it was a foreboding place. Mark said it was among the wild beasts (Mark 1:13).

Why did God the Father allow this, or worse, do this? Satan's temptation of Jesus Christ was planned by the Father, approved by the Father, and allowed by the Father, for a specific purpose. The testings that come to God's children are like that. For example, Job's test was not an accident, but it was God's plan that allowed Satan to test one of His choice servants. One day Satan reported to God that he had been walking around on earth. God asked Satan, "Have you considered My servant Job, that there is none like him on the earth, a blameless and upright man, one who fears God and shuns evil?" (Job 1:8). Why did God bring innocent, upright, Job into the picture? Surely if Job would have had a vote, he would have voted, "No!" God planned to perfect His servant through the testing process. Job proved that God's plan worked when he concluded that, "He knows the way that I take; when He has tested me, I shall come forth as gold" (Job 23:10).

Since Jesus Christ came to earth to be the Savior of humans, He too needed to face the kinds of temptation that people face. Actually, God the Son faced worse temptation than humans face. The Greek word translated *tempted* does not indicate whether any given test is toward good or evil. Some testing is toward good, such as a test used to determine the value of precious gems. Other testing is toward evil, such as a temptation to sin. Often the nature of the testing (good or bad) is determined by the one doing the testing. Satan is never interested in the good of God's people. Therefore, all testing designed by Satanic powers is toward evil because Satan seeks to make God's people fail.

In this case, Jesus was not tempted by the flesh nor was He besieged by a demon. He faced Satan personally. The title *devil* points out Satan's traits as an accuser and slanderer. Satan's design for the Son of God was to cause Him to fail which would allow him to accuse or slander the eternal Son to the Heavenly Father. Christ had to pass the test or He could not be the Savior of the people who trust God. Success was critical to assure Christ's work of redemption. The writer to the Hebrew Christians described the importance of Christ's victory over temptation:

> *Therefore, in all things He had to be made like His brethren, that He might be a merciful and faithful High Priest in things pertaining to God, to make propitiation for the sins of the people. For in that He Himself has suffered, being tempted, He is able to aid those who are tempted. (Hebrews 2:17-18)*

> *For we do not have a High Priest who cannot sympathize with our weaknesses, but was in all points tempted as we are, yet without sin. (Hebrews 4:15)*

Such passages leave little doubt that Christians will also face temptation. Most Christians will never know the severity of testing Christ faced with Satan. His temptation was an extreme test of His human nature (v. 2). Matthew said that He fasted. This does not mean that Jesus simply practiced a common dietary or health ritual. Rather, as the length of the fast indicates, Jesus went to the human limit of going without food because He was in deep communion with the Father. It is no wonder that at the end of forty days He was hungry. Lack of food for forty days will make any person hungry, or worse! People experienced in fasting report that after forty days the body's natural desires are often suspended. Therefore, Jesus' hunger would have added to the severity of the testing. This natural desire opened the door for Satan's first test.

Satan Tempted Jesus

About the time Jesus had reached the peak of extreme hunger Satan showed up. He confronted Jesus and dared Him to prove that He was Messiah by satisfying a legitimate physical need (vv. 3-4). Jesus was hungry. There were plenty of stones lying on the ground in that wilderness. "Why didn't Jesus of Nazareth just do a miracle and turn some of them into bread?" Satan queried. The Accuser insisted that if Jesus was really the Son of God, He could satisfy His own hunger through His own efforts (v. 3).

Hunger is a legitimate need for any person. Jesus was fully God, but He was also God in human form. As a human He understood legitimate human needs. Satan tempted Jesus to step outside God the Father's will and prove that He was more than human, that He was really God's Son. He could stop being hungry by doing a miracle on rocks. After forty days without food, being on the verge of delirium, did the stones look like loaves of bread? Was that Satan's strategy? Would the Father really care if the Son conceded to Satan on this small issue and met a legitimate human need? After all, Jesus really was God. What could be wrong with proving to Satan that He was actually divine? It was Satan's plan not God's. It is never right to yield to Satan's plan for anything.

At some point, Christians will also be tempted in this area of the desires of the flesh. In his first letter John warned that, "all that is in the world the lust of the flesh, the lust of the eyes, and the pride of life is not of the Father but is of the world" (1 John 2:16). Satan seems to have attacked Jesus in all three of these areas. This first attack was focused on a legitimate desire of the flesh. Not all desires of the flesh are legitimate. Many of the cravings of the flesh are rooted in greed, envy, or jealousy. Christians ought to be able to identify those wicked desires and abandon them immediately. But some desires of the flesh are legitimate. A wife's longing for her husband's affection is a legitimate desire. A parent wishing to have the respect of his child is proper.

Hunger is to be expected. Surely God wants His people to be satisfied in such things, doesn't He? Maybe the test is not whether God approves of satisfaction, but when the satisfaction will come. Trusting God's timing for the satisfaction of legitimate needs is often the real test. Who would not run ahead of God and fulfill the legitimate desires of the flesh if he had the ability to do it?

Jesus chose to trust the Father's timing (v. 4). He responded to Satan's challenge with complete authority. Satan tempted Jesus to turn stones into food. Jesus responded, " It has been written . . ." He did not argue. He did not attempt to reason. He appealed to the authority of the Old Testament scriptures which God has firmly established for eternity. Jesus understood that God the Father has already answered Satan's arguments with the authority of His Word. Christians must learn from Christ's example that human argument will not always stand against Satan's questions. This is a subtle danger of apologetics. Human logic is not a two-edged sword that pierces and divides between the thoughts and intents of the heart. God's Word is. A grasp and understanding of God's Word is a great defense against temptation.

Joseph Parker, a nineteenth-century preacher in London, pointed out some important features in Christ's answers to Satan. He noted that they were not the result of a keen intellect on the part of Christ to which mortals may not lay claim. He observed that they were not the outcome of ready wit nor of an unexpected flash of fire from friction that had not been counted on. They do not bear the marks of inventive genius. They were not answers that came on the spur of the moment as a result of His infinite wisdom. They were not metaphysical arguments elaborately stated and eloquently discussed. Jesus' answers were simple enough for the average child to understand. They were quotations from the Word of God on which He meditated day and night. They were authoritative, not in the form of submitted suggestions. Human reasoning and arguments are weak in conflicts with Satan because they lack authority.

Eve illustrated how powerless human reason is against Satan's testing. She faced the same tempter Jesus faced. Satan also confronted her with questions about God's Word. She responded to Satan's subtle questions by adding human reason to God's Word. She told Satan that God prohibited Adam and her from touching the fruit. She added that prohibition to God's requirement. Jesus responded with divine wisdom instead of human reasoning. God's Word alone was sufficient to answer the Great Accuser. His response proved His full trust in the Father's plan. Was bread a necessary item? Yes. Did food appear to be a necessary item right at the moment? Certainly. Most Christians will face pressing needs in life. At the moment of temptation God's child might be convinced that his need must be satisfied at any cost immediately. At those times the flesh cries out incessantly. It demands fulfillment of legitimate needs. But God determines the best time for meeting the needs of His people. When Christians wait for God's timing, they often discover the need was not as serious as they suspected. In those times God often opens the eyes of His people to the greater issues, the greater needs. Sometimes it is simply a test to determine if we trust God. Jesus, the Son of God, waited for the Father's timing instead of running ahead and meeting His need through His own power.

Satan's second temptation challenged Jesus to prove that He was Messiah by trusting the Father's promise (vv. 5-7). What could possibly be wrong with that? This test doesn't even sound like a temptation to sin. Satan claimed that if Jesus was really the Son of God, the Father would protect Him (vv. 5-6). That makes sense. Satan took Jesus to the pinnacle of the temple where he proposed that Jesus jump off in order to prove that He really trusted the Father to care for Him. The pinnacle of the temple could be interpreted as a "wing" of the temple. The southern wing on Herod's temple was built up from the valley below so that the top of the wing was 450 feet above the Kidron Valley. A jump from that height would be deadly for humans. Standing at that spot, (or some other spot of extreme height), Satan challenged Jesus to jump. He tempted the Lord to make a public spectacle in order to prove that He really trusted the Father's promise to care for Him. Surely there were people milling around the temple courts at that time who would see this miracle of survival. They would testify that Jesus was indeed Messiah. That sounds like a good thing to human reasoning.

The real issue in this temptation was whether Jesus could trust Scripture promises. The Deceiver actually quoted Psalm 91:11 as the basis of this test. Isn't Scripture authoritative? It is, but God does not approve of Satan's intentional misuse of Scripture. Satan proposed that when the people saw Jesus being born up by angels they would rush to make Him Messiah. The temptation appears to be directed at "the pride of life." Who does not want to be accepted by his peers.

Most people crave acceptance by others. That is the essence of the pride of life. While it is true that most people cannot resist this temptation, Jesus, the Son of God, chose to trust the Father's word (v. 7). If He would have yielded to Satan's pressure, He would have nullified God's promise. God is not required to protect His people if they seek to gain glory for themselves. It was not time for Jesus to become king of the earth. That will happen during the Millennial reign of Christ.

Satan's third test tempted Jesus to grasp the Father's promise outside of the boundaries of the Father's will (vv.8-10). Satan challenged Jesus to yield to him in worship. The prize for this worship would be that Jesus could gain the kingdoms the Father had promised and at the same time forego the pending suffering and shame of the crucifixion (vv.8-9). Satan supernaturally showed Jesus all the kingdoms of the world and reminded Him that he controlled those kingdoms. It is true that Satan is the prince and power of the air (Ephesians 2:2). It is true that during this age the world lies in his lap (1 John 5:19). Therefore, he really could have given the kingdoms to the Son of God in exchange for worship.

This test appealed to the lust of the eyes. Jesus could see the kingdoms. He knew that they would be His one day. He also knew that He would gain the kingdoms only after He endured the suffering of the cross. In the book of Revelation, the Lamb that had been slain receives the title deed to the kingdoms of earth. Satan forced Jesus to decide if He would submit to the Father's plan or circumvent the trouble of the cross and claim the prize according to Satan's terms. This was the boldest test because it required worship of someone other than God. God's people frequently face similar tests. The eye is the channel through which comes the temptation to give allegiance to something or someone other than God.

Jesus chose to trust the Father's will (v. 10). He reminded Satan that Scripture requires that we worship only God and serve only God. Jesus' three responses to Satan's temptation are very instructive. He appealed to the authority of Scripture. He insisted that He would trust the Father's will and the Father's timing. He chose to receive blessing from the Father's hand alone.

Jesus Withstood The Temptation

Jesus sent Satan away for a season. Satan had no choice but to obey Christ's command to leave. That does not mean that Satan never bothered Jesus again. The Gospel record indicates that the devil continued to try to circumvent the Father's will for the Son. Luke wrote that "when the devil had ended every temptation, he departed from Him until an opportune time" (Luke 4:13). Praise God, Satan failed! Jesus withstood the challenge.

Satan attacked Jesus Christ with temptation when He was most vulnerable. Christ resisted the temptation steadfastly. In response, God the Father sent angels to minister to Jesus. The supernatural beings, created by the Father to serve the Father, came to minister to Christ. The word translated "to minister" must include feeding, encouraging, and worshiping. Notice that the Father sent the angels. In His timing, the Father sent satisfaction to Jesus. Satan realized that Jesus, the man from Nazareth, was not just the son of a carpenter. He knew that Jesus came to earth to become the Savior from sin. Therefore, he threw all of his resources into attempts to make Jesus fail. The man from Nazareth withstood the tests. He is the Savior for everyone who confesses his sins and accepts His sacrifice, by faith, as the covering for his sins. If Jesus of Nazareth was not God in the flesh, why did Satan seek so diligently to cause Him to fail? The story is consistent with the rest of Scripture as it describes Jesus Christ and Satan's attempts to disrupt God's plan for the ages.

CHAPTER 3

TWO DISCIPLES REJOICED TO MEET JESUS

JOHN 1:43-51

Archimedes (287-212 BC), a gifted Greek mathematician and inventor, was the first scientist to recognize and use the power of the lever. He said, "Give me a place to stand and rest my lever on, and I can move the Earth." He also invented the compound pulley, the Archimedes' screw, and helped develop the science of geometry. He discovered that he could determine the purity of gold by applying the principle of specific gravity. It is reported that when he finally discovered this principle he cried, "Eureka," which means, "I found it." From this Greek word the English language derived the word *heuristic* which speaks of learning, discovery, or problem-solving through trial-and-error methods. The word refers to exploratory problem-solving techniques by utilizing self-educating methods. In other words, when a person has worked diligently, endured much trial and error, and then discovered what he had been searching for, he can cry out "Eureka!"

About twenty-five years ago, many churches throughout the south were swept up in the "I found it" campaign. This was an evangelistic outreach that involved, among many other things, a plethora of bumper stickers that declared, "I found it." The whole idea was that the one who displayed the bumper sticker, T-shirt, or button, declared that he or she had found God. Finding salvation in Christ is a wonderful experience. Did the people who found salvation cry "Eureka" because their much personal labor was rewarded with discovery? If so they misunderstood God's grace in salvation.

The Greek word *heurisko* appears three times in this text from John's Gospel. Jesus *found* Philip. Then Philip went out and *found* Nathanael and told him that they, (Peter, Andrew, John, Philip), had *found* the Messiah. Nathanael followed Andrew's advice to "come and see," and he met Jesus. He was immediately convinced by Jesus' words that He was the Son of God. No doubt these men felt like shouting, "Eureka." No doubt they were excited about their new discovery. But Jesus taught the excited disciples that they did not fully understand what they had found. He taught them a very important lesson about growth in the knowledge of Christ the Savior. In time they would learn that they were found by Christ. It is not sufficient to simply be introduced to Christ. It is necessary to grow in knowledge of the Christ after being found by Him.

Jesus Found Philip

This part of John's story about Jesus states that Jesus desired to go to Galilee. That simple, but important, statement sets the stage for the conversation. It implies that Jesus was still in Judea, where John had baptized Him, and near the place where Satan had tempted Him. In the previous paragraph (verses thirty-five through thirty-eight), John the apostle wrote that on "the next day" John the Baptist introduced two disciples (Peter and himself) to Jesus. The phrase "the next day," must speak of the day after Satan's temptation ended.

John introduced his two disciples to Jesus and they followed Him to the place where He was staying (John 1:38-39). The implication is that Jesus was staying in temporary quarters which might have been Bethany. By this time in His ministry, Jesus had already called three of the twelve apostles. He had called Andrew, Peter, (who Andrew brought to Christ), and John. However, John never mentioned his own name in his Gospel, but refers to himself by implication as the other one.

On this particular day, Jesus planned to walk up the western side of Jordan to the region of Galilee, located north of Samaria. Galilee was home for the first five disciples Jesus called. It was also the earthly home for Jesus because He grew up in Nazareth, a village in Galilee. Peter and Andrew were from Bethsaida, though later Peter lived in Capernaum. James, John, and Philip were also from Bethsaida according to John 1:44.

Probably while Jesus was on His way to Galilee He found Philip. Why were Philip and his friends so far from home? Surely it was the ministry of John the Baptist that drew these men south to the desert region near the Jordan River. They had traveled at least two days to get there. They traveled all that distance in order to be identified with John's baptism for the repentance of sins. Their determination indicates that Peter, John, Philip, and Andrew were already devoted to God even before they met Jesus.

The fact that Jesus found Philip in that place at that time was not a coincidence. The first five men Jesus chose to be His disciples were in the right place at the right time. But how did they arrive at that place at the very time Jesus was beginning His ministry? God the Father certainly ordained the men's journey having determined before the beginning of time who the apostles would be. Jesus acknowledged the Father's miraculous choice of these five men, as well as the other apostles. The night before the Romans crucified Him, Jesus prayed to the Heavenly Father:

> *I have manifested Your name to the men whom You have given Me out of the world. They were Yours, You gave them to Me, and they have kept Your word (John 17:6).*

> *I pray for them. I do not pray for the world but for those whom You have given Me, for they are Yours (John 17:9).*

Jesus knew that these exact men were the ones the Triune Godhead (of which He is the second person) had picked for the task of continuing His ministry. He found Philip by divine direction not by accident.

When Jesus found Philip He simply said, "Follow Me." It was a simple, direct, easy to understand command. It was much like the command He gave to John and Andrew a day earlier. When they had asked Jesus where He was staying, He simply said, "Come and see" (John 1:39). It was like the confirming call to Peter and Andrew a few days later when Jesus drew them from their fishing business saying, "Follow Me" (Matthew 4:19). It was the same kind of command Jesus used to call Matthew (Matthew 9:9). In each case the one who Christ commanded obeyed immediately. Here Jesus offered the divine invitation to Philip. At first this command appears to be an invitation to accompany Jesus on the journey back to Galilee. But these men would come to learn that Jesus' invitation was to walk in the path that He walked in order to learn how to continue His ministry. Has Jesus Christ found you? Has He invited you to follow after Him? Have you followed? What is the result?

Philip Found Nathanael

Jesus found Philip, and Philip, filled with joy at his new discovery, went out immediately to find Nathanael. He told Nathanael that he had found the One who Moses and the prophets had written about. Obviously, Philip was excited about meeting the Christ and was compelled to tell a friend about it. There is no doubt that Philip was convinced that this Jesus was the promised Messiah. Surely, Philip did not inadvertently meet Nathanael a few days later, and tell him about the Christ as a side note in the process of conversation. He did not accidentally run into this old acquaintance. He searched for him and found him so that he could tell him the good news. Philip must have known Nathanael since both of them were from the same geographical area, from a town called Cana.

It seems like these five God-fearing men had come to the desert together. If that is true, then Philip was aware that Nathanael was along with the other Galilean men who had come to Judea in order to participate in John's baptism. As quickly as possible, he went to find the other man from their group to tell him the good news that they had found Messiah. In light of Philip's response to meeting Jesus Christ, how should modern disciples of Christ react? Philip met Jesus from Nazareth, was convinced that He was the Christ, and immediately told a friend about it. Should that not be the expected norm for people who have been searching for the Christ? Christians ought to be astonished that Christ found them while they were wandering around in life searching for something or someone to offer satisfaction. People who find new life in Christ, people who are redeemed from spiritual deadness in sin, should be so grateful for their new found life that they share the good news willingly. The weak testimony of many Christians might indicate that they think that their discovery of Christ was due solely to their efforts. Do they believe that they found Christ only because they expended much effort in searching? It almost appears that some Christians are convinced that, through a process of trial and error, one day they stumbled across the answer to all of their spiritual problems. "Eureka!" After all of their labor and trouble they found the eternal answer. People who do not understand the amazing grace by which God finds lost and dying sinners, will not be quick to share the good news. One who thinks that he earned his salvation also thinks that he deserves it. The best that person can do is boast about his labor and accomplishments. Philip was not like that at all!

Philip found Nathanael and told him that the One promised by Moses and the prophets was none other than Jesus, the man from Nazareth. He asserted that Jesus was the same One Moses spoke about in the law. He was convinced that Jesus was the promised Seed who would crush Satan. Devout men like Philip and Nathanael would certainly remember that God promised in Genesis 3:15 to "put enmity between you [Satan] and the woman, and between your seed and her Seed; He shall bruise your head, and you shall bruise His heel." Devout, God-fearing men would remember how God had promised that the perfect Prophet who would be similar to Moses. Moses had told the Israelites many years earlier that, "The LORD your God will raise up for you a Prophet like me from your midst, from your brethren. Him you shall hear" (Deuteronomy 18:15). Philip was sure that this Jesus from Nazareth was the same One the prophets wrote about. God inspired Jeremiah to promise this One by saying, "Behold, *the* days are coming," says the LORD, "That I will raise to David a Branch of righteousness; A King shall reign and prosper, and execute judgment and righteousness in the earth" (Jeremiah 23:5).

Devout Jews anticipated this promised Prophet and King. They longed for the fulfillment of God's promise. One can be certain that people like these men who participated in John's ministry of repentance longed for and watched for the coming Messiah. Now Philip burst into

Nathanael's quiet meditation with the news that he had just discovered this Messiah! Indeed, Philip claimed that the promised Messiah was none other than Jesus, the son of Joseph, the carpenter, the man from Nazareth. It is possible that most people in that area of Galilee knew Joseph the carpenter or at least they had heard about his son Jesus. The people around Nazareth believed that Jesus was Joseph's son. Many of them knew about the young carpenter who was so wise and favorable to His peers. In light of such familiarity they would wonder how this fellow could be the Messiah.

It is not surprising that Nathanael doubted Philip's conclusion (v. 46). When Nathanael asked, "Can anything good come out of Nazareth?," he simply expressed doubt that Galilee could produce the Messiah. Maybe Nathanael's question stemmed from the fact that people in the neighboring regions denigrated the folks in Nazareth. History indicates that the people in Nazareth were generally poorer than the people who lived in Jerusalem. Then again, most of the villages in the countryside were poor. In truth, Nathanael's statement revealed more than a notorious class struggle. His words admitted that the people who lived in Judea denigrated all of Galilee. This was due partly to the fact that the region of Galilee was far to the north, many miles away from Jerusalem. Jerusalem, in Judea, was where all the important people of Israel lived. Galilee was home to fisherman, farmers, and country-bumpkins. Judea was where the priests, scribes, and other leaders lived. Even worse was the fact that Samaria, a region filled with people who were a mixed race of Jews and Gentiles, stood between Judea (Jerusalem) and Galilee. Someone as important as the promised Messiah would certainly come from Jerusalem. Certainly the One promised to fulfill the Davidic Promise would come from Jerusalem where David once ruled.

How should a devout believer respond to that kind of doubt? Philip's answer is a classic illustration of the proper response to doubters. He simply offered the invitation, "Come and see." This is still a good invitation. The simple presentation of the good news of salvation is often met with a plethora of excuses for not receiving Christ. Some sincere Christians attempt to use the arguments of human wisdom alone to convince doubters. But human wisdom often falls short in that attempt because doubts about the Christ is not a problem of the human flesh. Doubting the story of Jesus of Nazareth is a spiritual problem.

Doubt about Christ is ultimately a heart problem, not a brain problem. Therefore, the best argument to offer people who doubt Christ is the invitation, "Come and see." Come and see Jesus Christ manifested in the pages of His Word. Come and see Jesus Christ illustrated in the lives of His people.

Nathanael Found Jesus

Nathanael accepted Philip's invitation. He followed Philip, he met Jesus, and he was quickly convinced that the man from Nazareth was the Christ (vv. 47-49). His first impression was one of astonishment because Jesus perceived hidden truth about him (vv. 47-48). Nathanael had never met Jesus, the man from Nazareth, and yet this man described Nathanael's most secret characteristics. Jesus did all of that while Nathanael was still approaching. They had not even engaged in conversation yet.

Who was Nathanael? What does the Bible say about him? Matthew, Mark, and Luke do not list him with the other disciples. Was he one of the original disciples? Was he ever listed among the apostles? The answer to the question might be discovered in the fact that the other three Gospel writers list Bartholomew in the parallel passages where John listed Nathanael. Bartholomew is a family name which is not normally used to identify a person. Therefore, one can be quite certain that when Matthew, Mark, and Luke wrote about Bartholomew, they wrote about the same man whom John called Nathanael.

Jesus observed that Nathanael was an Israelite without deceit. It was a significant compliment. It is rooted in the fact that all Israelites came through the lineage of the man named Israel. Israel was the name God gave to Jacob after his conversion at Peniel. Jacob had been a deceiver all of his life up to that point. His name actually meant "supplanter." When Jacob was leaving Canaan, after he had deceived his father and robbed his brother, God met with him and promised to care for him and bring him back home. Then, many years later, when Jacob was returning home to Canaan, God met with him again. This time Jacob wrestled with God, but could not prevail. Finally, after a long wrestling match, God humbled Jacob and changed his name from "supplanter" to "prince," — which means power with God and power with man.

Jesus said that Nathanael was an Israelite with no guile. The compliment means that even though Nathanael was born in the lineage of the converted deceiver, he himself was sincere and honest. Jesus Christ described Nathanael as being frank, open, and honest. He had no hidden agenda. Of course, Nathanael was amazed at Jesus' words. His response to the Lord was not disrespectful, but as one would expect based on Jesus' observation, open and honest.

Nathanael had never met Jesus. Maybe he thought that Philip had told Jesus all about him. He asked Jesus, "How do you know me?" That is the kind of question sinners ought to ask God. Sinners prefer to keep their failures hidden and many of them are bothered to think that the God of heaven knows their deepest secrets. People who are so bothered, might even deny that there is a God who knows them so thoroughly. They prefer to think of God as a Divine patsy who is selectively ignorant; One who only knows the good things about them.

Nathanael was even more amazed when Jesus went on to describe his activity in detail. Jesus told him that He had seen him sitting under the fig tree. It is a picture of Nathanael resting, sitting down, lost in thought. What was he contemplating? Was this Israelite, born in the lineage of Jacob, thinking about the story of Jacob's ladder? Was he thinking about Messiah, through whom God would meet with man?

At this point, Nathanael was fully convinced that this man from Nazareth was indeed the Messiah (v. 49). He declared that Jesus is the Son of God, acknowledging the fact that He was at least a divine being. He concluded that Jesus was like an angel. But Nathanael also concluded that Jesus is the King of Israel. This term pointed directly to the fact that Jesus is the promised Messiah. That was a true and honest conclusion, but what does all of that entail? What if this "Man" was divine in nature? What if He was the Messiah? Nathanael thought he knew all the ramifications of such truths. He was probably quite sure that this meant that the man standing in front of him was, even then, preparing to gather and army together, defeat the Romans, and renew the Theocracy in Israel. Nathanael thought that he knew what Messiah entailed. He was like people who talk about Jesus Christ as their King. To what extent is He king? Over what does He rule? How precise is His rule? Or is it possible that the average religious person's view of Christ as king is more like the opinion that Christ is their personal genie?

Jesus taught Nathanael that he was did not fully understand all that he had found (vv. 50-51). He promised that Nathanael would see great things (v. 50). There is no doubt that this was a reference to the many miracles which Jesus would do in the disciples' presence during His earthly ministry. Very soon after this event Jesus would begin those miracles at a wedding feast in Cana. Seeing Jesus confirm that He was Messiah by doing miracles would certainly be encouraging to Nathanael. People naturally like to see divine wonders in order to convince themselves, and others, that Jesus is the Christ.

However, Jesus promised something more important than signs and wonders. He also promised that Nathanael would learn the fullness of the term "Son of Man." This is a veiled reference to Jacob's ladder. In Jacob's dream, the divine beings were sent from the Father to minister to people on earth. Therefore, Jesus expanded Jacob's vision to be a reference to God the Father proving and affirming Jesus Christ's divinity. Nathanael would see the divine ministers (angels) affirming the deity of this Christ.

The term "Son of God" indicated Jesus' divinity and the term "Son of Man" pointed to His vicarious atonement. That was a concept that Nathanael could not fully grasp even though he was convinced that Jesus was the Christ. It would take him about three years to understand what Jesus meant by the Father's affirmation of His title "Son of Man." In time, Nathanael did come to understand Christ's work of atonement for sin. He proved his conviction by giving his life. Tradition holds that he went to India as a missionary with the gospel. The story claims that people who hated the gospel flayed him to death. It is good to respond like Nathanael. It is good to be excited that you have found the Christ. But what have you found? Nathanael proved that he understood Christ by giving his life for Him. What does your life prove about your knowledge of Christ?

CHAPTER 4

NICODEMUS LEARNED WHO JESUS WAS

JOHN 3:1-21

Jim was a good co-worker. He was prompt, dependable, and always did his share of the work. He was not obnoxious or odd, but he did have one noticeable idiosyncrasy. Jim was an avid ham radio builder and operator. He was more than just a builder and operator—he was fanatic. Jim spent all of his spare time with his hobby and spent most of his spare money on new equipment. It was no surprise that Jim enjoyed talking about his hobby when anyone would listen to him. He loved ham radio, knew much about it, and could not understand why the rest of his co-workers did not share his love.

Most people have a quirk like Jim's. Some folks talk endlessly about their cars, others about girlfriends, or boyfriends, or clothes, or gadgets, or books. People talk about what they love, and often that love becomes the sole focus of life for them.

Jesus, the man from Nazareth, also illustrated His sole purpose in life through His words. The good news that He came to provide eternal life for all who would trust Him was the point of many of Christ's conversations. A perfect example of this practice is found in His conversation with Nicodemus. Nicodemus, a leader among the Jews, desired to gain eternal life. His interest is shared by, or at least considered, by most people at some point in their lives. According to John's story, Nicodemus barely opened the conversation with Jesus when the man from Nazareth quickly laid out one of the best explanations of salvation found in the Bible. His conversation with the Jewish ruler is one of the most significant statements about this most important matter of eternity. To understand Jesus' explanation to Nicodemus is to understand the eternal purpose of the triune God fulfilled in God the Son.

Nicodemus Was A Religious Man Looking For Answers

To say that Nicodemus was a religious man is an under statement. John stated in this story that Nicodemus was a Pharisee. Pharisee is a title that identified members of a philosophical or religious party in Israel. Pharisees were not elected or appointed. Individuals chose to associate themselves with the party. No one became a Pharisee by birth or by accident. Nicodemus chose to be associated with other men of this religious party who, like him, were devoutly committed to keeping God's Law.

The Pharisee party originated during the time of the Maccabeans in reaction to a secular drift among many of the Jews. Some of the devout Jews saw this drift as a wholesale forsaking of God's Law, and they determined to do all that they could to stop the ongoing abandonment. They were determined to keep the people aware of the demands of God's Law at all times. Probably there were never more than 6,000 members in the party at any one time. Sparse numbers mattered little to the Pharisees. They were convinced that the Pentateuch, the first five books of the Bible, was the most important possession God's people could have. Because of this focus, when a man joined the party of the Pharisees, he took a pledge to keep the Law scrupulously.

Every Pharisee, and most Jews who were not Pharisees, could clearly define God's Law. All Jews agreed that the Law was contained in the first five books of the Bible where God laid down the requirements that His people must meet in order to please Him. For example, one of the most obvious statements from the Law is, "Remember the Sabbath to keep it holy." The requirement, by itself, is plain and simple. But when the Pharisees explained how to put the requirement of the Law into practice, things got complicated. The requirement to remember the Sabbath meant, "Do no work." That application is obvious from the statement in Exodus 20:10 where God wrote through Moses, "But the seventh day *is* the Sabbath of the LORD your God. *In it* you shall do no work: you, nor your son, nor your daughter, nor your male servant, nor your female servant, nor your cattle, nor your stranger who *is* within your gates" (Exodus 20:10). But what constitutes work?

At this point the party of the Pharisees began to wander away from the clear facts to embrace the product of man's imagination. Indeed, it took twenty-four chapters in the *Mishnah* to define "work." As a result, these devout keepers of the Law concluded that work meant tying knots. What kind of knots? Well, for a camel driver, or a sailor to untie knots they had tied on a previous day, was to do work. That was forbidden. However, if a camel driver or sailor could untie the knot with one hand, that was not work. The average citizen was allowed to tie a knot in his sandal or her skirt, but they had better not think about tying a knot in the rope attached to the bucket they dropped into the well to get water. Even more imaginative was the scribes' requirement that a woman should not look in the mirror on the Sabbath because she might see a grey hair. Apparently, ancient Jewish women were like modern American women who, when they see a grey hair are tempted to pull it out. Not on the Sabbath. That was work which would profane the Lord's Day.

One can easily see how attempts to explain God's law became ludicrous. Many of the common people concluded that attempts to keep the scribes' explanations of God's law were foolish. Then why did the Pharisees, men like Nicodemus, pledge themselves to do this? They believed that keeping the Law (especially their own rules which explained the Law) was the means for gaining eternal life. That explains why, on another day, a young Jewish ruler asked Jesus, "What good thing must I do to inherit eternal life?"

Human nature tends to seek ways to earn salvation from God. Nearly all false religions teach that peace with God is gained through personal sacrifice or labors. A quick review of modern religious teachings indicates that most religions propagate the need for people to do many good works in order to gain salvation. Even Protestant Christian groups teach this error, either overtly or covertly. Many gospel songs and folk songs confess the need for sinners to do something in order to win God's favor. Several years ago a popular country hit declared, "I hope my feet are clean enough to walk on streets of gold." Human nature is arrogant enough to think that it is able to buy off God. The error of eternal salvation gained by works of the flesh did not die with the demise of the Pharisees.

Nicodemus was a Pharisee. He was wholly given to doing good works. He was also a ruler of the Jews. The term *ruler* means that he was a member of the Sanhedrin. He was one of seventy select leaders who governed the religious matters for Israel. The overruling government of Rome permitted the Sanhedrin to have limited, but important, authority over the Jews. Nicodemus was one of the select rulers.

This select ruler of the Jews believed that Jesus was a gifted teacher (v. 2). Therefore, one night he came to Jesus seeking information about eternal life. Why did he meet Jesus at night? The common explanation is that Nicodemus, being a ruler of the Jews was afraid to meet with the man from Nazareth in broad daylight. He might have feared the ramifications of associating with this Teacher who had become so hated by the members of the Sanhedrin. Maybe Nicodemus came at night because Jesus was so busy ministering to the people during the day that it was impossible for them to meet.

Regardless of the reason, the fact that Nicodemus came to Jesus proved that he was confident that the Teacher could help him. He even expressed a certain amount of faith in Jesus when he called Him "Teacher." Actually, Nicodemus admitted that Jesus was more than a teacher. He confessed that He was a teacher come from God. His confession indicates that Nicodemus had taken note of Jesus' many wonders and signs. Those miracles manifested Jesus' divinity. Even the rulers had to admit that, at the least, this Jesus from Nazareth must have come from God. Nicodemus agreed with the majority of people in the world today who conclude that, at the very least, Jesus was unique. Whatever He was, whoever He was, He had some kind of God-given approval.

Jesus Explained The New Birth To Nicodemus

Jesus' reply to Nicodemus' greeting appears to be abrupt. Right away Jesus told the ruler that he needed to be born again. In fact verse three begins with the words, "Jesus answered." Those words seem to be out of place since, up to this point in the story, Nicodemus had not asked anything. He didn't need to ask because Jesus knows the deepest secrets of every heart. Jesus of Nazareth was God in the flesh. He knew why Nicodemus sought Him out. He fully understood that this ruler of the Jews sought an audience with Him for the same reason the rich young ruler sought an audience with Him. According to Matthew's account, the young ruler asked, "Good Teacher, what good thing shall I do that I may have eternal life?" (Matthew 19:16b). That is what Nicodemus wanted to know. But before he could even pose the question Jesus told him that he needed to be born again in order to enter the kingdom of God.

Nicodemus wondered about eternal life and Jesus explained entrance into the kingdom of God. What is the connection? The kingdom of God is where the King, God, reigns supreme. God's kingdom is where His will is done. That is why Jesus taught His followers to pray, "Your kingdom come. Your will be done on earth as *it is* in heaven" (Matthew 6:10). The believer begins to enjoy eternal life as soon as Jesus becomes King of his heart. Jesus becomes King of the repentant sinner's heart the moment he is born again. The idea of being born again really confused the ruler of Israel (vv. 4-6). It still confuses sincere seekers of eternal life.

Nicodemus wondered what Jesus meant by telling him that he needed to be born again. The key for understanding this truth is found in the meaning of the word *again*. That word might mean 1) from above, a higher place; or 2) all over, radically new; or 3) from the beginning. Luke used the third meaning of this Greek word in the prologue of his Gospel. He wrote, "It seemed good to me also, having had perfect understanding of all things from *the very first*, to write to you an orderly account, most excellent Theophilus" (Luke 1:3). Obviously, Jesus did not mean that Nicodemus needed to be born from the very first. Rather, He taught that sinners need to experience a radical change that comes from above. The radical change is like being born again.

People generally struggle with that idea. A supernatural rebirth that comes from heaven is too unbelievable to the human mind. That is why many folks naturally conclude that doing any number of good works in exchange for eternal life makes more sense. Undergoing a miraculous, supernatural change doesn't make any sense at all. Where does one go to get such a miracle? How does the sinner even go about asking for it? Nicodemus expressed typical, natural, confusion very well when he told Jesus that the idea of a new birth makes as much sense as getting back into his mother's womb!

It was obvious that Nicodemus could not accept Jesus' teaching. Therefore, Jesus continued to instruct the man. He taught the ruler that the new birth is critical. First, He explained that a person must be born of water before he can enter the kingdom of God. That could have been a reference to the common process of being born in the flesh, through the water sack. Later, in verse six, Jesus also contrasted the flesh and the spirit. However, the reference to water could have been a reference to identification with John's baptism for repentance, which was water baptism.

However, the second part of Jesus' instruction is the most important. He told Nicodemus that it was not enough to be born of water, but that he must also be born of the Spirit. In other words, no one inherits eternal life unless he or she is birthed through the Holy Spirit. Paul explained to pastor Titus that no one is regenerated, "by works of righteousness which we have done, but according to His mercy He saved us, through the washing of regeneration and renewing of the Holy Spirit" (Titus 3:5). To be born of the Spirit is to experience regeneration through His power. It is to be identified with His work from that point on.

One can imagine that Nicodemus, the teacher and ruler, looked dumbfounded as Jesus explained this wonderful truth to him. Therefore, Jesus told him that he should not be incredulous (vv. 7-10). In fact, Jesus pointed out that in another area of life Nicodemus readily accepted the work of the unseen by faith (vv. 7-8). Why do people marvel at the idea of God creating a new heart through the Holy Spirit (v. 7), when the same people regularly accept things they cannot explain? Jesus reminded Nicodemus that he could not see the wind, but he did not doubt that there was wind because he saw its effects. Most people do not question the existence of wind even though they cannot grab a handful of it. Most people do not doubt the presence of electricity in their houses. Folks take the existence of electricity for granted all the time. They do not have to explain it to appreciate it.

Likewise Jesus told Nicodemus to trust the promise of the new birth. He told the ruler that he, of all people, should understand this matter of being born again because he was the teacher of the people

(vv. 9-10). Here was one of the chief religious leaders of God's people who freely admitted that the whole idea of the new birth eclipsed his human understanding (v. 9). Good! That is a wonderful conclusion for a very religious person to reach. It is good for people, who teach a religion that consists of trying to please God by keeping rules, to learn that eternal life is gained only through the supernatural new birth.

Jesus Taught The Principles Of Eternal Life

Having established the need for the new birth, Jesus continued by telling Nicodemus that God Himself provided the means for experiencing the new birth. God provided the only acceptable means for entering eternal life (vv. 11-16). In fact Jesus taught this teacher that God had revealed His plan for a long time (vv. 11-14a). Nicodemus had approached Jesus by saying that he and all the wise men of Israel (we) knew that He was a teacher come from God. Jesus told Nicodemus that *We* spoke what *We* knew and saw (vv. 11-13). His response implied that Nicodemus and his friends knew very little (v. 11). The term *We* in verse eleven refers to the Trinity. God the Father, God the Son, and God the Holy Spirit speak, testify, and reveal truth. But Jesus explained that, you people (plural) do not receive Our witness. The rulers of Israel did not trust God in the most obvious things, how could they trust the secret things (v. 12)? Where there is no trust, there is no relationship! Who has gone to heaven to be an eyewitness of God's plan and returned to explain it to a needy world (v. 13)? Far better for the needy citizens of this terrestrial sphere to believe the Messenger from heaven, Jesus Christ, the man from Nazareth.

Jesus told the teacher of Israel that he should have understood God's means for entering eternal life because God had given instruction and illustration of it throughout the Bible. Where? There was the clear example of Moses lifting up the serpent (v. 14a). That story reveals how the people of God had sinned. God sent deadly serpents into the camp to judge the unrepentant rebels. After several of their friends and relatives were killed by the snakes, the remaining sinners cried out to God for help. God told Moses to put a bronze serpent on a pole and raise it up in the center of camp. Then God told the people to look on the serpent and trust Him (God) to heal them. Everyone who trusted God's instruction enough to act—to look at the serpent—was saved. Could people not learn about the importance of faith from that example?

Surely Nicodemus, a teacher of the Law, was aware of God's message to Ezekiel. God challenged the people, through His prophet Ezekiel, to "Cast away from you all the transgressions which you have committed, and get yourselves a new heart and a new spirit. For why should you die, O house of Israel?" (Ezekiel 18:31). How would they get a new heart? Later God explained, "I will give you a new heart and put a new spirit within you; I will take the heart of stone out of your flesh and give you a heart of flesh" (Ezekiel 36:26). That is the miracle of the being born again. Nicodemus should have understood God's Word.

Jesus taught the teacher that God had kept the promises He recorded in the Old Testament. God Himself revealed the means for getting a new heart, for experiencing the new birth, which is to gain eternal life. Eternal life is found in Jesus Christ, the man from Nazareth (vv. 14b-16). Christ is the fulfillment of the entire picture. The Old Testament sinners believed God, not the serpent on the pole. Modern sinners believe the Christ who hung on the tree (v. 15). They must trust His finished work alone for eternal life. Why? Because God loved the world of sinners so much that He provided Christ as the only acceptable sacrifice to cover sins (v. 16). Believe what God said about Him.

Jesus taught that God made all of the necessary provision for eternal life. He also explained the amazing reality that, in spite of God's provision, people condemn themselves (vv. 17-21). God did not condemn the world through Christ. Christ did not come to bring judgment (v. 17). The second time Christ comes to earth He will bring judgment. But the first time He came to accomplish the work of salvation. In verses eighteen and twenty-one Jesus taught that He came to earth so that sinners could have faith in His finished work. Therefore, sinners must believe in Christ alone for salvation (v. 18). There is no middle ground. Isn't that exactly what Jesus taught Nicodemus from the beginning of their conversation? Earlier Jesus taught, "You must be born again." Indeed, "We all must be born from above."

When a person truly believes Jesus' teaching, his faith will be obvious in his life (v. 21). Jesus told Nicodemus that the one who finally grasps the truth about the new birth and receives Christ's finished work as the payment for personal sin, has no problem allowing God to investigate his secret life. Born again people are supposed to live according to truth. Real believers live according to God's truth. Sinners prefer to avoid the light of God's truth. They do deeds outside of a relationship with God. Outside of a relationship with God is spiritual darkness. Sinners are comfortable there. They reject Christ because He is light and light makes their sin look bad. In fact, if the Light had not come at all, sinners would have an excuse. But Christ the light has come. Nevertheless sinners continue to reject Him. The idea of receiving the gift of eternal life by faith through grace is non-sensical. They refuse God's gift of salvation and continue on in their deeds of darkness, thus proving that they hate light (v. 20). Many try to hide their wicked deeds through deception or denial. They express their rejection in statements like the one on a bumper sticker that said, "I was born okay the first time." People like that don't think that "earning" salvation is evil. They refuse to trust something or Someone they don't understand. Jesus invites sinners to, "Ask, and it will be given to you; seek, and you will find; knock, and it will be opened to you" (Matthew 7:7). God's desire is that sinners from all levels of life would trust His plan for eternal life. He longs to give the gift of eternal life to those who have offended Him by their sins.

CHAPTER 5

JESUS EXPLAINED WHO HE WAS TO A SAMARITAN WOMAN

JOHN 4:4-42

For several weeks after the terrorists attack on September 11, 2001, religion, God, and the future were hot topics of conversation. In light of the devastating destruction of life and property, many people wondered where God was, who God is, and what God was doing. For a brief period of time it seemed like nearly everyone had an opinion about God and the future.

Maybe tragedies flush out the fact that many people in this culture still have a certain amount of knowledge about God. Maybe people retain some thoughts about Jesus Christ and some sort of second coming of Christ. In that sense, maybe a majority of the American culture could agree with the Samaritan Woman's statement: "I know that Messiah is coming." Millions of Jewish people are still watching and waiting for Messiah to arrive on earth the first time. Christians of every stripe believe that one day in the future He is coming back to earth for the second time. Even many cults teach that Jesus the Messiah will come to earth. But a mere confession that Messiah will come is not proof that the person making the confession has experienced the new birth that Jesus described to Nicodemus.

Nicodemus was a ruler of the Jews, a Pharisee, one of the most strict religious people. The woman in Samaria was his contrast. She was notoriously sinful. Nicodemus purposely came to meet with Jesus at night. This woman did not plan to meet Jesus at all. But Jesus planned to meet her. Nicodemus wondered how he could enter the kingdom of God. It appears that entering the kingdom of God might have been the furthest thing from this woman's mind. Jesus taught Nicodemus the difficult truths that a ruler of the Jews would be expected to know or understand (cf. 3:10-12). Jesus taught this woman a simple spiritual truth, and yet, one that was similar to the truth He taught Nicodemus. After Jesus explained the simple truth to this woman, He went on to explain some pointed but practical matters about the woman's life. Different hearts require different responses. Jesus' conversation with the woman in Samaria illustrates some of the most important principles for sharing the gospel. It is good to understand that the same method is not successful for every case or person. It is imperative to learn from Christ to respond according to the recipient's heart. He, being God, assessed each heart perfectly. He knew how to explain His divinity to each person He engaged in conversation.

Particular Circumstances Preceded Jesus' Meeting With The Samaritan Woman

Jesus left Judea in order to go through Samaria (vv. 1-5). It was necessary for Jesus and the disciples to leave Jerusalem at this time because of the unfavorable attention that suddenly surrounded Him (vv. 1-3). This event took place about nine months after Jesus began His public ministry. By this time many followers had gathered around the wise and benevolent Teacher from Nazareth. The multitudes of people were constantly amazed by His teaching, and they were astonished by His ongoing miracles. Many of them wanted to identify with His ministry through baptism. One might conclude that such attention heaped upon Christ was a good thing. But the timing of the attention was not a good thing.

John 2:13-22 indicates that Jesus had driven the merchants and traders out of the temple about fifty days before this. That action would certainly attract a lot of attention from the religious leaders—and the attention was not good. Jesus' actions raised the rulers' ire. According to this first verse of the text, the Pharisees were well aware of Jesus' work. The religious leaders quickly developed a poor opinion of Jesus from Nazareth who disrupted their trade and cost them money. They certainly planned to resist Jesus' work. Ultimately, their resistance went to the extreme of crucifying the only perfectly innocent man who ever lived.

That is why Jesus had to leave Jerusalem for a while. It was not yet time for the crucifixion according to the Father's plan. The time would be right only when it was determined by God the Father. He had previously determined His plan and timing and it would not change. A few days before this meeting in Samaria, Jesus had told Mary that His hour was not yet come (2:4). Therefore, it was necessary for Him to move away from the hotbed of religion and go back to the more pastoral region of Galilee. Most of Jesus' ministry took place in the quiet hillsides of Galilee and on the banks of the Sea of Galilee.

Not only was it necessary for Jesus to leave Jerusalem, but it was also necessary for Him to go through Samaria (vv. 4-5). That statement could mean that the shortest route from Judea to Galilee was through the region called Samaria. Samaria was located between Judea and Galilee. There were three roadways leading from Judea to Galilee. One could take the western road and travel up the coast on the western side of Samaria. That route was somewhat direct, but it required the traveler to pass through Samaria. Devout Jews were not interested in doing that. They preferred to walk out of their way, cross the Jordan River and take the eastern road, thereby avoiding Samaria altogether. Taking the road that ran right through the center of Samaria was the shortest route but it was also the road less traveled by Jews.

Jesus had to pass through Samaria, but not because of the roads. This statement means that Jesus was determined to go through Samaria — and that was not a normal Jewish response at all! In Jesus' day there was a centuries-old problem brewing between the Jews and the Samaritans. Samaria had been home to the capital city of the ten tribes of Israel after the division caused by King Rehoboam, son of Solomon. The people in those tribes were stubbornly determined to live in sin. In response to their rebellion God sent the Assyrian king to defeat Israel. In 720 BC the Assyrians captured the nation and sent the best people of the land into exile (2 Kings 17:24-41). The Assyrians realized that it was not wise to leave a few poor people to care for the conquered land. Therefore, in an effort to break up the camaraderie of the remnant, the king of Assyria repopulated the land with people from Babylon, Cuthah, Ava, Hamath, and Sepharvaim.

Human wisdom dictates that this was a stroke of genius. As one might expect, the Jewish people intermarried with the Gentiles. The result was that a mixed race inhabited that portion of the Promised Land. That was unacceptable to devout Jews who lived in the regions of Judah and Benjamin. And things got even worse. After the land was repopulated, a renegade Jewish priest moved to Samaria and combined pagan worship with the true worship of Jehovah (2 Ki. 17:28-36). This was an utter abomination to loyal Jews.

About 130 years after Assyria had defeated and reestablished the land of Israel, the mighty nation of Babylon overran Judah and took the people into captivity. The result of this captivity was different than what Assyria did to Israel. The Jews from Judah stubbornly maintained the purity of the Jewish race even while they were in exile. Seventy years after Nebuchadnezzar had captured the land and deported the inhabitants, Cyrus, the king of Persia, allowed the Jewish people to return to Jerusalem. Under the leadership of men like Ezra and Nehemiah the Jews rebuilt the city walls, and the temple, and repopulated Jerusalem. The mixed race of Jews and Gentiles came to be known as the Samaritans. When the pure race of Jews returned to rebuild Jerusalem the Samaritans became enraged because the Jews would not allow them to help with the restoration project. Because the Jews refused their help, the Samaritans built their own temple on Mount Gerizim. Devout Jews, led by the Maccabeans, destroyed that temple in 129 BC. Nevertheless, the Samaritans remembered their temple for years.

Another major religious difference between the Jews and the Samaritans was that the Jews maintained regular reading and study of the Law, the Prophets, the Historical books, and the Poetry. Conversely, the Samaritans had their own Bible which consisted of only the first five books of the Old Testament. Because of these differences, the Jews despised the Samaritans and the Samaritans had similar feelings for the Jews.

Jesus understood this mutual animosity, but He still had to go through Samaria. He had to go into that society of people who despised His earthly heritage. Why? Jesus was God. He knew that He had a preordained meeting with a woman in Samaria. Sometimes it is difficult of God's people to allow Him to be God. He knows, He arranges, He ordains. Often He accomplishes His will in matters that appear to be abnormal or unacceptable in normal life. God's people must maintain such close fellowship with their Master that it will be easy to follow the way that He leads in order to bring honor to Him.

Jesus went into a city of Samaria and sat down at Jacob's well (v. 6). He was weary, tired and thirsty. He was tested in His human nature the same way all people are tested. He understood the needs of the flesh. It was the sixth hour which might mean that it was noon, or it might have been about six o'clock in the evening. Either time would allow for Jesus to be tired after a long, dusty walk. He would need to sit and rest for awhile.

Jesus chose to sit down by Jacob's well on purpose. Jacob and his sons dug this very well many years earlier on property Jacob had purchased from Hamor (Genesis 33:19). The well was originally 100 feet deep, and it might have been fed by a spring rising up from beneath. Not far from this site Joseph's relatives had buried his bones after they brought them out of Egypt. The well was located at the foot of Mount Gerizim. Mount Gerizim was an important mountain in the history of Israel and Samaria. It is located one-half mile south-southwest of Sychar, the old city of Shechem, a city rich in Jewish history.

Jesus sat alone at the well of Jacob because the disciples had gone into Sychar to buy much needed food. While it is true that the Jews and Samaritans despised each other, they were still able to transact business deals, such as buying food. Money has a way of tempering personal dislike of others. Jesus planned to sit alone at the well because He needed to counsel with a visitor.

The Woman Did Not Fully Grasp The Wonderful News

Probably Jesus did not sit at the well very long before a woman came along to draw water. When she arrived at the well, Jesus asked her for a drink of water (vv. 7-9). That would not be an unusual request in most cultures. But for several reasons, it was an astonishing request in Jesus' day (v. 7). First, as a general rule, travelers carried their own leather water bottle which was attached to a cord so that they could draw water from the wells along the journey. Where was Jesus' bottle? Second, a Jew never asked a Samaritan for a favor. Third, a good Jew would not have been caught dead talking to a woman of such ill repute. In fact, if another devout Jew witnessed a Rabbi talking to a woman like this, it would have ruined his career. This was a very unusual situation indeed!

In light of the circumstances it is not surprising that the woman was surprised (v. 9). She understood that it was not right for this Jewish man to ask a Samaritan for a drink. Her surprise is explained more by John's comment that "the Jews have no dealings with the Samaritans." But if the Jews have no dealings at all with the Samaritans, why did the disciples go to Sychar to get food? A more accurate translation of that phrase points out the fact that a Jew would never, ever, use a Samaritan's drinking vessel.

Why did Jesus ask for a drink from this particular woman? Why did He put her on the spot? Jesus intended for His first statement to open the woman's heart so that she would listen to Him. He set a good example for everyone who seeks to tell the Good News to others. Asking a person to do a favor often opens the door of communication if that person is willing to help. It makes the person feel needed and helpful and makes the person making the request appear to be dependent. Most people respond favorably to such a request. Hopefully the request will present an opportunity to tell the Good News of salvation to the person who is truly needy. Asking for a favor is much like the importance of doing a kind, but unexpected, deed for someone. Finding opportunities to present the gospel message is just that simple. One wonders why more of God's people are not actively creating such opportunities. Maybe Christians are not very concerned to tell sinners the Good News?

The woman responded to Jesus' request for a drink, and that gave Him the opportunity to tell her about living water (vv. 10-12). He told this needy woman that living water was a gift from God (v. 10). The poor, uninitiated woman did not understand what Jesus meant by living water. Who does? The Man from Nazareth had actually offered the Samaritan woman a running stream or spring, a cool spring that runs forever. Naturally if a person heard these words, he would think of fresh, cool, pure water. That was certainly not the kind of water that filled Jacob's well. If Jacob's well was typical, it was filled with water that seeped through the veins of rock. At best, it might have been dug into a spring, which would provide a kind of "living water" at the very bottom of the well.

However, Jesus did not offer this woman a literal spring of fresh water. That is what normal people would think about, but Jesus spoke about eternal life. Did the woman grasp that meaning? In light of her lifestyle one wonders if this woman ever had much opportunity to hear about or read the many Old Testament references to living water. Probably she was not very aware of the promises of God-given, refreshing, living water. She had probably not gone to Sunday School as a child and memorized, "As the deer pants for the water brooks, so pants my soul for You, O God" (Psalm 42:1). She probably did not know the promise, "He shall be like a tree planted by the rivers of water, that brings forth its fruit in its season, whose leaf also shall not wither; and whatever he does shall prosper" (Psalm 1:3). Because this woman only had the Pentateuch for a Bible, she did not know that God promised, "Therefore with joy you will draw water from the wells of salvation" (Isaiah 12:3). Nor did she know that God promised, "I will pour water on him who is thirsty, and floods on the dry ground; I will pour My Spirit on your descendants, and My blessing on your offspring" (Isaiah 44:3).

The woman at the well was very much like many people in modern America who are unaware of the great promises in Scripture about eternal life. Why are they unaware? Jesus explained to this woman that if she understood what He offered she would have asked for it. She did not ask for the gift because she did not perceive the truth. She was like all sinners who walk in darkness until God opens their eyes to the light of truth. Paul described sinners as people, "whose minds the god of this age has blinded, who do not believe, lest the light of the gospel of the glory of Christ, who is the image of God, should shine on them" (2 Corinthians 4:4). What a hopeless situation! But because God is gracious the story does not end on a hopeless note. Two verses after describing the sad condition of sinners Paul declared that, "it is the God who commanded light to shine out of darkness, who has shone in our hearts to *give* the light of the knowledge of the glory of God in the face of Jesus Christ" (2 Corinthians 4:6).

God longs to give light. God longs for people to desire the living water. But this woman didn't ask for the gift. She was so typical of sinners. Why didn't she want eternal life? The woman was confused.

She was confined to thinking in human terms (vv. 11-12). She reminded Jesus that the well was deep, that He had no bucket or rope, and therefore, could not understand where He planned to get the fresh running water or how He could get it. Mere humans must think in human terms.

Jesus did not argue with the woman about logistics. Instead He told her about the advantage of living water (vv. 13-15). He taught that the living water He offered is eternal (vv. 13-14). The experience of millions of Christians affirms that the person who drinks of Christ's water will be satisfied. Indeed, satisfaction with Christ is self-perpetuating for eternity. It never ends. That kind of satisfaction is the great need of the modern American culture that is enslaved to sin. It is sad to observe foolish Christians flirting with sin because they have forgotten how satisfying Jesus Christ is. What kind of testimony is that to sinners whose sin leaves them spiritually parched? Christians who forget the refreshing nature of fellowship in Christ will seldom encourage sinners to be refreshed in Jesus.

Jesus also explained the benefit of eternal life to this needy woman. He told her about everlasting satisfaction, but this poor woman was still concerned with temporal matters (v. 15). She desired only physical satisfaction. Her whole life was focused on temporal things. While Jesus spoke of eternal spiritual satisfaction, the woman could only think about the relief of not having to travel a half mile every day to satisfy her physical thirst. This is a common response for sinners. Most people are not interested in a new birth that will make them different than they are and different than their peers. They want satisfaction within their current circumstances. Why are they unable to grasp an understanding of eternal satisfaction? They do not understand how thirsty they really are. Jesus showed how to deal with that lack of understanding.

Jesus Revealed The Truth

Jesus, the man from Nazareth, offered the woman eternal refreshment through salvation. The woman could not see beyond her temporal need. What can one say to awaken such a person to her real need? Jesus accomplished that task by revealing the truth about the woman (vv. 16-18). This woman was a notorious sinner and Jesus put His finger right on the problem (vv. 16-18). Out of the blue (it seems) Jesus said, "Go call your husband." What did that have to do with the conversation? Everything! It was obvious that the woman was trying to conceal her sin. Apparently she had practiced that lifestyle for years. She lived in denial, but Jesus uncovered the truth. He pointed out that she was guilty of sin and explained the extent of her sin. He detailed the fact that over the years the woman had five different husbands and was, at that time, living with a different man out of wedlock (v. 18). Many people would accuse Jesus of being terribly unkind to the sinful woman. Today people wonder why Christ was not more tolerant of her sin. The Christian who honestly loves sinners will be compelled by love to uncover the truth that illustrates how thirsty those sinners really are.

It is interesting to compare Jesus' conversation with Nicodemus and His conversation with this woman. He did not need to tell Nicodemus that he was a sinner. The teacher of the Jews came to Jesus looking for answers about the kingdom of God because he was aware of his needy condition. This woman was blind to her need. The gospel message is one message of hope for sinners. But the messenger must take each sinner's condition into consideration when he shares the good news. All needy people do not have the same background or the same knowledge.

The good news is that this woman faced her condition —sort of (v. 17a). She responded to Jesus' accusation with a very brief answer. Up to this point the woman had been quite conversational, but suddenly her answer consisted of three words (in the Greek). "I am having no husband" was a feeble attempt to cover the reality of her condition. She could have bluntly confessed what Jesus already knew, but human nature chaffs at exposure of sin.

Jesus revealed true worship (vv. 19-24) to this needy sinner. The woman tried to deflect the truth (vv. 19-20). Her feeble efforts to side step the truth failed because the Prophet who knows the secrets of every heart was her inquisitor. She willingly acknowledged that Jesus was very discerning, and yet she did not confess her sins to Him. In fact, it appears that the woman tried to change the subject (v. 20). She suddenly introduced the difference of worship methodology between Jews and Samaritans. She was obviously trying to change the subject away from her sin, trying to deflect Jesus' penetrating knowledge of her heart. At the same time, her question about worship might have been evidence that the woman was searching for the solution to her sinful lifestyle.

Jesus taught the important lesson that true worship occurs in the heart (vv. 21-24). The place of worship is not the key (v. 21). God's creation must worship God according to His nature. God is true, so our worship must be rooted in the truth of His Word (v. 23-24). God is spirit, so our worship must flow from obedient hearts, not simply be outward expressions (vv. 23-24). True worship is the result of salvation (v. 22). Since God is seeking people to worship Him He must also desire for all people to be born again (v. 23).

Finally, Jesus revealed the only hope for the sinful woman (vv. 25-26). In light of His teaching about worship, the woman wondered about Messiah (v. 25). Probably someone had taught her about Messiah. Maybe she had heard about John the Baptist's message that described Messiah as the anointed servant of God. Whatever else she understood, this woman was sure that Messiah would have the right answers about worship. She sounded like many people who are looking for that magic formula, that special person, that unique religion that will open their understanding.

This woman longed for the One who would unfold the truth about all matters. Jesus kindly introduced her to Messiah, the One with the answers (v. 26). Why did she not discern from their conversation that the man from Nazareth was Messiah? He promised eternal life, and she didn't get it. He uncovered the secrets of her heart, and she didn't get it. Did she ever receive Jesus Christ as her Savior? When she testified to the men of the town, she still wondered if this was Christ (v. 29). There is no clear statement regarding her salvation. Her testimony, recorded in verse thirty-nine, does not prove salvation. Complete faith in Christ alone (v. 42) proved that the men of the city had been born again. They were saved because they believed in His word (v. 41). Maybe this woman was like many other people who hear the good news. They hear it, they are impressed for awhile, but the cares of this world choke out the word. Too often Satan snatches away the seed of the gospel, or it drys up and withers away because it does not find root. In spite of rejection or unconcern, the word of the gospel stands true. The fact that Jesus of Nazareth alone is the eternal hope of a world held fast in the grips of sin never changes. He is the only hope for sinners to assuage their spiritual thirst because He is God.

CHAPTER 6

JESUS REVEALED THE COST OF FOLLOWING HIM

MATTHEW 8:18-22 (LUKE 9:57-62)

During the War Between the States, the armies from the North and the South had to deal with the problem of desertion. It seems that when the war began, thousands of young Southern boys jumped on the bandwagon to pull their states out of the union. At the same time, thousands of young Northern boys rallied to keep their southern friends from seceding. No doubt their young hearts thrilled as they heard the bands play, participated in the rallies, and watched the soldiers marching past dressed in new uniforms and carrying shiny new weapons. An enthralled heart might cause a young man to join the military in any age. Youngsters were quick to join their respective armies, but once the rigors of war set in, many of the boys changed their minds. Apparently, many of those young men believed the war was going to last only a few months. Most of their political leaders had told them that would be the case. When it became obvious that the war was going to drag on for a long time, hundreds of young soldiers abandoned the armies.

The glitz and glamour of marching armies can be impressive. But an army of young men and women who only want to wear neat uniforms and carry shiny rifles is not going to be very effective in war.

This picture leads one to question how many people there are in churches today who are happy to wear the uniform of Christianity, but who are not willing to do battle for the Lord's army. Maybe these faint-hearted Christian soldiers were recruited by super-salesmen who told them that joining the Lord's army would add meaning to life. Maybe someone promised that being in the Lord's army would pave life's road with ease. Maybe they joined in order to gain wonderful rewards. Faint-hearted Christian soldiers might wear the uniform of the Lord's army, but they are seldom prepared for a lengthy conflict and they are seldom willing to endure to the end. The overwhelming evidence throughout the past few years seems to indicate that when the spiritual war clouds begin to form on the horizon many of these would-be soldiers go AWOL.

That being true, one must wonder if people who are not willing to face difficulties associated with following Christ are truly born again. Jesus dealt with the issue of faithful followers who do faithful service during His ministry. Matthew and Luke recorded an incident where three different people seriously considered the possibility of becoming Christ's disciples. However, when the man from Nazareth explained His expectations, the would-be disciples walked away never to be heard from again. Jesus Christ `never soft-peddled the gospel nor its requirements. Many modern soul winners inadvertently teach that Jesus' method of recruiting followers was flawed. He made it difficult for people to follow Him because He told them the truth, the whole truth, and nothing but the truth. Christ's conversation with these three would-be disciples should cause all professing Christians to reevaluate their dedication to Him. Are we really in the Lord's army or are we just wearing the uniform. If Jesus of Nazareth was just another man, people would be foolish to sacrifice for Him. If, as it is, Jesus was God in the flesh, no cost can be too great to deter us from following Him.

Following Christ Is Not Always Convenient

The first volunteer Matthew wrote about (Luke also recorded this story) was a scribe. He willingly volunteered to follow the Christ, the man from Nazareth (vv. 18-19). This scribe approached Jesus about joining His followers and becoming a disciple at about the same time

Jesus was preparing to go to the less populated, and less friendly area of the Gergesenes (v. 18). It is important to remember that a move to a less friendly area is the context for these conversations about discipleship.

Probably in the days just prior to this event, Jesus had been ministering in Capernaum. During that time, He healed Peter's mother-in-law, healed many other sick people, and cast out many demons. Matthew rightly saw this part of Jesus' ministry as a clear fulfillment of the promise God gave through Isaiah regarding Messiah. Isaiah foretold that Messiah, "has borne our griefs and carried our sorrows; yet we esteemed Him stricken, smitten by God, and afflicted" (Isaiah 53:4). Matthew's insight and application of that promise sets the stage for the question of discipleship. How ironic that at a time when Jesus of Nazareth could have been accepting men's praise, He was instead associated with sickness, pain, and sorrow. Jesus understood His ministry well and knew what He should be doing. He had taught his followers that, "The Son of Man did not come to be served, but to serve, and to give His life a ransom for many" (Mark 10:45). His ministry was a work of giving, serving, and suffering. His glorified reign will come later.

Furthermore, when the scribe stopped Jesus in order to offer his allegiance, Jesus was preparing to go to a foreboding region (Matthew 8:28-34). Ministry in such a place fits well with the context of Jesus' suffering and rejection by many. The country of the Gergesenes was a desolate place. According to verse twenty-eight in this chapter, when Jesus and His entourage arrived on the shores of that region, He went among the tombs. He went to that unwelcome place for the express purpose of healing two demon possessed men (vv. 29-32). He met the two men and quickly released them from the power of Satan. Immediately, the men showed clear evidence that their lives had been changed. But after Christ healed the men, the townspeople raised their voices in protest and begged Jesus to leave their area. Matthew wrote that, "The whole city came out to meet Jesus. And when they saw Him, they begged Him to depart from their region" (Matthew 8:34). That is incredible! It is a revelation of the nature of fallen humanity. The sorrow, disappointment, and pain of fallen humanity; the context of suffering and trial, is the environment of service for discipleship.

Would a scribe actually be willing to go with Jesus to a barren region where He was not welcome? It was amazing that a scribe even volunteered for service to Jesus Christ (v. 19). He obviously held great respect and esteem for Jesus of Nazareth. It is significant that the scribe addressed Jesus as "Teacher." That is a surprising address because the scribe was a teacher himself. In fact, he was a chief of teachers. The people considered scribes to be among the chief authorities in Israel. Scribes taught Israelites how to live and how to love God. Scribes really believed that they, and the people, could fulfill the Law of God. Therefore, most of the scribes were offended when Jesus claimed that they could not possibly fulfill God's law through their human strength and wisdom. There is no doubt that the majority of this scribe's coworkers were stringently opposed to Jesus' work. Eventually the scribes as a whole joined efforts with other Jewish leaders, (Pharisees and Sadducees), in order to kill Jesus.

Nevertheless, a scribe, who was quite different than his peers, addressed Jesus with the highest term of respect. His words proved that he saw Jesus as the teacher's teacher. Was he kidding? Was he just trying to trick Jesus or discover what it took to be a disciple? Not at all. The story reveals that this scribe was very sincere about volunteering to work in Jesus' ministry. No one coerced him to volunteer. He came willingly. He not only sought out Jesus and willingly volunteered for service, but he even volunteered to go anywhere.

Surely, the Lord needed this man's help. A teacher of the people of Israel would certainly add much credibility to the little band of Jesus' followers. The Man from Nazareth must have been very happy to see this scribe step out of the crowd and volunteer for service. Actually, that thought expresses the limitations of human thinking. Human wisdom recruits the important people, the successful people, the people who can do the most for the organization. However, human wisdom also requires a trimming of the gospel's demands in order to make it more palatable to people like the scribes or the movers and shakers in modern society.

Because Christ is God, He thinks on the divine level. He knows the heart of each person which means that He knew the thoughts and motives the scribe harbored in his heart. Jeremiah 17:9 teaches that the God understands our hearts better than we who own the hearts. Because of this knowledge Jesus' response to the willing scribe seems almost rude or uncaring. Because the Christ is omniscient, and because He knew the scribe's most secret motivations, His response was perfectly correct.

Jesus warned the willing scribe that discipleship is inconvenient (v. 20). He reminded the man that while animals have homes, He did not own a place to sleep. No doubt the scribe was already familiar with the habits of foxes and birds since they were plentiful in that region around Galilee. Everyone was aware of the general habits of the animals. When the bystanders heard Jesus' answer to the scribe, they might have wondered what the habits of foxes and birds had to do with a sincere offer for service.

The Lord's response hit the nail on the head. He taught this willing scribe that the follower of Christ would be affected by the Son of Man's homeless status. Unlike the animals of the wild, Jesus never owned a home. The records of Matthew, Mark, Luke, and John reveal that Jesus of Nazareth spent time at Peter's home in Capernaum, at Lazarus' home in Bethany, and that He even spent some nights out in the open air as He communed with the Father (e.g., on the Mount of Olives, John 7:53-8:1). Not only was Christ homeless during His ministry, but He was despised and rejected as well. A few verses after this story about the volunteers, Matthew recorded that the Gergesene people asked Jesus to leave their region (v. 28). Later in the ministry the people in Judah rejected Him (John 5:18). Even the people in Galilee, the place where Jesus spent most of His time, eventually cast Him out (John 6:66). The people in Samaria refused Him lodging (Luke 9:53). Ultimately, rejection by the whole world was voiced by the mob when they shouted, "Crucify Him!" (Matthew 27:23).

The scribe was sincere. He promised, "I'll follow You wherever You go." Jesus replied, "You don't seem to understand that the Son of Man doesn't even own a bed." Chronologically, this is the first use of the term "Son of Man" in the New Testament. The title carries important ramifications regarding the Lord's character and ministry. This term alone is sufficient to define the cost and rewards of discipleship. On the one hand, it points to humiliation and sacrifice. For example, Jesus taught the twelve disciples, "that Elijah has come already, and they did not know him but did to him whatever they wished. Likewise the Son of Man is also about to suffer at their hands" (Matthew 17:12). In a similar way, Jesus frequently used the term "Son of Man" in connection with His pending humiliation and suffering.

On the other hand, the title, "Son of Man," speaks of Jesus' exaltation. The first time the title is used in the Bible is in Daniel 7:13

where Daniel described how he, "was watching in the night visions, and behold, One like the Son of Man, coming with the clouds of heaven! He came to the Ancient of Days, and they brought Him near before Him." Daniel's vision guarantees that this same Son of Man, who suffered humiliation and shame at the hands of the wicked crucifiers, will return to earth and reign in supreme power. Jesus Christ also confirmed this truth when He responded to the High Priest's accusation at His trial by saying, "It is as you said. Nevertheless, I say to you, hereafter you will see the Son of Man sitting at the right hand of the Power, and coming on the clouds of heaven" (Matthew 26:64). The Son of Man, who appeared to be weak while He was on earth, will be mighty in eternity.

Jesus attempted to help the willing scribe understand that anyone who followed Him would be affected by that stigma of humiliation before there would be any exaltation. That is the same lesson Jesus taught the disciples. He warned them that, "if the world hates you, you know that it hated Me before it hated you" (John 15:18). The same principle applies to every disciple of Jesus Christ in every age. Paul warned Christians that "all who desire to live godly in Christ Jesus will suffer persecution" (2 Timothy 3:12).

Did the scribe join up? It doesn't appear that he did. Instead it appears that the man left! There is no record that the man joined the ranks of the disciples even though Jesus did not forbid him from following. He volunteered not to follow because it was too difficult to be closely associated with the man from Nazareth who would be despised and rejected. It still is.

Following Christ Is Not Always Financially Profitable

Shortly after the scribe left another disciple stepped forward and volunteered to follow Christ—with a provision (v. 21). If this man was a disciple, why was he not already following Jesus? In this verse, Matthew used the term disciple in a broad sense. Often the term "disciple" referred to a person who had forsaken everything and everyone in order to become just like the teacher. It gained that meaning during the age of Greek philosophers when men gladly abandoned all relationships and goals in life in order to spend every minute with the famous teachers. That was the cost for becoming just like the teacher. Therefore, the term disciple would most appropriately describe the people who followed Jesus. It is still an appropriate word to describe His devout followers.

However, the same term can also describe a person who followed a teacher or a movement loosely or at a distance. In that case, the word "disciple" referred to the people who followed Jesus simply because He fed them or because His miracles excited them or entertained them. Sadly, this shallow use of disciple is the most accurate way to describe many people who call themselves Christians in this age.

The disciple in this story was thinking very seriously about giving up all to follow Jesus. Probably he expressed a legitimate desire to follow Jesus. He really wanted to follow Jesus, but before making an all-out commitment to Christ, he wanted to go home and bury his father. What could possibly be wrong with that? The disciple simply expressed a desire that everyone in that culture held to be most noble. Unlike the ancient Egyptians and modern Americans who embalm their dead, the Israelites buried their dead immediately after the person passed away. Jewish teachers taught that burying a dead relative ranked as the highest expression of kindness. Surely Jesus would let the man go home and take care of this matter!

In response to the man's offer for service, Jesus warned that to be His disciple he would have to forsake potential financial gain (v. 22). What did financial gain have to do with burying the dead? Actually when this man expressed the desire to bury his father, he meant more than appears on the surface. His conditional offer really required that he go back home and wait until after he had collected his inheritance before following Jesus. In several ancient cultures, the phrase "bury my father" commonly referred to waiting until the father died. When the father died, the rightful heirs buried him, and then they collected their inheritance.

Is that really what this disciple wanted to do? Remember that he lived in a culture that buried their dead immediately. If this disciple's father had just died, why was he among the crowd that was with Jesus? If his father had actually died he would have been at home burying him. It is more likely that this disciple used the common phrase to talk about going home and waiting until Dad died so that he could get the rightful inheritance. That could have taken years.

Jesus knew the man's heart and realized that he was not ready to sacrifice all things in order to follow Him. At this point it is important to remember that Jesus Christ does not give the same test to everyone. He does not make "staying at home waiting for the inheritance" a test for every disciple anymore than He requires everyone to sell all that they have and follow Him. That was the Lord's response to the young rich man (Luke 18:18-23). Jesus knows each servant's heart. He is fully aware of any idol, any false god, that interferes with full service for Him. Our Lord knows that idol that keeps us from full surrender. Each servant's test of dedication will be directed at that individual's idols. What are you unwilling to give up in order to serve Christ fully? That is the pressing question.

Jesus told the disciple that spiritually dead people are concerned with financial well-being. It seems that financial gain was the idol that kept this disciple from genuine service. Therefore, Jesus told the man to let the people who are spiritually dead spend their lives waiting for financial rewards. Spiritual life demands better. Spiritual life compels the disciple to forsake all and follow the Lord. This is a difficult test to pass. Following Christ demands a break with the natural desires of the flesh first. Jesus did not tell this man to go away. He pointed out the cost of following and then left it up to the man to make the decision. It appears that this man also left. An honest assessment about the demands of the gospel leaves very few honest disciples to follow Christ.

Following Christ Is Not Always Popular

Luke's account of Jesus' ministry included a third man in this scenario (Luke 9:61-62). This man volunteered to follow Christ, but only after he took care of common courtesies (v. 61). This man called Jesus from Nazareth, "Lord." That is a pretty clear indication that he had already decided to follow Jesus. The title reveals that the man recognized Christ's authority. The use of the title alone does not always prove that the one calling Jesus "Lord" is fully committed to follow Him. It's possible for religious folks to recognize Christ's authority over nature, or over others, but not over them. Admitting that Jesus deserves to be Lord is not the same as allowing Him to be Lord of our lives.

This man, like the previous two would-be disciples, volunteered to follow Jesus Christ apart from an invitation or any coercing from Jesus. Such a willing volunteer must represent a person who is truly born again! Not necessarily. Notice that this would-be follower expressed the desire to go home and bid farewell to family before he followed the Lord in earnest. What could be wrong with saying, "Good-bye" to family and friends? Jesus' response pointed out how dangerous it is to put any kind of qualification on following Christ. It is true that most Christian leaders would be delighted to have three volunteers like these fellows offer their services. But Jesus fleshes out true motives first.

Jesus did not give this man a position on the roster either. He warned the man that looking back disqualifies volunteers (v. 62). He told the man that his desire to go back home disqualified him, and He used a common illustration of the plowman to drive the point home. A farmer can plow a straight furrow only as long as he keeps his eye on a target at the end of the field. When he removes his eye from that point of focus, the furrow he is plowing will almost certainly get crooked. A crooked furrow is obvious to everyone. Jesus used that simply illustration to reveal that this man's desire to go back to his family was an indication that he was already taking his eyes off the goal of devout service.

Jesus' lesson was plain. Discipleship costs everything. Jesus' call to follow writes a completely new chapter in the disciple's life. Everything must change. All of his or her plans and desires must come into conformity with the Master's will. Attempts to hang on to the old way while doing the new task are like a person quitting a job but still trying to work for the old boss. It cannot work. True discipleship requires the death of self. Are we willing to pay the extreme price? The three volunteers thought that they were, but Jesus knew their hearts.

Jesus knew that this third volunteer would yield to the pressure of his family in the time of testing. God loves the family but also warns that unspiritual family members can deter a servant from following. God gives many instructions about establishing a strong, God-honoring family. At the same time God also warns about the danger of interference from family. Jesus warned:

Do not think that I came to bring peace on earth. I did not come to bring peace but a sword. For I have come to set a man against his father, a daughter against her mother, and a daughter-in-law against her mother-in-law; and a man's enemies will be those of his own household. He who loves father or mother more than Me is not worthy of Me. And he who loves son or daughter more than Me is not worthy of Me. And he who does not take his cross and follow after Me is not worthy of Me. (Matthew 10:34-38)

It appears that this man walked away too. How sad. He demonstrated a scenario repeated too often. What could be sadder than people who sit before a preacher, exposed to the Bible, having heard many warnings and invitations, and still walk away from Christ? Are you really a disciple of Jesus Christ, or have you placed stipulations on your offer? There is a stigma attached to being one of Christ's true disciples. The world thinks that suffering with Christ is a terrible thing, but His faithful servants know that it is a wonderfully encouraging thing. It marks the servant as one of Christ's. It would indeed be fool hearty to sacrifice everything in life to follow a zealot who made such wrong choices that he ended up getting crucified. It is a different story altogether to sacrifice everything in order to follow the God of creation who gave Himself to save us from the penalty of sin. Complete sacrifice to follow such a God is wise and rewarding.

AD 28

CHAPTER 7

JESUS CHALLENGED JOHN'S FAITH

MATTHEW 11:1-6

Yogi Berra is credited with saying a lot of things that seem senseless at first. One of his pithy sayings was, "It ain't over till it's over!" That makes sense. Essentially, the master of understatement meant that we need to be careful not to draw conclusions too quickly because the story might not end in the expected way. Unexpected things do happen.

Some Bible statements affirm the same practical wisdom. In ancient Bible times Ben-Hadad, the king of Syria, gathered his forces together and besieged Samaria, the capital of Israel. He ordered king Ahab to surrender because he didn't stand a chance against the mighty Syrian army. Ahab replied, "Tell him, 'Let not the one who puts on his armor boast like the one who takes it off'" (1 Kings 20:11). Solomon taught, "Do not boast about tomorrow, for you do not know what a day may bring forth" (Proverbs 27:1). He also observed that, "under the sun that the race is not to the swift, nor the battle to the strong, nor bread to the wise, nor riches to men of understanding, nor favor to men of skill; but time and chance happen to them all" (Ecclesiastes 9:11).

Solomon's conclusions taught the reality of human finiteness. No one really knows what tomorrow holds. We make plans and draw conclusions based on the evidence on hand, but sometimes that evidence is insufficient. Is that to conclude that everything is left to chance? Actually, Solomon's conclusion at the end of Ecclesiastes acknowledged that all things are not a matter of chance but are determined by God. Life is not a matter of fate, but a matter of God's sovereign control. Therefore, it is wise to look to God for wisdom and guidance in life. Sometimes life gets confusing and it becomes difficult to understand what, if anything, God is doing. However, genuine faith in God leaves Him to accomplish what is best. Real faith in God helps explain how all things work together for good for those who love God and are called according to His purpose.

Time is always on the side of truth. Those who wait patiently on God will eventually understand how He always acts according to His word. His word expresses His wisdom. When God's wisdom comes to bear, His people are glad they trusted Him.

John Doubted

John the Baptist sent representatives, some of his disciples, to Jesus in order to discover if He was really the Messiah he himself had introduced (vv. 1-3). He couldn't go to Jesus himself because he was in prison (vv. 1-2). It must have been difficult for John to sit in prison while Jesus was busy teaching and preaching in the cities in Galilee. That alone would be enough to make John wonder if he had misunderstood something about Jesus from Nazareth. Sometime during Jesus' lengthy ministry in Galilee, John needed to know the truth about the man from Nazareth.

It was important for Jesus to do much of His ministry away from the attention of main-city Jerusalem and in areas where the authorities would not expect to find Messiah displaying His power and mercy. The movers and shakers of the day would have expected to find Messiah in the key metropolitan areas, especially in Jerusalem, the capital city of God's people. But Jesus was working in the rural region of Galilee where He called people to make right decisions, exhorted them to come along side His standard, and challenged them to enter the kingdom. Those are all characteristics of good preaching. While John was sitting in prison he heard that Jesus went to the cities to preach.

In ministry, Jesus also unfolded the truths about God's Scriptures (the Old Testament) and applied those truths so that the people understood how they should live. That is the word teach. John also heard that Jesus went to the cities to teach.

John must have also heard that Jesus was doing many other good works such as healing the sick, raising the dead, casting out demons, and calling sinners like Matthew and his friends to repentance (9:9-13).

News of Jesus' ministry caused John to wonder what was wrong. Jesus was preaching, teaching and doing good, while he, Messiah's forerunner, was sitting in prison. Herod Antipas had placed him there. Matthew 4:12 states that Herod put John in prison, and Matthew 14:1-12 explains why. The extra-biblical story says that at some point Herod Antipas (the Tetrarch) had visited his brother Philip in Rome. While he was there, Antipas fell in love with Philip's wife, Herodias. He returned home, divorced his own wife, and then lured Herodias away from Philip and married her. John was a preacher of righteousness. When he saw how this guy who was ruling over God's people disregarded God's law, he boldly confronted the king with his sin. Herod, like most sinners, did not appreciate John commenting on his private life, and put John in prison at the palace at Machaerus. This palace was located on the eastern shore of the Dead Sea. John never left the prison. Eventually Herod had him beheaded in order to satisfy the wrath of his wife Herodias.

John sat in prison in the desert hearing about all the wonderful things Jesus was doing, and he began to wonder. He began to doubt that Jesus was really the Messiah (v. 3). Why? John had faithfully preached the arrival of the kingdom. His conscience was clear on that matter. Matthew wrote that, "In those days John the Baptist came preaching in the wilderness of Judea, and saying, 'Repent, for the kingdom of heaven is at hand!'" (Matthew 3:1-2). He had cried out against sin telling the crowd of seekers, "Even now the ax is laid to the root of the trees. Therefore every tree which does not bear good fruit is cut down and thrown into the fire" (Matthew 3:10). He had faithfully uncovered the religious hypocrites. "But when he saw many of the Pharisees and Sadducees coming to his baptism, he said to them, 'Brood of vipers! Who warned you to flee from the wrath to come?'" (Matthew 3:7). John was so sure about God's standard of righteousness that he even exposed the king's sin. He "said to Herod, 'It is not lawful for you to have your brother's wife'" (Mark 6:18).

John had thundered the standard of righteousness. Now he was confused! He had cried out to announce the King, His kingdom, and repentance, but landed in jail. How could he explain that? The King he introduced to the world had been going about freely for the past year doing good things, teaching, and preaching. What kind of king was that? Where was Messiah's army that would free God's people from Rome? Where was the kingdom? Where was justice?

John truly misunderstood God's timetable. He believed that Messiah would establish the actual kingdom of Israel as soon as He showed up in Jerusalem. That was not the case. John did not understand that God has a different plan. He has been working from the time of Messiah's advent until this present day to establish the spiritual kingdom. There are still many sinners for God to redeem and add to His people. Messiah came to provide the means for people to enter His spiritual kingdom (i.e. salvation). The literal, physical kingdom of Israel will come later during the Millennium.

Who would be the first person to step up and accuse John for having weak faith? Who is not like him? God's people are limited to observe all of God's work within their own little timetable or their own meager scope of time. God sees all of human history against the backdrop of eternity at one moment. Far better for near sighted Christians to allow for the unseen and unknown. Great reward is found in realizing that God sees and knows all things all the time. Trusting God when circumstances do not make sense helps weak faith grow strong. Growing faith becomes great faith, but only through difficult circumstances.

John's representatives stated John's questions to Jesus, and Jesus sent them back to John with good news (vv. 4-6). He told John's disciples that He was busy doing good works (vv. 4-5). Surely that was not new information to them. They must have heard about Jesus' mighty works. Everyone seemed to know that He was a powerful preacher and teacher. Jesus told John's friends to tell John that He was doing exactly what God promised the Messiah would do. God had promised through Isaiah the prophet that, "In that day the deaf shall hear the words of the book, and the eyes of the blind shall see out of obscurity and out of darkness" (Isaiah 29:18). Isaiah had promised seven hundred years earlier that when Messiah came, "The eyes of the blind shall be opened, and the ears of the deaf shall be unstopped. Then the lame shall leap like a deer, and the tongue of the dumb sing" (Isaiah 35:5-6a). He had promised that Messiah would rightfully claim, "The Spirit of the Lord GOD is upon Me, because the Lord has anointed Me to preach good tidings to the poor; He has sent Me to heal the brokenhearted, to proclaim liberty to the captives, and the opening of the prison to those who are bound" (Isaiah 61:1). John needed to know that Jesus from Nazareth was doing precisely what the prophets said Messiah would do.

When John preached in the wilderness near the Jordan River, he had helped the people see the reality of their sins. Jesus helped those who acknowledged and confessed sin to see great hope in the good news. Both John and Jesus exposed sin. But Jesus' ministry made God's mercy more obvious. Both of those traits describe the ministry Jesus left with His people. The Christian's ministry must expose sin and, at the same time, reveal God's mercy. It is foolish to offer God's mercy to people who do not understand that their sins have offended the holy God. It is just as foolish to expose a person's sin without offering hope that God will forgive him.

Jesus sent John's disciples back to him with a blessing (v. 6). One could easily conclude that Jesus should have rebuked John because his faith was weak. In fact, Jesus did rebuke John gently. He rebuked His friend for being offended. He also promised John that he would receive a blessing if he did not get offended by Jesus' work.

Jesus Praised John

As John's disciples were leaving, Jesus told the crowd that John was a great success. Maybe John's representatives heard His words while they were leaving. Jesus reminded the people that they themselves had affirmed John's greatness (vv. 7-9). Their response to John's preaching proved that they had pursued a great man (vv. 7-8). The people did not leave their homes and jobs and travel for two days into the dusty desert to see a wavering reed. Thy flocked to hear the preacher who stood firm like an oak tree in his convictions. John was not like chameleon preachers who preached whatever was expedient at the time. He was unlike some of the religious leaders who purposely preached to please the masses. Jesus assured the crowd that John was not a softy. Many of the religious leaders concluded that he was radical. Matthew's description of John's appearance and practice reveal how radical John was. "And John himself was clothed in camel's hair, with a leather belt around his waist; and his food was locusts and wild honey" (Matthew 3:4). They went out to see the preacher who lived in the desert. By today's standard, it would be an understatement to say that John lived an austere lifestyle. He was serious about his work. The people flocked to hear him and many were identified with his ministry through baptism. Jesus reminded the crowd that John was not a waverer.

Many of the people in the crowd had affirmed that John was a success because they had acknowledged that he was a prophet (v. 9). They trekked out into the desert to listen to a man who spoke God's message. History proves that Herod Antipas was reticent to harm John because he feared the masses who considered John to be a prophet (Matthew 14:5).

But John was more than just another prophet. Jesus said that he was the greatest of prophets (vv. 10-15). He was the prophet God had promised to be Messiah's forerunner (vv. 10-11, 13-14). John was the special prophet God had promised through the Old Testament prophet Malachi (3:1). Jesus even said that John was the greatest person born of women. Jesus was the greatest man ever born, but His birth was not normal since Mary was a virgin. John was the greatest human born through normal means (v. 11). John's ministry was the capstone of all the prophecies in the law and the prophets (v. 13). Everything in the past had pointed to Messiah's arrival, but John introduced the Messiah to the people. John was the second Elijah (v.14). When the angel foretold John's birth to his father Zacharias, he promised that John would, "also go before Him [Messiah] in the spirit and power of Elijah, to turn the hearts of the fathers to the children, and the disobedient to the wisdom of the just, to make ready a people prepared for the Lord" (Luke 1:17). The people needed to accept John as the messenger God sent. Why?

John was so important because he plainly announced the invitation to enter God's kingdom (vv. 12, 15). God used John to pave the way for the kingdom (v. 12). That entrance is amazing. Verse twelve indicates that it involves great vigor or zeal.

However, before we get excited about entering the kingdom, we need to know what the kingdom is. Which kingdom did John announce? The term kingdom, as it is used to refer to God's kingdom in the Bible, has a future literal aspect and a present spiritual aspect. In both cases, the kingdom is where Christ the King reigns supremely. The literal kingdom will be viable during the millennium when Christ will reign from an actual throne in Jerusalem. The spiritual kingdom is viable right now where Christ reigns as king on the throne of His people's hearts. The present spiritual kingdom is manifested in the universal Church. In John's day and in Jesus' day, the kingdom of God was a spiritual kingdom, a matter of salvation, like it is today. Therefore, Jesus said that from the time that John introduced the kingdom until the time He was speaking, Christ's work of redeeming sinners from sin is pressing on. He promised that no power from hell can stop it.

Jesus also taught that everyone who enters the kingdom does so vigorously. No one enters the kingdom of God accidentally. In other words, no one is going to be surprised to be in heaven. The person who would enter heaven must be vigorous to that end. No one will enter heaven without vigor because the way is too difficult. Jesus taught that we must, "Enter by the narrow gate; for wide is the gate and broad is the way that leads to destruction, and there are many who go in by it. Because narrow is the gate and difficult is the way which leads to life, and there are few who find it" (Matthew 7:13-14). The New Testament reveals evidence of the vigor that accompanies entrance into the kingdom of heaven. On Pentecost, Peter preached the good news of salvation to sinners who he indicated were responsible for crucifying the Christ. Peter taught that their sins were the reason that Jesus Christ was crucified. That principle is still valid. The people who heard Peter realized the gravity of their sins and responded with vigor. Luke recorded that when they heard Peter's message, "they were cut to the heart, and said to Peter and the rest of the apostles, 'Men and brethren, what shall we do?'" (Acts 2:37). They were shook to the depths of their souls by the message of the kingdom. Likewise, when the Philippian jailer was under great conviction of sin through God's grace, "He called for a light, ran in, and fell down trembling before Paul and Silas. And he brought them out and said, 'Sirs, what must I do to be saved?'" (Acts 16:29-30). Those are illustrations of entering the Kingdom through great vigor.

69

Jesus challenged the crowd to listen to John's message. God sent him and that meant that he was a special preacher. God still longs for sinners to hear His message. Everyone who can hear ought to listen (v. 15). But most people choose to ignore God's message. This temporary life on earth is too attractive to people. There is so much to enjoy and experience that people do not take time to consider God's invitation to enter the kingdom of heaven for eternity. People in Jesus' generation responded in a similar way.

Jesus Rebuked His Generation

Jesus told the crowd that their generation was incorrigible (vv. 16-19). More precisely Jesus meant that the people in the crowd that day were incorrigible. He pictured them as children playing in the marketplace (vv. 16-17). That was a common illustration of fickle-ness with which all of the listeners would have been familiar. They understood what Jesus meant. They had observed their own children entertaining themselves while the parents shopped and visited with friends in the marketplace. It is possible that playing wedding and funeral were some of the kids' favorite pastimes since those were also the biggest social events of life. On any given day, some of the children wanted to play wedding and begin piping happy music on the flute. But other children preferred not to play wedding. So the kids turned to playing funeral instead. Then there were the stubborn kids who did not want to play either wedding or funeral. Jesus' story illustrated the fact that nothing pleases all of the people all the time, and that some folks are never pleased any of the time.

The people should have understood the story. In order to assure that the people in the crowd did not miss His point, Jesus applied the principle of fickleness to their own contradictory responses to God's messengers (vv. 18-19). Jesus of Nazareth explained to the people that they had gladly accepted John until they realized that he required them to confess and forsake sin. When they discovered that confession of sin was required, they concluded that John was unnaturally austere, maybe even demon possessed (v. 18). In similar fashion the crowds rallied around Jesus instead, because He did compassionate works. But after awhile the religious leaders convinced them that the man from Nazareth could not really be righteous and reach out to sinners at the same time (v. 19). So the multitudes rejected Him too. Was this unimportant? Was it just a matter of fads or passing popularity? Not at all. A proper response to Jesus and His gospel is the most important decision each person must make in life. It is a decision with eternal ramifications.

John had introduced the man from Nazareth to the multitude, telling them that He was Messiah. Within a few months he wondered why Messiah was not overthrowing Rome. He doubted. The multitude clamored after John until he required a commitment from them. They turned to the man from Nazareth who taught well and did magnificent works. But when Jesus rebuked them for their fickleness, they would abandon Him also.

The people proved that time always reveals the truth. Jesus confronted them with that important principle according to verse nineteen where the Bible states that He taught that wisdom is justified by her children. He drew a picture of children praising wisdom. Proverbs 31:28-31 says that the excellent wife's, "children rise up and call her blessed; her husband also, and he praises her" (v. 28). Since that is true, others are admonished to, "Give her of the fruit of her hands, and let her own works praise her in the gates." (v. 31). In other words, the excellent wife's fruits will eventually tell the truth about her. The resulting works of wisdom always justify or verify the presence and exercise of wisdom.

Jesus, the man from Nazareth, is the Christ. The Christ is God's wisdom incarnate. The modern world scoffs at Jesus' teaching just like the people in Jesus' day scoffed at Him. The world still denies the reality or the purpose of Jesus' divinity and sacrificial death. The world proves their disdain for Jesus by using His name almost exclusively for cursing. But, in His wisdom God chooses that which the world calls weak to accomplish His glory (1 Corinthians 1:26-31). The world mocks Jesus' teaching and works, but one day those who scoff will regret their response. In the end the mockers will wish that they could benefit from Jesus' work of redemption, the very works they belittled throughout life. When a sinner stands before God's judgment bar it will be too late to change his or her mind. In the end, everyone will agree that Jesus is the Messiah who takes away the sins of the world. The Lord encouraged John with those words. Truly wise people are still encouraged by the same message.

CHAPTER 8

JESUS SET ASIDE HUMAN TRADITIONS

MATTHEW 12:1-8

On any given Sunday morning, people who drive past the many different kinds of church buildings can observe crowds entering or leaving the buildings. Do they ever wonder what those people do inside the buildings or why they gather together every Sunday? That is a foolish question for Christians. Surely every reasonable person knows that Sundays are for going to church. Even many irreligious people understand that God-fearing people, or at least people who claim to be Christians, will meet in church buildings on Sundays. Who made that rule? Some very religious people attend public services on Saturday. Who decided that Sunday is the only acceptable church day? Or is that just the non-negotiable rule? It has always been this way hasn't it? It is true that church going is a tradition. Our grandparents taught the tradition to our parents, and our parents taught it to us. So in the end, it really doesn't matter where a person has been all week or what he has done in the previous days, as long as he shows up for services on Sunday. Attendance at the local, family assembly, means that a person is generally okay in the eyes of fellow church goers.

If the foregoing argument is true, then the opinion of other believers becomes the sole authority for Christian habits. If tradition or habitual ceremony are the reasons for attending public church services, it would be tempting to stop participating. Maybe that is why so many former church attenders are former church attenders. If the religious observance of a rule such as church attendance is rooted in human law, people who try to keep the law will become frustrated and disillusioned. Eventually they become inconsistent, which deepens their frustration, and then they quit altogether. There must be a better reason for doing religious things. Jesus, the man from Nazareth, zeroed in on this issue regarding the religious leaders' view of the Sabbath. He uncovered their wrong reasons for observing the Sabbath and taught important lessons about living for God's glory. He taught the difference between living according to God's governing principles and living according to man's overbearing rules. No one would understand the difference better than God incarnate. No one could explain the difference better.

God Ordained The Sabbath

The religious leaders took Jesus to task because His disciples were breaking the Sabbath law. At least, it was their opinion that the disciples broke the law. They argued with Jesus on the basis of rules that God had established regarding the Sabbath. They were quite sure they understood God's regulations, and that they were the authorities in such matters. It is true that God had set down rules about the Sabbath in the law He gave to Moses. God ordained the Sabbath as a day of rest. In fact, God established the general rule for the Sabbath many years before He gave His law to His people. In order to assure that His people understood, God plainly stated His regulations for the Sabbath in the law He gave Israel at the inception of the nation.

During the subsequent forty years of wilderness wandering, (after Israel received God's law), God illustrated the concept of Sabbath rest by withholding manna on the seventh day of each week. Moses relayed the Lord's instruction to the people regarding the collection of manna. He told them that the Lord had said, "Tomorrow is a Sabbath rest, a holy Sabbath to the LORD. Bake what you will bake today, and boil what you will boil; and lay up for yourselves all that remains, to be kept until morning" (Exodus 16:23). God intended for the people to collect extra manna on the sixth day so that they would not need to collect food on the seventh day. Why? Because generations earlier God had established that the seventh day was holy to the Lord. Did the average Israelite understand that God had a special plan for the seventh day?

A quick review of the Ten Commandments proves that God was serious about the Sabbath. His law required His people to "Remember the Sabbath day, to keep it holy." He told the people they should do all of their work in six days, but the seventh day was to be the Sabbath of the Lord their God. No one, including visitors in Israel, were allowed to do any work on the Sabbath (Exodus 20:8-10). According to God's requirement, His people were to set aside the seventh day each week as a holy day, a day dedicated unto God. God held this rule to be so important that He listed it right along with other rules such as do not steal, do not murder, and do not commit adultery. Good Jews did not doubt that the Sabbath law was an important law.

All of the Ten Commandments convey God's character. Through those ten statements people can get a glimpse of what God is like. Through those requirements, a person can begin to understand what it takes to maintain a relationship with his Creator. The law regarding the Sabbath was one of the significant ten.

No doubt the expression of God's character is obvious in rules like, don't steal, don't lie, and so on, but what part of God's character is revealed by prohibiting work on the Sabbath? The command reveals that God chose to make that day holy. Since the day was holy, (i.e., set apart for God), all normal activity, such as work, was supposed to cease. A day without work provided the opportunity for God's people to meditate on Him. The Sabbath was a day when God's people could sit around and contemplate what "holy" means. That sounds unbelievable in the context of today's busy culture.

God also set apart other special days in the year or for special occasions during which His people were supposed to set aside normal activities in order to reflect on Him. Celebrations like the Feast of Trumpets were holidays when God expected His people to cease normal activities in order to focus on God's merciful care.

God was serious about these Sabbath days. He required that the leaders of His people would punish anyone who offended the Sabbath rules. His law required:

"You shall keep the Sabbath, therefore, for it is holy to you. Everyone who profanes it shall surely be put to death; for whoever does any work on it, that person shall be cut off from among his people." (Exodus 31:14)

Since death was the punishment for breaking the Sabbath law, people would certainly be careful not to do any work during those days. But someone was bound to ask, "What constitutes work?" That was a very important question. Someone with authority needed to determine what work was. Actually, God Himself hinted at what He meant by work when He warned, "You shall kindle no fire throughout your dwellings on the Sabbath day" (Exodus 35:3). A fire for cooking or staying warm was one of the basic necessities of life. But building a fire was work and God prohibited that on the Sabbath. Even picking up sticks on the Sabbath resulted in capital punishment for the offender (Numbers 15:32-36). God was very serious about Sabbath observance.

God established the rules for observing the Sabbath, then He gave the reason for His rules. He said that the people needed to cease work on the Sabbath in order to commemorate His work of creation. The connection is unmistakable. Immediately after requiring the Sabbath observance God's law reads:

"For in six days the Lord made the heavens and the earth, the sea, and all that is in them, and rested the seventh day. Therefore the Lord blessed the Sabbath day and hallowed it." (Exodus 20:11)

God said that the seventh day should be a time to reflect on His wonderful work. That naturally extended to mean that every Sabbath (holy day) was an opportunity to reflect on the works of God's mercy that He had done in behalf of His people.

Furthermore, God taught that the Sabbath was a time for rejuvenation. When Moses rehearsed this law to the Israelites, he ended the statement about observing the Sabbath by explaining that the reason for not working was so that, "your male servant and your female servant may rest as well as you" (Deuteronomy 5:14). God really wanted His people to rest once in awhile. Fortunately, Christians in this age don't need to rest like ancient Israelites did. Or do we?

The Religious Leaders Perverted God's Law

God stated His law in clear terms. However, several hundred years after God gave His law, religious leaders attempted to explain what God really meant to say. They claimed that they were sincerely concerned about God's law and just wanted to help God's people keep the law successfully. The leaders who were most concerned about God's law were the scribes and the Pharisees. The Pharisees, a group that originated around 134 BC, saw themselves as the official guardians of God's law. The first scribes in Israel were known to have existed as far back as 450 BC when Ezra was specifically called a scribe. During the intervening years the scribes became the self-appointed teachers and interpreters of God's law. Probably, in the early years, the scribes and Pharisees were very devout and sincere. However, as time wore on their interpretations of God's law grew in number, until the leaders finally gave there interpretations of God's law equal authority with God's law. By the time Jesus was ministering in Israel, the interpretations given by the religious leaders took precedence over God's law.

The scribes and Pharisees sincerely believed that it was their responsibility to decide what constituted work so that the Jewish people could avoid breaking God's law regarding the Sabbath. They identified thirty-nine basic actions that constituted work. More than that, they explained each one of those thirty-nine actions with thousands of other actions. As a result one section of the Talmud has twenty-four chapters which describe only the Sabbath rules. How could it take twenty-four chapters to define work? One simply needs to consider the scribes' definition of carrying a burden in order to answer that question. Carrying a burden was definitely work. And God's law prohibited carrying a burden on the Sabbath because it was work. But what is a burden? The scribes concluded that a Jew broke God's law when he carried anything that was heavier than a dried fig. Anything lighter than a dried fig was not a burden. However, that same Jew could carry an object that weighed half as much as the dried fig twice and not be guilty of desecrating the Sabbath. They concluded that people could pick up some things in the wide place and set it down in the free place and be completely within the law. However, no one could agree on the interpretation of wide places and free places— and we don't even understand what they were talking about.

The religious leaders determined that travel was also work. Therefore, they needed to define travel so that sincere Jews would not inadvertently break God's law. The scholars decided that travel should be limited to a distance of 3,000 feet from home. However, an Israelite who was determined to keep God's law, could put food at a place 3,000 feet from his house on Friday (the day before Sabbath). Then, on the Sabbath, the person could travel to the place where he put food on Friday, eat it, and continue to travel an additional 3,000 feet further without breaking God's law. How did that avoid breaking God's law? They reasoned that when the Israelite ate the food where he had placed it on a previous day it made the place of eating an extension of his home. Since the law allowed travel 3,000 feet from home, the fellow could also walk 3,000 feet beyond the logical extension of home. Along the same lines, the leaders decided that if a person connected a building across the street from his house by a rope, that building also became an extension of his house and he could travel 3,000 feet from that place without breaking God's law.

The scribes' laws became so immense in number (because they added new laws quite frequently) that people never knew for sure what they were allowed to do on the Sabbath. It got so confusing that some women would not look in the mirror on the Sabbath because if a woman saw a grey hair she would be tempted to pull it out and that would be work. As a result, the scribes and Pharisees created an unbearable burden for the people. It became impossible for God's people to obey God's clear requirement about the Sabbath. God simply wanted His people to make the seventh day each week a special time for rest and reflecting on Him. The religious hypocrites made it a day of frustration, anxiety, and focusing on rules.

The ramifications of the scribes' foolishness were painful. The Roman army was able to overrun Jerusalem with ease in AD 70 because they built their siege works on the Sabbaths, knowing full well that the Jews would not resist them on those days. Also, many people died unnecessarily because providing medical aid on the Sabbath was considered to be work. Ultimately, the masses were frustrated with religion. That is not the result God desired from Sabbath observance.

Jesus Taught A Proper View Of The Sabbath

Jesus did not make Sabbath observance a burden. He interpreted the law in it's most basic form, which did not correspond with the teaching the religious leaders had given. His view caused several conflicts with the religious leaders regarding the Sabbath (vv. 1-2). One such conflict happened on a day when the religionists accused Jesus' disciples of harvesting grain on the Sabbath. Matthew wrote that the disciples picked a few grains and ate them while they walked through the grain fields. It was a common picture. A group of men picked a few heads of grain and ate them while they were walking along a path that ran between adjoining fields. Anyone living in Israel in those days would have seen the same picture repeated many times during the harvest months of April or May. On the other hand, it might not have been so common to see men strip a handful of grain from a few stalks on the Sabbath.

How far from the house were Jesus and the disciples? It seems quite certain that they were at least 3,000 feet from home, which meant that they had also broken the Sabbath rule regarding travel. Even more curious is the fact that the Pharisees were near enough to see the so-called transgression of the Sabbath. Why were the religious leaders so far from home on the Sabbath? Were they also breaking the rule? Maybe they had special permission to desecrate the Sabbath because they were in charge of spying on rule-breakers that day.

Actually, the disciples broke several aspects of the Sabbatical law according to the Pharisees' opinions. Luke described the scene by saying that, "His disciples plucked the heads of grain and ate them, rubbing them in their hands" (Luke 6:1). First, picking the ripened heads of the grain off the stalks was tantamount to harvesting. That was never allowed on the Sabbath. Second, the disciples rubbed the grains in their hands in order to separate the husks from the grain. That was winnowing and winnowing was also never permitted on the Sabbath. Third, they blew away the chaff which was the same as sifting the grain. Sifting was work, and therefore, disallowed on the Sabbath. The Lord's followers were such wretched sinners in the eyes of the Pharisees. They clearly breached the leaders' rules. But did their actions breach God's law? That is the important question.

In other cases, the authorities accused Jesus of law-breaking because He did good works on the Sabbath. For example, the leaders confronted Him because He cast a demon out of a man on the Sabbath (Mark 1:21-28). They viewed Him with suspicion because He healed a man's withered hand on the Sabbath (Mark 3:1-6). He was suspect because He loosed a woman from a spirit of infirmity on the Sabbath (Luke 13:10-17). Also on the Sabbath, Jesus had healed a man with dropsy (Luke 14:1-6), healed the lame man at Bethesda (John 5:5-15), and He healed a blind man (John 9:7). It almost appears that Jesus enjoyed trying to teach the religious leaders important lessons about the real meaning of the Sabbath. They didn't get it. In fact they concluded that, "This Man is not from God, because He does not keep the Sabbath" (John 9:16a).

The disciples picked grain on the Sabbath, and the religious leaders complained to Jesus that they broke the law. Jesus employed illustrations and principles to explain to the religious leaders His relationship to the Sabbath (vv. 3-8). He tried to make the men see that there were exceptions to the elders' traditions (vv. 3-5). For example, their hero David clearly stepped outside the established law regarding the shewbread in the tabernacle (vv. 3-4). The shewbread consisted of twelve loaves of bread that the priests laid out on a gold table in the holy place each day. This table was located very near the Holy of Holies where God's presence dwelt. The shewbread, which represented the twelve tribes of Israel, illustrated fellowship between God and His people. God's law forbade everyone except the priests from eating that bread. It was exclusively for the benefit of the priests who took care of the tabernacle ministry. But one day when David and his men were escaping from Saul, they were hungry and ate the shewbread in the tabernacle. God never condemned David's action in that case. David did other things that God soundly condemned, but God seemed to turn a blind eye to David's breaking of the shewbread law. Obviously, God allowed an exception to His law.

Second, Jesus pointed out that the priests in His day continually breached the religious leaders' rules in that they killed animals on the Sabbath (v. 5). They were certainly doing work when they lifted the sacrifice up and placed it on the fire they maintained on the altar. Indeed, God required twice as many sacrifices on the Sabbath than He did the other days of the week. This, meant that the priest actually did double work on the Sabbath. And God required it! Jesus' lesson to the religious leaders illustrated the fact that whenever we try to live by specific man-made rules, we will eventually become inconsistent. Even God Himself makes exceptions to His rules. How then shall we live? We shall love God with all of our heart, soul, and strength; and we shall love our neighbor as ourselves.

Having pointed out the exception to the religious leaders' rules, Jesus finished His conversation with them by teaching important principles about the Sabbath (vv. 6-8). He said that He, Jesus, the man from Nazareth, superseded law (vv. 6, 8). He said that He was greater than the temple (v. 6). In three quick statements, Jesus pointed out that the priests worked on the Sabbath in the temple, and that was according to God's plan. He explained that the temple was God's manifestation of His character to the people, and, that Jesus of Nazareth was the Christ, the person of God in the flesh! Wow! This statement shocked the Pharisees because they believed that nothing was more important than the temple. Just in case they missed His point, Jesus told Pharisees that He is Lord of the Sabbath (v. 8). The Pharisees knew that only God was Lord of the Sabbath. Therefore, Jesus of Nazareth claimed to be God.

The Pharisees misunderstood God's law because they misunderstood God. They did not grasp what God really desires from His people. Jesus taught that God desires mercy over ceremony (v. 7). When religious people go beyond God's desires they will make rules and ceremonies that become a burden. God commanded sacrifices that would always remind the one offering them that one day the Lamb of God would offer the final sacrifice. Old Testament sacrifices were supposed to point to the finished work of Christ. People who love God with all their heart will seek to do what pleases God. The Old Testament saints loved God and did the sacrifices, but God never desired for the ceremony to become more important than the people. Likewise, people who love their neighbors as themselves keep the rules of ceremony in their place. They do not allow the ceremony to become an end in itself.

According to Mark's Gospel Jesus said that God made the Sabbath for man's benefit (Mark 2:27). The Sabbath was an opportunity for people to rest from work and to think about God. Both are beneficial to the human soul. Rules are necessary for maintaining order in any setting or society, but the keeping of rules does not win God's favor. Too much focus on rules distracts our attention from God's desires. A strong desire to keep rules for the sake of keeping rules takes our focus away from our love for God and our love for others. At that point rules become a detriment to pleasing God. A wrong view of rules will make a rule keeper proud and arrogant instead of helpful. Jesus showed how to keep the proper focus. Because He was God, He understood and explained the principle perfectly. His people need to apply it.

CHAPTER 9

JESUS ILLUSTRATED FORGIVENESS

LUKE 7:36-50

Religion can be a beneficial thing. People who are born into a religious environment, or who grow up in a Christian setting, often escape much of the sin that influences people who are not so privileged. Part of the benefit of living in protected circumstances lies in the fact that sin always leaves memories and scars. Sin is like a plow that plows furrows in the mind. It takes many years to cover those furrows, if they are ever covered at all. Children who grow up in guarded circumstances often do not fall prey to gross sins, and therefore, escape many of the consequences such sin leaves. It is encouraging to observe children who learn about Christ's sacrifice for sin at a very early age, receive Him as their personal Savior from sin, then learn to obey and serve Him in the home, through Christian education, and in the local church. Many children in this culture grow up in such enviable situations.

However, there is another scenario that looks very similar to this enviable situation, but which brings far different results. It is common for children to be born into environments that are more religious than they are Christian. Those children learn at an early age to live according to a set of rules. They learn how to gain the approval of their parents and leaders and how to stay out of trouble by keeping the rules. They live life in a Christian home, gain a Christian education, and experience a Christian church without facing much conflict. But when these children become adults and leave home, they are never quite able to express genuine dedication to the things of God. They always appear to live on the ragged edge somewhere between the worlds of sin and Christianity. They know the right words to say, and they know how they should act, but real sacrifice for Christ never enters the equation of their lives. They do that which is convenient in the realm of "Church," but inwardly they think and feel just like unsaved people think and feel. Such people find it impossible to delight themselves in the Lord.

Both of the foregoing descriptions present religious people. But there is a major difference in the lives of the individuals illustrated. Religious people are satisfied to be religious. True Christians are only satisfied when they live out their love for Jesus Christ. True Christians have discovered that talking about love for Christ and living out love for Christ are quite different. They have learned that the motivation behind each response is radically different. Simon the Pharisee was a religious man. He believed that Jesus of Nazareth was a good teacher. On the other hand, the sinful woman in this picture loved Christ. She believed He was God, and therefore, able to forgive her sins. The two people illustrated a major difference in motivation in their relationship to the man from Nazareth.

A Sinful Woman Honored Jesus

One day, while Jesus was still ministering in Galilee, a Pharisee invited Him to, what appeared to be, a formal dinner. In that setting a most remarkable thing happened. Luke recorded that a sinful woman walked into the house and anointed Jesus' feet (vv. 36-38). A couple of things about this event make it a remarkable. First, according to verse thirty-six, the woman did this while Jesus was reclining at a meal. Second, she did it while Jesus was at a meal in the home of a Pharisee. One cannot be absolutely sure where the event occurred, but it was almost certainly while Jesus was in Galilee.

At the outset it seems strange that Jesus was in a Pharisee's house. On the one hand, it is not odd that Jesus was eating with a

Pharisee, because He was a friend of sinners. Many of the religious leaders insulted Jesus because he ate with tax collectors and sinners. In Luke's account, Jesus spoke of the religious leaders' accusations shortly before He went to eat at Simon's house. (Luke 7:34) Obviously, it was not unusual for Jesus to be with a sinner, but the Pharisee's did not consider themselves to be sinners.

On the other hand, this was a strange setting because the Pharisee invited Jesus of Nazareth to eat with him in his house. Why? Maybe this staunchly legalistic man was honestly curious about this teacher who came from the village in the hills of Galilee. If so, the man was not alone in his curiosity. Many people tried to figure out who Jesus really was during the early years of His ministry. Possibly this Pharisee wanted to see if this man from Nazareth really was a special prophet from God. It is also possible, and maybe more likely, that the Pharisee was looking for an opportunity to trap this teacher whose teaching angered the Pharisees down in Jerusalem.

The text says that Jesus sat down to eat. The Greek word translated "sat down" refers to the typical posture one assumes when eating. For modern Americans that posture is sitting upright in a chair. In Jesus' day, especially at a formal meal, the words "sat down" would mean that the guest was lying on a couch on His left elbow. With Jesus in that position, one can easily see how this woman could anoint His feet which would be sticking out in plain view.

Thus, the story begins with the teacher from Galilee reclining at a special meal given by an important Pharisee. It was a formal occasion and probably there was a certain amount of tension surrounding the event. There was probably tension simply because of the formality of the event. There was also tension, no doubt, because everyone who lived in important circles, like this Pharisee did, was aware of the ongoing conflicts between Jesus and the Pharisees in Jerusalem.

Into that setting walked a sinful woman who showed great honor to Jesus (vv. 37-38). How did she, an uninvited guest—a sinful woman at that—get into the Pharisee's house? It was common in that culture for uninvited visitors to attend meals where a dignitary or celebrity was eating. These people would sit around the walls of the room, or even outside the room, where they would listen to the teachers in order to catch bits of the conversation. Sometimes these uninvited guests would interrupt or try to engage the teacher in conversation. If this Pharisee was a wealthy man, he would have lived in an expensive house, which almost certainly would have included a courtyard in the center. Often, especially during temperate weather, the owner hosted formal dinners in the courtyard. If this was the case, it would have been quite easy for this woman to walk into the dinner. When she did, everyone present must have held their collective breath. This particular woman had a reputation. Everyone knew that she was a sinful woman.

Even more astonishing is what the woman did after she barged into the dinner as an uninvited guest. The woman, whom Luke labeled as a sinner, knew that Jesus was at the meal. The implication is that she took this risk because she also knew something about the teacher from Nazareth. The broader implication is that she had already heard Him teach. That being true, it is possible that the woman had already expressed faith in the Christ and had already been redeemed from sin when she showed up at the meal. The verb in verse thirty-seven actually says that she "had been a sinner."

One can imagine how all of the guests and the Pharisee gasped in disbelief when this woman entered the house. But there really was nothing to gasp about. This woman, who had been a sinner, simply wanted to show tremendous respect and thankfulness to Jesus. Luke said that she broke the neck of an alabaster flask of costly perfume, she wept profusely washing Jesus' feet with her tears, and then she wiped Jesus feet with her hair which she had let down. This was a radical thing to do according to her culture. On her wedding day, a Jewish woman would bind up her hair and from that day on she never let it down in public. This woman soaked Jesus' feet with her tears of gratitude and then dried His feet with her own hair. Then she anointed Jesus feet with costly perfume from the alabaster flask. In a final act of love and honor, the woman kissed Jesus' feet.

Three very important observations are in order at this point. First, this woman sacrificed her pride in that she, a known sinner, entered the self-righteous Pharisee's house. She not only went into the pompous man's house, but she also wept publicly and let down her hair. The woman did not feel it necessary to guard her pride. She had been a wicked sinner who found grace in Jesus Christ. Pride was a thing of the past. Second, the woman sacrificed what little possession she had when she anointed Jesus with costly perfume. Third, she sacrificed dignity when she wiped Jesus' feet and kissed them.

What drove this woman to make such a sacrificial display of love and honor for Jesus? Would modern disciples ever consider making such sacrifices of dignity, self-respect, possessions, and the opinions of others in order to honor Christ? Probably not!

It is possible that while this woman was showing her love and respect for Jesus, Simon the Pharisee was reclining on a couch nearby with his mouth hanging open in disbelief. He was certainly offended by the event because he was sure that the woman was a great sinner (v. 39). Luke makes the point quite clear that this woman had been a notorious sinner. Everyone knew that she had been a prostitute. Where did we get that interpretation? Actually, the text does not identify the kind of sin for which this woman was famous. The text does not identify her as a harlot at all. She could have been guilty of any number of sins. For all we know she might have counterfeited Roman coins. She was just a sinner who had been redeemed. That is all the text says or implies.

Simon was offended because he knew in his heart that this was a wicked woman. Furthermore, he concluded from Jesus' response that the man from Nazareth was certainly not a prophet. He knew that if Jesus had been a true prophet He would have discerned the woman's sinful heart, and He would have rebuked the sinful woman. However, it is obvious that Simon arrived at his conclusion on the basis of human wisdom which is often insufficient for ascertaining the deep secrets of the human heart. Jesus knew this woman far better than Simon did. In fact, Jesus knew Simon far better than Simon did. Simon judged both himself and the woman on the basis of human religious standards. It is very important to understand that verse thirty-seven clearly states that the woman was (imperfect tense) a sinner. Contrast that fact with Simon's conclusion in verse thirty-nine that "the woman is (present tense) a sinner." Jesus judged both the woman and Simon on the basis of God's righteousness. What is our standard of judgment? Do we also disdain forgiven sinners because they were once sinners? What were we before Christ saved us?

Jesus Explained the Significance of the Woman's Action

In response to Simon's wrong conclusion, (about the woman and about Jesus), Jesus presented a simple but graphic picture to the self-righteous Pharisee (vv. 40-43). The teacher from Nazareth told a story about two debtors who owed different sums of money to a creditor (vv. 40-42a). One man owed the creditor fifty denarii. The denarius was a Roman coin which was equal to a day's wage for an average worker. Compared to today's values, the story says that this man owed his creditor the equivalent of $5,000. The other debtor was in far deeper trouble because he owed five hundred denarii. That would be equivalent to 500 day's wages or $50,000. However, the creditor forgave both debts.

This little story proved that Jesus of Nazareth really was a prophet (vv. 42b-43). The story proved that Jesus knew Simon's heart. Isn't that what Simon thought prophets should be able to do? Like a good prophet, Jesus drove home the truth of the story to Simon. He asked him which of the forgiven debtors had the most reason to be thankful. Jesus the prophet knew that lack of thankfulness because God had forgiven his sins was Simon's problem. He knew what Simon was thinking. He also knew the woman's heart because that is what prophets knew. Amazingly, Simon answered Jesus' question without (apparently) realizing that Jesus had just uncovered his heart.

Simon answered Jesus' question by saying that the man who had been forgiven most would love the forgiver most. Jesus explained that true forgiveness always produces expressions of love (vv. 44-50). At that point, Jesus drove the principle home to Simon by illustrating how little love or concern he had shown the Christ, God in the flesh. From the time Jesus came to his house Simon refused to show Him any honor. First, he did not give any water to wash Jesus' feet. That was one of the most common acts of respect shown in ancient Israel. Because people wore sandals and the roads were dusty, almost any guest could be sure that a servant would wash his feet. Surely a teacher like Jesus could have expected at least that much honor. At the very least, water was commonly offered to guests so that they could wash their own feet. Hosts typically offered that courtesy to common people. If Simon really believed that Jesus was "Rabbi" (teacher), he would have offered water for His feet, if not a servant to wash His feet.

Second, Simon did not kiss Jesus on the cheek. Another common greeting of respect was for the host to place a hand on the guest's right shoulder and then plant a kiss on the guest's cheek. This was certainly the normal greeting for a distinguished guest like a teacher, but not for Jesus.

Third, Simon did not anoint Jesus' head with oil. It was also common for a host to show honor to his guest by burning a pinch of incense or by placing a drop of perfume on the guest's head. Simon did neither of those things. Why not? Jesus said that Simon showed little love because he knew little forgiveness (v. 47b).

Outwardly Simon was far more religious than the woman. In fact, everyone in town looked to men like Simon to set the standard of righteousness in life. No one who wanted to pursue righteousness would follow a sinful woman's example. Simon assumed that he had the ability to judge whether Jesus of Nazareth was actually a prophet sent from God. Why shouldn't he be able to cast that judgment? He was one of the most devout men in Israel. He kept God's law and the elders' traditions meticulously. But in all of his rule-keeping, Simon did not understand the need for forgiveness of sin. He really believed that he could gain favor with God through his multiplied good works. Therefore, he was content to keep man-made rules. Simon was like so many modern religionists who are satisfied to attend church fairly regularly, to do good deeds, and to avoid strong drink, tobacco, and all those other nasty habits. They think that such a restricted life-style is enough to gain God's favor. They are sure that such disciplines of life are sufficient to get them into heaven.

People like that are as mistaken as Simon was. They know some rules and try to keep them, but they are not even willing to make the smallest, insignificant, sacrifices for Christ. They spend more time and money trying to impress friends or business clients than they do to honor Jesus. They love Jesus little because they have little understanding of the forgiveness of sins. They have little forgiveness of sin because they do not understand who Jesus of Nazareth was. They become consumed in good deeds that benefit the social well being of needy people because Jesus was a good man. The thought of confessing their sins to a dead man from Nazareth is ludicrous to them. They love little because they have been forgiven nothing.

The person who knows the joy of sins forgiven is quite the opposite of Simon the Pharisee. The formerly sinful woman lavished honor on Jesus. She showed many expressions of love in that she washed Jesus' feet with tears (v. 44), she wiped Jesus' feet with her hair (v. 44), she kissed Jesus' feet (v. 45), and she anointed Jesus' feet (v. 46). Jesus said that she did these many good things because she loved much (v.

47). Simon showed little love because he understood little forgiveness. This woman, who had been sinful, understood the tremendous forgiveness God gave her. She understood so she loved much.

As Gustave Doré was putting the finishing touches on the face of Christ in one of his paintings, an admiring friend stepped quietly into the studio. She looked with bated breath at the painting. Doré sensed her presence and said graciously, "Pardon, madam, I did not know you were here." She answered, "Monsieur Doré, you must love Him very much to be able to paint Him thus!" "Love Him, madam?" exclaimed Doré, "I do love Him, but if I loved Him better I would paint Him better!" If we loved Christ better, we would indeed serve Him better.

The former sinful woman's acts of love toward Jesus were an expression of her condition. Jesus told Simon that the woman's many sins had been forgiven (v. 47). This is a perfect tense verb that speaks of an action that was completed in the past but has continuing results. Jesus also announced to the woman the good news that her sins had been forgiven (v. 49). Again He used the perfect tense verb to declare that forgiveness had already taken place in the past. It was Jesus' public announcement of the fact to the people. Furthermore, Jesus said that her faith had saved her. Again, He used a perfect tense verb which indicates that it was not the woman's expressions of love at the moment that saved her from God's wrath against sin. Her expressions of love were rooted in the fact that she had already experienced forgiveness.

The woman had heard Jesus teach, she believed what Jesus had taught, and she accepted Him as her Savior by faith. Therefore, Jesus said that she could go in peace. The woman who had been a sinner had something the Pharisee could not claim. She had been justified by faith, and therefore, she was living by faith. That principle is found repeatedly in the Bible. It appears first in Habakkuk 2:4 where the prophet said, "Behold the proud, His soul is not upright in him; but the just shall live by his faith." Paul applied the same principle in Romans when he wrote to the Roman Christians that he was not ashamed of the gospel because, "in it the righteousness of God is revealed from faith to faith; as it is written, The just shall live by faith." (Romans 1:17). The same principle appears in the letter to the Christians living in the Galatian region where Paul wrote, "that no one is justified by the law in the sight of God is evident, for the just shall live by faith."

(Galatians 3:11). The forgiven woman showed expressions of love because she knew that she found forgiveness through Jesus Christ.

People who understand that God the Son, Jesus Christ, has forgiven their sins, cannot help but show acts of love for Jesus Christ. It is natural to love Him and then to love His people as well. Religious people tend to be self-centered and concerned mostly with their own needs or the needs of their families. The idea of sacrificing so that others might know about Christ, or might know Christ better, is out of the question. People who have not grasped the concept of forgiven sin lose much joy that is found in living for Christ alone.

AD 29

CHAPTER 10

JESUS' WORDS WERE ALWAYS FITTING

MATTHEW 15:1-20

The same answer is not appropriate in every situation. That is a natural fallacy of human laws. Why is it that as soon as the government passes a new law, or the work place makes a new rule, or the family sets down a specific standard, someone will come up with an exception to that rule?

The same principle holds true in matters of conversation. Peter admonished believers to always be ready to give an answer or a defense for the hope they have in Christ (1 Peter 3:15). Does that mean that the same answer will be appropriate for every question in every circumstance? According to Jesus' example, an appropriate response to questions considers the uniqueness of the questions and the uniqueness of the individual asking. Jesus Christ responded to people according to their special circumstances. Those circumstances might have included the person's emotional state (whether he or she was happy or sad, calm or agitated), physical condition, or especially his or her spiritual condition.

In the story recorded in this text, Jesus responded to the religious leaders' accusation regarding a spiritual principle. Jesus gave four different responses to four different people or groups of people. He gave each party exactly what they needed. The leaders needed rebuking, the multitude needed to learn a general principle, the disciples needed more specific teaching, and Peter needed a precise explanation of the principle. Jesus illustrated how important it is to give a response that is appropriate for each question and for each person who asks the question.

Jesus' Words To The Pharisees

Once again, while Jesus was teaching in Galilee, He faced Pharisees who were deeply concerned about the elders' traditions (vv. 1-2). In this case a contingent of religious leaders from Jerusalem confronted Jesus (v. 1). The incident probably took place at about the time of the Passover celebration. That being true, it is obvious that whoever these leaders were, they were very intent about their work. Being in Galilee, they were in danger of missing the Passover celebration. It was a long trip from Jerusalem to Galilee. These scribes and Pharisees were not local clerics, but were representatives from the ruling council in Jerusalem who traveled to the rural area of Galilee. Obviously, the inquisitors were very important people on a very important mission.

The scribes were the official teachers of God's law and of the elders' traditions in Israel. Most of the scribes belonged to the party of the Pharisees which was the most conservative religious sect in Israel. These particular scribes and Pharisees must have been sent by the Sanhedrin in Jerusalem to lay traps in an attempt to catch Jesus of Nazareth teaching something that was contrary to their traditions. They did not travel all the way to Galilee to determine if the Sanhedrin would be interested in supporting this new teacher from Nazareth. The Sanhedrin had already passed judgment against Jesus. The religious leaders were already opposed to Him. They had been strongly opposed to Jesus of Nazareth since the earliest days of His public ministry because He regularly uncovered their hypocrisy.

Jesus taught what is commonly known as the Sermon on the Mount at about the half-way point of His ministry. The principles of that sermon expose many of the basic errors of the elders' traditions. Surely, Jesus had taught the same principles since the beginning of His ministry. Surely, the scribes and Pharisees heard Jesus from Nazareth teach the people, "that unless your righteousness exceeds the righteousness of the scribes and Pharisees, you will by no means enter the kingdom of heaven" (Matthew 5:20). Such strong accusations would not sit well with the religious leaders. Furthermore, Jesus taught, "when you do a charitable deed, do not sound a trumpet before you as the hypocrites do in the synagogues and in the streets, that they may have glory from men. Assuredly, I say to you, they have their reward" (Matthew 6:2). That was rather pointed. It's no wonder the religious leaders were opposed to Jesus from the beginning.

The scribes and Pharisees described in this text appear to be concerned about the disciples' sin (v. 2). They complained to Jesus that the disciples stepped outside the elders' traditions. Every Israelite was familiar with elders' traditions. The scribes and chief men of Israel had been compiling the various traditions for at least 400 years before this event took place. The chief men of Israel did not set out to create a plethora of rules that would contradict the Old Testament Scriptures. Their goal was to explain and apply God's law in simple terms so that the unlearned people would know how to obey God and please Him. Their traditions taught that God gave the law to Moses who passed it on to the elders. The elders, who were the teachers of Israel, were to meditate on God's law and apply it to people's lives. They were also expected to train future generations of teachers who could continue the tradition of "building a wall" around the law in order to protect it. This wall became their collection of traditions.

Unfortunately the wall became so huge that it obscured the law it was supposed to protect. The scribes compiled most of these rules in the Talmud. This collection is divided into sixty-three different Tractates, or volumes. Each Tractate deals with a particular matter such as Sabbath keeping, offerings, divorce, and so on. The traditions included thousands of rules that were often contradictory. By the time this particular group of leaders confronted Jesus, the scribes and Pharisees considered the traditions to be superior to God's law. In Jesus' day, it was a greater offense to break the elders' traditions than it was to break God's law.

The specific problem that the leaders pointed out to Jesus was that His disciples were eating without washing their hands. Most mothers teach their children simple rules of hygiene. Washing their hands before eating is one of those rules. However, concerned mothers do not teach hand washing like the Pharisees taught hand washing.

Physical hygiene was not the issue for the scribes and Pharisees. In fact, they were not even concerned that the disciples broke one of God's regulations about ceremonial cleansing. Most of the Mosaic laws that dealt with cleansing were for the priests who were engaged in offering sacrifices at the tabernacle or the temple. Certainly they needed to maintain ceremonial purity.

The scribes had decided that the same purity laws that applied to the priests should apply to the common citizen of Israel. Therefore, they were upset that the disciples broke the elders' rule about ceremonial cleansing. They taught that every Jew should be careful to cleanse himself ceremonially before he ate. Why was such cleansing so important? The leaders taught that God's people faced constant danger throughout the day of becoming ceremonially impure. This could easily happen if a Jew accidentally touched something that was ceremonially unclean such as a Gentile or a pig. Some teachers even taught that it was possible for a person to get a demon named Shibtah on his hands. This posed a serious problem because the demon would enter the affected person while he was eating. Ceremonial hand washing was critical since these and many other such dangers of impurity were lurking. Some teachers went so far as to teach that eating with unwashed hands was a sure way to forfeit eternal life. They were serious about ceremonial washing!

The hand-washing ceremony was clearly described in the elders' laws. It was a specific process that required every home to have ceremonial water available. The amount of water for washing was roughly equivalent to the amount required to fill one and one-half egg shells. The person held his hands out with the fingers pointed upward, then water was poured over the fingers and the hands running off at the wrists and taking all ceremonial impurity with it. Then the person turned his hands with the fingers pointed downward, and the water was again poured on the hands, and it ran off the finger tips. The next step was for the person to rub the fist of one hand in the palm of the other and vice versa. A devout Jew did this between each course of a meal. The disciples didn't do it before they ate, which means that they clearly broke the rule! The religious leaders complained to Jesus about His followers' reprehensible behavior.

Jesus' response to the leaders' complaint exposed their hypocrisy (vv. 3-9). He revealed that they were actually the ones who broke

God's law (vv. 3-6). Because they insisted on keeping their own traditions, the leaders actually stepped over God's law (v. 3). Jesus did not hesitate to confront the accepted religious authorities of His day with the reality of their transgression. He accused them of breaking God's law which was the very law they thought they were protecting.

Surely the religious leaders recoiled at such an accusation. Therefore, Jesus proved through an illustration that they actually broke God's law (vv. 4-6). He pointed out that God's law required that they honor their parents (v. 4). However, the scribes created the tradition of Korban (vv. 5-6), which virtually nullified God's requirement. According to their tradition, a person could pronounce "korban" over all of his possessions. This announcement was a vow for the person to dedicate everything he owned to God's service. Once the man had dedicated all of his possessions to God, he could not use them for mundane matters. That also means that he could not use his possessions to benefit mere humans, like his mother and father. Devout Jews who pronounced the vow of Korban would not dare break their vow to God even if it was to help mom and dad. Incredibly, the same tradition allowed the person who pronounced all things "korban" to turn around at a later time and pronounce them "korban" again, which would release his possessions from dedication to God so that he could use them for himself.

Jesus uncovered the truth that only a wicked heart would allow for such hypocrisy (vv. 7-9). The religious leaders were hypocrites. They only pretended to serve God. They were very sincere about their religion, but their religious practice overruled God's clear commands. Their testimony, their claims, seemed to indicate that they drew near to God, but in reality their hearts were far from God. The hypocrites could not draw near to God because only a regenerated heart can truly worship God. A regenerated heart is cleansed from unrighteousness. A regenerated heart loves God wholly and loves his neighbor as himself.

Hypocrisy still abounds among religious people. Multitudes of religious people really believe that as long as they go to church on Sunday they can think anything they want to think during the week. They are convinced that they can do anything or say anything without fear of God's judgment, as long as they take care of the external traditions. As long as they confess sin before communion, they think they are in fellowship with God. They carefully choose their words to prove to their peers that they are in fellowship with God, but their hearts prove that they are far from God. Such people need to face the truth. It is right to point out their hypocrisy and to challenge them to be honest with God.

Perfect judgment in every case escapes the child of God. It is possible to misjudge another person's motives or actions, and wrongly conclude that he or she is a hypocrite. Jesus never erred in judgment. He always knew who was a hypocrite and who was sincere because Jesus of Nazareth was God in the flesh.

Jesus' Words To The Multitude

The multitude gathered to hear Jesus (v. 10.). It is interesting to read in this text that Jesus invited the crowd to Himself. His invitation presents an obvious contrast because it is clear that Jesus did not invite the religious leaders from Jerusalem to gather around and listen to Him. They invited themselves in order to attack Jesus from Nazareth. The crowd had already been gathered around Jesus by the time the hypocrites arrived. The multitude gathered around Jesus for noble reasons. According to 14:34-36, there were many people in the crowd who had come to Jesus for healing. It is also likely that there were people in the crowd who were looking for free food, like the food the disciples had recently passed out to the crowd of 5,000 (14:13-21). No doubt there were people in the crowd who simply wanted to hear Jesus teach.

These people were already nearby when Jesus invited the crowd to learn from Him. The crowd consisted of folks who were often ignorant or naive, but they were not hardened hypocrites like the leaders. Mark wrote that when Jesus saw the multitude of needy people He "was moved with compassion for them, because they were like sheep not having a shepherd. So He began to teach them many things" (Mark 6:34). He wanted to teach them.

Jesus still invites everyone to hear Him and gain understanding from His Word. Still people respond to the Lord's invitation in various ways. That is the principle Jesus taught in the parable of the Sower and the seed. Various kinds of ground produce various amounts of fruit. There are still people who reject God's Word in the same way that stony ground does not respond to good seed. They still prefer their church's religion over the clear teaching of Jesus.

When the people gathered around Jesus, He explained the general principle of defilement (v. 11). He taught them that food does not defile the real person. To defile means to make common, and therefore, to render unclean. Actual food might make a person sick, or physically polluted, but the issue here is spiritual pollution of the real person, the heart. A person can eat food that might pollute his body. But Jesus taught that whatever comes from the heart defiles more than just the body. On a different occasion Jesus taught that a person's words reveal what is in his heart (Matthew 12:33-37). The sins that are harbored in the heart are self-defiling, and they will defile other people when the sinner expresses them.

Therefore, it is more important to be concerned about what we think, what we place in our hearts, than what we eat and place in our stomachs. The religious leaders proved that this principle is true. They took great care not to allow imaginary demons to get into their physical bodies, while at the same time they continually broke God's law through hypocrisy. Their words and actions proved that their hearts were terribly polluted.

Jesus' Words To The Disciples

After Jesus explained the simple principle of defilement to the multitude, the disciples complained that His teaching had caused a problem. They were concerned that Jesus had hurt the Pharisees' feelings (v. 12.). It was obvious from the text that the religious leaders were offended when Jesus exposed their hypocrisy. A literal rendering of the disciples' complaint shows that they believed that Jesus' exposure of the leaders had thrown something in their path and caused them to stumble. That is the basic meaning of the word offend. In the disciples' opinion, Jesus was guilty of putting "something" in the leaders' path, and it caused them to stumble. Why did they say this?

What made the disciples think that they had the authority to point out Jesus' supposed errors? Jesus had taught that His disciples are supposed to guard against causing others to stumble or be offended. Maybe they tried to apply the same principle to Jesus that He had taught them. However, sometimes it is not the speaker who causes someone to stumble, but it is the truth the speaker conveys. Paul affirmed this principle. He taught that the truth of God's Word offends everyone who rejects. He confessed that, "we preach Christ crucified, to the Jews a stumbling block and to the Greeks foolishness" (1 Corinthians 1:23). God's truth about Jesus' work is a stumbling block.

The disciples were concerned about the effect Jesus' words had on the respected leaders. They knew that Jesus' explanation of defilement offended them. Was Jesus unaware that His words offended? Of course not. Then why did He say something that He knew would cause offense? Jesus of Nazareth was God. God always intends for His truth to cause sinners to stumble so that they will carefully consider what it was that caused them to trip. Stumbling is a good thing when it causes a person to stop and learn what caused him to stumble. A person is well nigh hopeless when God's truth does draw him up short!

The disciples were concerned, but not for the right reason. Therefore, Jesus of Nazareth explained the principle of non-interference (vv. 13-14). He reiterated a principle that He had taught on a previous occasion in the parable of the wheat and tares (Matthew 13:40-42). In verse thirteen of this conversation, Jesus explained to the disciples that there will always be pseudo-righteous people (v. 13). He illustrated that kind of person in the parable of the enemy who sowed the tares in the field of God, thus doing the work of Satan. The tares are already sown, and they will continue to grow until God sees fit to remove them. Therefore, because of Satan's deceptive work, false teachers will always be present. Because false teachers and false believers will always be in this age, there must also be times when it is best to avoid them (v. 14). Jesus never invited dialogue with the hypocrites. They approached Him regularly with attempts to trap Him, but He rebuked them. It is not wise to dialogue with those who are spiritually blind because they are going to fall into a spiritual pit. You do not want to share the pit with them. An occasional reminder that they are denying truth, or an infrequent confrontation with truth might be useful. But ongoing dialogue with a hardened false teacher is both unscriptural and unwise.

Jesus' Words To Peter

The Pharisees claimed to know God's truth, but refused to obey it. The multitude learned that the most critical kind of defilement is spiritual not physical. The disciples erred to think that it was wrong for Jesus to offend hypocrites with the truth. And Peter did not understand what Jesus meant, and he admitted it (v. 15). Peter's response is a good example to follow. He told Jesus that he wanted to understand the principle of defilement. That was an honest, sincere response. Surely, the Teacher from Galilee would kindly instruct him.

In fact, it almost appears that Jesus' response to Peter's question was uncaring. He chided Peter for failing to grasp the truth. He asked, "Are you also still without understanding?" That response seems to imply that Peter should have grasped the meaning and that he was wrong not to. Contrary to the way it appears, Jesus was not being mean to Peter. His response really was not a rebuke. Rather, Jesus challenged Peter to move up to a higher plain of understanding. Human nature requires frequent challenges in order to make progress in godliness. It is good for us to be challenged to learn more about Christ, walk closer with Christ, and to understand Him better. That is one of the activities of God's Word. Real Christians cannot read the Bible very long without being chided to move up a few levels in dedication and fellowship with the Lord. We should be thankful when the Lord chides us or, as the writer to the Hebrews put it, when He chastens us in love (Hebrews 12:6).

Jesus explained the principle of the defiled heart to Peter (vv. 16-20). He explained that food does not defile the real person (vv. 17, 20). Rather the sins that people harbor in their hearts cause the most serious defilement (vv. 18-19). The heart is the source for all kinds of sins that harm us and others. That is why God's Word frequently warns His people to guard their hearts diligently. Christians must carefully guard what they allow to pass through their eyes and ears and into their minds.

The challenge does not require the creation of more rules in an effort to corral sins. Rather it requires a change of heart. Experience has taught us that it is easier to make rules than to change hearts. How can a person do that? How do the important changes of the heart happen? What can God's people do about it? Is it even a possibility for Christians? Actually, only God can change a heart. Therefore it is vitally important for Christ's followers to plead with Him to point out our deficiencies and correct them. Wisdom pleads with God to make the changes necessary so that our hearts are not full of defiling things. God promised through Jeremiah that He would "put [His] law in their minds, and write it on their hearts; and [He] will be their God, and they shall be [His] people" (Jeremiah 31:33). He promised the same kind of heart-changing work through Ezekiel: "Then I will give them one heart, and I will put a new spirit within them, and take the stony heart out of their flesh, and give them a heart of flesh" (Ezekiel 11:19). God moved the writer to the Hebrews to record this same principle as it applies to Christians: "This is the covenant that I will make with them after those days, says the LORD: I will put My laws into their hearts, and in their minds I will write them" (Hebrews 10:16).

Changed hearts gladly receive Jesus' teaching. Religious people are satisfied to set up human rules and to imagine that God is pleased when they successfully keep them. Religious people are not concerned that their hearts are defiled with sin while at the same time they work diligently to maintain an outward pretense of rule keeping. Confused people do not understand that what a person thinks in his heart will govern his words and actions. Errant followers of Christ do not understand that God's truth is supposed to offend sinners. God designed His truth to cause sinners to stumble in order to gain their attention. Sincere people, like Peter, want to be taught by Jesus' truth. Sincere believers learn that God changes the heart so that they will no longer desire to be polluted with sin. People who have Peter's attitude never wonder if Jesus of Nazareth was God. We are fully convinced that only God can teach such lessons.

CHAPTER 11

JESUS COMMENDED GREAT FAITH

MATTHEW 15:21-28

A young man had worked for years to establish himself as a peach grower. He had invested all of his money and energy in a small peach orchard which bloomed bounteously. Then came the frost and he lost the entire crop. The fellow didn't go to church the next Sunday, or the next, or the next. His minister went to hunt him up and inquired the reason for his recent absence from church. The discouraged young fellow exclaimed: "I'm not coming to church any more. Do you think I can worship a God who loves me so little that he will let a frost kill all my peaches?" The old minister looked at him for a moment in silence, and then replied kindly: "Young man, God loves you more than he does your peaches. He knows that while peaches do better without frosts, it is impossible to grow the best men without frosts. His object is to grow the best men, not peaches."[1]

God used several severe tests to shape and mature Job's faith. Was God unfair to Job? If Job could stand and testify today, he would no doubt proclaim that the testing God allowed to overtake him was the most valuable experience in his life. His own confession to God after the testing was, "I know that You can do everything, and that no purpose of Yours can be withheld from You" (Job 42:2). Job gained superior faith because he endured the test that God allowed.

The same kind of testing often accompanies birth into God's family. Sometimes babies are born into this life with physical difficulties that hinder their early growth. They are smaller than other children or not as well developed as other children. However, as they age, these children often outgrow the early problems and actually surpass in size, stamina, or intellect, their peers who entered life easily and normally.

This text teaches that the same principle is true regarding spiritual birth. It sounds strange to hear Jesus teach that the spiritual kingdom, salvation, is taken through violence. Why did He teach that people agonize to get into the kingdom? That is a simple description of the fight of faith that some people experience in the process of being born again. How many sinners, who eventually were born again, wrestled for months or years with the supposed impossibility of free salvation? How many Christians had a hard time accepting God's offer of redemption through Christ alone? Many people heard the gospel when they were children, made an intellectual decision to accept that good news, but experienced only a little subsequent spiritual growth. Little faith results in little spiritual growth. But later in life, when these same people come to grips with the exceeding sinfulness of sin and the incredible magnitude of God's grace, they are literally overwhelmed with the reality of what God accomplished for them.

When God puts our faith to the test, we realize the greatness of God's gift of faith. The Canaanite woman proved this truth when God the Son put her faith to the test. A mere man would have no purpose in testing this woman the way Jesus did. God, on the other hand, presents Job-like tests frequently so that mere people will learn to trust Him.

Jesus Withdrew From Galilee

A comparative study of the four Gospel accounts proves that, up to this point, Jesus had been engaged in a lengthy ministry in the Galilean region where He had been dealing with Jewish people. The people who experienced His ministry had responded in various ways. There were multitudes of people who followed Him for one reason or another. Many of them clamored to hear Him teach because they never heard such teaching. When Jesus taught at the synagogue in Capernaum, "they were astonished at His teaching, for He taught them as one having authority, and not as the scribes" (Mark 1:22). The people who heard Jesus of Nazareth teach the Sermon on the Mount at the beginning of His ministry said the same thing. They were amazed at His teaching. That explains why some of the people in the ever-present crowds followed Jesus.

Other people in the multitudes followed Jesus because they wanted to see more miracles. Some of those people were motivated by selfish goals and desired to be awed by the supernatural. They were like modern Americans who pay thousands of dollars annually for tickets to see spectacular things. Humanity loves to be entertained. Some of the people in the crowds said to Jesus, "What sign will You perform then, that we may see it and believe You? What work will You do?" (John 6:30). At the same time, there were miracle seekers in the crowd who had legitimate reasons for wanting to see a miracle. They longed for healing for themselves or for friends or family members.

Some of the people in the multitudes followed Jesus around Galilee because they wanted free food. Jesus confronted people like that when He said, "Most assuredly, I say to you, you seek Me, not because you saw the signs, but because you ate of the loaves and were filled" (John 6:26). Those people didn't even try to hide their carnal desires for getting food without work. Unrighteousness is often expressed in brazen arrogance.

Some religious leaders also followed Jesus. They generally hung around in order to hound Him. They hated Jesus of Nazareth because His teaching exposed their hypocrisy. By this point in Christ's ministry, the scribes and Pharisees seemed to be on hand continually. It appears that they were driven by the constant desire to test Him in order to trap Him in an error or inconsistent teaching.

Common sense says that the continual pressure of dealing with such people is sufficient to justify a respite. Who wouldn't need a vacation from that kind of pressure? It was fitting for Jesus to withdraw from Galilee and take a break. He needed to move out of the area where He was so well known, in order to find protection for awhile. Many of the people in the multitude were ready to make Jesus of Nazareth the king of Israel. But Jesus did not come to set up the earthly kingdom at that time. He came to earth to open the way to the spiritual kingdom through His sacrifice on Calvary. It was still too early in the ministry to stir the wrath of Rome regarding His kingship. He knew that when Rome got involved it would end in His death. That was all part of the Father's plan for redemption, but it was not yet the Father's time for that to happen. The Son of God was determined to stay within the boundaries of the Father's timing.

Furthermore, it was a good time for Jesus to withdraw from Galilee because the religious leaders had already decided to kill Him. They clearly rejected Him and His teaching. They hated the Teacher from Nazareth so much that they accused Him of exercising Satanic power (Matthew 12:22-37). They were offended because He often rebuked them (Matthew 15:1-12). The leaders were not alone in their rejection of Jesus. Even His own towns people were so offended by Him that they tried to kill Him (Matthew 13:53-58). Then there was king Herod who ruled the region that included Galilee. He was growing wary of Jesus because of all the things he had heard about Him. Herod had murdered the innocent preacher John the Baptist in order to appease his wicked wife. He knew that he was wrong and his guilty conscience led him to believe that Jesus might be John the Baptist resurrected (Matthew 14:1-2). Because of this mounting pressure Jesus needed to withdraw from the conflict in Galilee for a season.

Maybe the most important reason for Jesus to withdraw from the Galilean ministry for awhile was that He needed to rest. On the one hand He was fully God, but on the other hand He was wholly man. His humanity was necessary if He was going to be able to identify with human weaknesses. One of those natural weaknesses is the tendency to become tired and weary after long hours and days of intensive labor. We are not robots or machines. Neither was Christ. We get tired. So did Christ. We're supposed to get tired. So was Christ. Because He possessed this human trait, Jesus occasionally separated Himself from the crowd. Sometimes He went away from the crowd to pray (Matthew 14:23). In this case He simply wanted to escape attention. On this occasion Jesus, "arose and went to the region of Tyre and Sidon. And He entered a house and wanted no one to know it, but He could not be hidden" (Mark 7:24).

It is interesting that Jesus left Galilee of the Jews and went to a Gentile region. The area where He and the disciples went was once a part of the famous region called Phoenicia. The city of Tyre was forty miles northwest of Capernaum where Jesus had been ministering for many days. Tyre was called "The Rock" because it was built on a rock formation that jutted out into the Mediterranean Sea. This formed one of the most natural and safe harbors in that part of the world. The safe harbor allowed Tyre to become a world famous port through which many goods and travelers passed. Sidon was sixty miles northwest of Capernaum. Although once part of Phoenicia, at this time Tyre and Sidon were independent of each other. Each city had its own king, own gods, and own coinage.

Jesus went into the region near those two cities. As one might expect, the area was completely pagan. The citizens of the region had descended from the ancient Canaanites whom God had commanded Israel to destroy because of their idolatry. Before God permitted Israel to possess the Promised Land, He gave them final instructions through Moses. Moses told the people to "utterly destroy them: the Hittite and the Amorite and the Canaanite and the Perizzite and the Hivite and the Jebusite, just as the LORD your God has commanded you" (Deuteronomy 20:17). However, the people in Joshua's day did not fully obey God. Joshua wrote that, "when the children of Israel grew strong, that they put the Canaanites to forced labor, but did not utterly drive them out" (Joshua 17:13). The disobedience of ancient Israelites meant that descendants of the pagan Canaanites were still around Tyre and Sidon when Jesus went there.

Therefore, it is almost certain that the woman, who is the focus of this text, grew up worshiping Astarte, a licentious, powerless goddess, or some similar powerless gods. Jesus, God the Son, left Galilee and went into a wicked region where people opposed God's righteousness.

Jesus Tested A Woman's Faith

At some point after Jesus arrived at His destination, one of the pagan women in the area came to Him with a request: "Have mercy on me, O Lord, Son of David! My daughter is severely demon-possessed." Jesus did not answer the woman. It appeared that He was going to ignore her request completely (vv. 22-23). How could God in the flesh ignore something so amazing? Here was a Gentile woman who lived in a pagan environment, expressing faith in Messiah (v. 22).

Matthew specifically stated that she was descended from the ancient Canaanites. Matthew's story paints a beautiful picture of God's long-suffering and grace. Here was a woman living in a pagan culture who was privileged to see and talk to God's Son. Indeed, she would receive the Savior's benefit. She would receive God's blessing in spite of the fact that God had commanded the Jews to destroy her ancestors centuries earlier. There should not have been any Canaanites alive in Jesus' day. But there she was, asking Jesus for help. The story is a reminder that God is not willing that any should perish (1 Peter 3:9).

The woman cried for mercy. More accurately, she kept on crying out, kept on asking for mercy. Mercy is the help that someone who is superior offers to a person who is helpless. This woman acknowledged that she was the one with a need. She acknowledged that she was helpless, and that is why she cried for mercy. Her confession of need begs a question: "How can God help the self-sufficient?" How can God help anyone who does not understand or acknowledge his or her need? Helpless people experience God's help most when they admit their helplessness.

The needy woman cried out to Jesus of Nazareth because she respected Him. The religious leaders over in Galilee, from which Jesus had just come, essentially called Him the Devil. This woman who lived in pagan Phoenicia called Him Lord. It was a title of respect at the very least, and possibly it was a reference to His position as Messiah King. It seems clear that this pagan woman actually believed that Jesus of Nazareth was the Jew's promised Messiah. She called Him "Son of David." That was a precise Messianic title.

It is amazing that a pagan Gentile would even know such truth. How did she know this? Where did she learn that truth? Obviously, God had revealed this to her. Maybe she had Jewish friends or acquaintances who told her about the Messiah God had promised. Maybe they had confided that they were waiting for Messiah. Maybe this woman had heard about Jesus of Nazareth and believed that He fulfilled God's promise for the Messiah. The important matter is that she believed it. Ultimately, God gave her the opportunity to believe in the Messiah, much like God revealed to Peter that Jesus is Messiah. Shortly after this event, Peter confessed that Jesus is the Christ, the Son of the living God. Jesus responded, "Blessed are you, Simon Bar-Jonah, for flesh and blood has not revealed this to you, but My Father who is in heaven" (Matthew 16:17). Maybe this woman who lived among pagans had become convinced of the same truth Peter knew, by the same means that Peter knew.

She who believed in the Messiah had a need that only God could meet. Her daughter was severely demonized. She confessed that she did not trust the false religion of her hometown to help her. She was in a wonderful situation. She had given up on herself and on false religion. She turned to the Savior. She had faith that He could help her. She expected Him to help. The majority of people in the history of the human race never come to this wonderful point in life. It's too humiliating!

At first it appears that Jesus did not even care about this woman's problem (v. 23). He never answered the woman, which would have been the very least acknowledgment of Her plea. In fact, the disciples read Jesus' response as an indication that He didn't want to be bothered, so they urged Jesus to get rid of the woman. They were so much like Christians who fail to recognize God's special work with unregenerate people who need His help. How do we respond to people who are faltering, halting, and struggling in faith? Do we find it easy to cast them aside or make them go away because they are not making enough progress? It is too easy to assume that unsaved sinners are not interested in Christian things and, therefore, we should not waste time trying to make them interested.

Things got worse for the needy woman when it seemed like Jesus chided her for making a request (vv. 24-26). Finally, He responded to the woman's continuing cry for mercy by telling her that the Heavenly Father sent Him to benefit the sheep of Israel (v. 24). It is true that God the Father sent the Christ, God the Son, to the Jew first. Therefore, it is also true that salvation began with the Jews. Paul emphasized this truth when he admitted, "I am not ashamed of the gospel of Christ, for it is the power of God to salvation for everyone who believes, for the Jew first . . ." It is good to discover that the verse does not end there, but Paul goes on to say, ". . . and also for the Greek" (Romans 1:16). This woman was a Greek. She had reason to hope!

The testing intensified when Jesus said that the Father sent Him to give food to the Father's children (vv. 25-26). He said this because the woman would not give up. When He told her that He was sent to the Jews, the woman worshiped Him, which probably means that she fell prostrate before Him. This was a sign of full dependence on the man from Nazareth. Obviously, she realized that Jesus was more than a mere man. She expressed to Him the attitude of one who truly trusts in Jesus Christ alone. Falling down and worshiping, she begged for help. What a wonderful expression of selflessness! Should we feel sorry for this woman whom Jesus forced into such submission? More to be pitied is the man or woman who has never been so dependent on Christ.

Jesus told her that it would not be proper to give the children's food to dogs. In this case, "the children's food" referred to the Lord's mighty works which benefited the Jews. That is a significant issue, but it is not the point that stands out prominently. The thing that is so astonishing about His response is that Jesus virtually called the woman a dog. The English New Testament translates two different Greek words "dog." One word refers to the roving packs of dirty, mean, homeless beasts that fed on garbage. That is the word Jesus used in Matthew 7:6 when He warned His followers not to give what is holy to dogs. But here, Jesus used that word that speaks of household pets. He said that compared to the Jews, who are God's children, this woman was a household pet. Did she give up? Did she walk away discouraged and hopeless?

Jesus Commended The Woman's Faith

The woman responded to Jesus' direct statements by willingly acknowledging her humble position (v. 27). She admitted that she was not one of the children. She admitted that, in God's plan, she was no better than a household pet. What sinner could claim a better position by nature? Every person is a sinner by birth, an enemy of God by nature. Every person is guilty of thinking and doing that which offends the Holy God. No person can claim a higher station than any other person before salvation. All have sinned, and all have missed God's mark of righteousness. Admitting our natural, fallen, needy condition, is a difficult thing to do. It is the essence of humility. The inability to acknowledge sin and failure is probably the most common impediment standing between sinners and salvation.

The Canaanite woman was determined to receive God's blessing and she was wise in her pursuit of it. She admitted to Jesus that she was not a child of God by birth, but she also acknowledged that even non-children are recipients of the Father's provisions. Her statement affirms that God's grace is abundant toward everyone. Even the most wicked sinner receives God's favor every day in the form of rain, sunshine, water to drink, air to breath, and on and on the list goes.

In the end, the woman received God's favor through faith (v. 28). Upon her statement affirming God's abundant kindness to those who do not deserve it, Jesus praised her great faith. Where did she get such faith? How did a woman who lived among pagans and who worshiped false gods, exercise faith in Jesus Christ the true God? Even this woman's faith was a gift from God. She confessed that God is gracious to care for the lowest of His creatures. Did she understand that one measure of God's grace is the gift to believe? True Christians cling to the promise that, "by grace you have been saved through faith, and that not of yourselves; it is the gift of God" (Ephesians 2:8). Faith to receive Christ as Savior is not generated by sinners who are dead in their sins. It is the gift of God. No redeemed saint can take credit for being wise enough or shrewd enough to confess sins and become born again. How could a true believer, take credit for his own faith when, "to you it has been granted on behalf of Christ, not only to believe in Him, but also to suffer for His sake" (Philippians 1:29). God's grace grants faith so that sinners can believe. That is why God the Son praised the results of God's gift of faith to this woman.

She endured the trial of her faith to God's glory. Her responses illustrate the principles Jesus taught in the Sermon on the Mount. She was poor in spirit. Jesus promised that people like that would receive the Kingdom of Heaven (Matthew 5:3). She kept on mourning and was comforted just like Jesus promised (Matthew 5:4). She hungered and thirsted for righteousness and Jesus satisfied her with it (Matthew 5:6). She kept on asking, seeking, and knocking, so Jesus granted her request (Matthew 7:7).

The man from Nazareth healed the believing woman's daughter. Did the woman really believe it? Mark 7:30 states that when Jesus told the woman that her daughter was healed, she did not argue, she did not hesitate, she just went her way because she believed Jesus' words. That is the response of God given faith. Faith that rests in God's Word alone takes His promises for granted. True faith never doubts all that God said. True faith may not always comprehend the depths of the

Lord's teaching and promises, but it always assumes that He is true. That kind of faith is the reward of humble submission. Humble submission opens the door for believers to present their requests to God. It begins by acknowledging personal sin against God. It believes that God can cover those sins with Christ's blood and that He will forgive. It trusts that God will do what He promised. That is great faith. Great faith walks away from a conversation with Christ, confident that He always does what is best, and always tells the truth. Only great faith can accept the truth that Jesus of Nazareth was God in the flesh.

CHAPTER 12

JESUS REVEALED THAT HE IS THE BREAD OF LIFE

JOHN 6:22-40

Thaipusam is celebrated in the Hindu month of Thai, usually around the last week of January or the first week of February. During the celebration about 50,000 Hindu devotees make a procession, escorting a statue of Lord Maruga, from the Sri Maha Mariamman temple to the Batu Caves. They work themselves up into a spiritual frenzy, indulge in masochistic acts of self mutilation and body piecing, and drag heavy weights and beautifully decorated structures attached to various parts of their bodies. One devotee confessed that he completed his conversion to the Hindu faith by piercing himself through the cheeks with a quarter-inch thick, four foot long steel rod, and pulling a chariot for two miles by ropes attached to his back and chest by steel hooks. Others walk through long pits of fire. These disciples have undergone a month-long ritual cleansing process to prepare themselves for the feats of endurance. During this time they deny themselves alcohol, tobacco and sex and meditate regularly. Why? According to some interpretations of Hindu doctrine, sacrificial works are required for the candidate to achieve salvation.

Mormon teaching requires people to do a number of good works throughout life in order to obtain heaven in the end. The person who aspires to ascend to the highest orders in heaven must dedicate at least two years of his life to an austere missionary endeavor. While they acknowledge the atoning sacrifice of Jesus Christ, they also teach that people cannot appropriate Christ's expiation of sin apart from individual efforts manifested through faith, repentance, and continued works of righteousness.

The Jehovah's Witnesses teach a penance doctrine. They also accept the fact that the perfect man Jesus Christ gave His life as a ransom for sin. However, only those who are "recovered from blindness have a full chance to prove, by obedience or disobedience, their worthiness of life eternal."[2] Again, obedience to prescribed laws is the prerequisite to salvation.

The Roman Catholic Church teaches that acceptable works are essential if a person would go directly to heaven at the point of death. They teach that a sinner must first respond to God's grace and then confess faith. Confessing faith, according to church doctrine, is firm acceptance of the major doctrines taught by the church and summarized in her creeds. Furthermore, the confessing sinner must do good works, and then, upon proving his worthiness, he or she is baptized by the church. Justification takes place only after the penitent sinner meets all of the foregoing requirements.

A strict Armenian theology in the Protestant Church requires that sinners do good works in order to gain salvation. Then the redeemed saint must continue to do good works at the risk of losing his salvation. One of the required good works is faith in Jesus Christ. But faith in Christ alone is insufficient.

A thorough investigation of every religion or sect in the world today is not necessary in order to discover that they share a similar principle. The point where nearly all religious creeds or organizations depart from the standard of God's Word is in the matter of works for salvation. Nearly all religions agree that a person's good works supersede faith in Christ alone for gaining and maintaining salvation.

Jesus Christ taught otherwise. He taught that faith in Him alone is the only acceptable means for salvation. This conversation (John 6:22-40), between Christ and a multitude of people reveals how natural it is for folks to insist on doing good works in order to please God.

This conversation also shows how unnatural it is for people to trust Christ alone for spiritual satisfaction.

The Multitude Sought Jesus

In these verses, John painted the picture of a mass of people who were confused because they observed something that was hard to understand (vv. 22-24). The event took place the day after Jesus miraculously fed 5,000 men plus women and children. That same evening He had walked across the tempestuous sea in order to encourage the disciples who were struggling in a small boat on that sea. The multitude witnessed the feeding, but only the disciples saw both miracles—Jesus feeding the multitude and walking on the water.

Now, on the following day, the people gathered again somewhere near the village of Capernaum. It is logical to assume that they gathered at the dock on the Galilee Lake. The people came back together after they had scattered to their various homes or places to stay, after eating the miracle bread and fish the day before. They came to Capernaum because they were looking for Jesus. Most of the folks had come from Tiberias (v. 23), and now stood on the shore by the dock in Capernaum wondering what had happened (v. 22). What was the problem? What caused them to wonder? They saw only one boat, other than the boats they brought themselves. They knew that Jesus had not gone with the disciples when they left Tiberias the day before. They naturally wondered how Jesus got to Capernaum without a boat.

Eventually the people found Jesus and asked Him about this matter that troubled them (v. 25). They wondered when or, more specifically, how Jesus got to the town. John paints a telling picture of these people who seemed to be consumed with this very practical but unimportant matter of life. The picture of people consumed with trivial matters about Jesus of Nazareth is still a common picture of life. The masses run hither and yon searching for the Christ. When they find Him, the questions they want to ask have to do with the temporal, unimportant, matters of life. They are consumed to know about the mundane matters of life instead of learning about the important issues. That is so human! Even devout Christians search for Christ through prayer, asking Him questions like, "Where should I live?" or

"What job should I have?" or even more foolish, "Is my team going to win?"

Is the Lord of all creation concerned about such things? The things that seem so important to Christ's followers are generally silly and of no consequence to fellow believers who live in different cultures or who lived at different times. And yet Jesus promised that God even numbers the hairs of our heads (Matthew 10:30). He also said that God invites His children to ask whatever they will (Matthew 21:22). God hears His children ask their questions about the unimportant and insignificant matters. But the seasoned saint, the Christian who has spent many hours in communion with his Lord, knows that there are far more important matters to ask about. Untried believers tend to neglect the important matters in favor of the mundane.

Jesus' answer to the questioners uncovered the real motivation behind the peoples' questions (v. 26). In fact, He never really answered their question. Maybe His response indicated that He thought their question was not important. It seems that there are times when Christ treats the requests of His sincere followers the same way. Our requests might appear to be unanswered because we tend to ask for things, and about things, that are so foolish in light of His eternal plans that they do not deserve an answer. Most Christians are familiar with receiving a "no" answer from God when they present Him with their requests. Most people who pray regularly have learned how to live with requests that never come to fruition. Part of the Christian maturing process is learning what is important in God's plan.

The people asked when Jesus came to Capernaum. He told them that they were seeking Him not because they saw the signs. Does it appear that the conversation is convoluted at this point? First, Jesus' answer did not deal with the peoples' question. Second, the people did see the signs. In verse fourteen of this same chapter, John wrote that the men saw the sign of the miraculous feeding of 5,000 and drew a conclusion about what it meant. "Then those men, when they had seen the sign that Jesus did, said, 'This is truly the Prophet who is to come into the world'" (John 6:14). Jesus fed the 5,000 men, plus women and children, on purpose. He intentionally performed the miracle in order to grab peoples' attention. He needed to get their attention in order to teach them something. God ordained many miraculous signs during

Jesus' ministry so that people would pay attention to His Son, God in the flesh, the man from Nazareth.

The people were astonished when Jesus fed more than 5,000 people with five loaves of bread and two small fish. They should have been. That was God's plan. No doubt the people saw the event with their own eyes, but did they believe it? As a result of the miracle they concluded that Jesus of Nazareth was the promised Prophet, the Messiah. Does this mean they were born again? No. The same kind of response has been common in every age since Jesus' ministry on earth. Many people today conclude that Jesus was a unique prophet, the Christ, the Messiah who came to save people from their sins. But for a sinner to draw a right conclusion about Jesus of Nazareth does not necessarily indicate that the sinner has gained salvation.

The important question is, "What did the people think about the Prophet concept?" Did they believe what God promised? They might have concluded that Jesus was the Messiah, but what did Messiah mean to them? Many people in this age admit that Jesus was the Christ, but they have an unbiblical view of what the Christ is or does.

Jesus accused the people of following Him for carnal reasons. He said that they followed Him not because of what the sign of feeding 5,000 proved, but in order to satisfy their basic desires. They did not grasp what the miracle really proved. They saw it with their eyes, but they did not perceive the true meaning in their hearts. Therefore, they followed the Prophet because He gave them free food. How many people lay claim to the title "Christian" because of fleshly motivation? One day when it seemed like life could not get any more discouraging, someone told them to become a Christian. They expressed some kind of belief in Christian teaching, and things seemed to level out. Was the person born again? Probably not. In many such cases, once life levels out the person who made a decision was no longer found among God's people. The person claims to be a Christian but he or she is never found in church, never prays, never reads the Bible, and really does not care to have Christian fellowship. In the Far East missionaries describe people like this as "rice Christians." They have discovered that these people are glad to be Christians as long as the missionaries are handing out free rice. But as soon as the rice runs out most of the "Christians" are also gone.

Jesus challenged the people to pursue higher goals (v. 27). He said that people should not labor for perishable food. What they sought for would leave them in want again because the pleasures of the flesh never fully satisfy. In spite of that deficiency in fleshly things, the great focus of most people is on temporal things. Therefore, Jesus taught that wise people labor for everlasting food. This text unfolds one of the important tensions in the Bible. On one hand, everlasting food, salvation, is the free gift of God. On the other hand, it is appropriate for sinners to labor toward salvation. Jesus expressed this same tension when He said that, "from the days of John the Baptist until now the kingdom of heaven suffers violence, and the violent take it by force" (Matthew 11:12). He meant that salvation is taken by those who are aggressive to pursue it. Jesus also expressed the concept of personal responsibility when He warned, "Do not lay up for yourselves treasures on earth, where moth and rust destroy and where thieves break in and steal" (Matthew 6:19). His teaching means that the individual is responsible for where he or she lays up treasure. Wise people heed Jesus' teaching and accepts His challenge to, "seek first the kingdom of God and His righteousness" (Matthew 6:33). Jesus challenged people to seek after salvation the way a treasure hunter seeks for hidden treasure. He illustrated the search for salvation with the picture of "a merchant seeking beautiful pearls, who, when he had found one pearl of great price, went and sold all that he had and bought it" (Matthew 13:45-46). All of these passages draw the picture of a person laboring to enter or gain the kingdom.

Jesus' teaching coincides with the many similar challenges in the Bible from God's evangelists for sinners to do something. For example, Peter told the religious sinners who were attending Pentecost in Jerusalem to, "Repent . . . and be converted, that your sins may be blotted out, so that times of refreshing may come from the presence of the Lord" (Acts 3:19). Paul said a similar thing in his testimony when he confessed that he, "declared first to those in Damascus and in Jerusalem, and throughout all the region of Judea, and then to the Gentiles, that they should repent, turn to God, and do works befitting repentance" (Acts 26:20). Sinners, who understand that their sin offends God, need to respond to the revelation of God by doing the right thing.

Jesus of Nazareth said that the highest goal toward which people should work is eternal life. He said that eternal life is available from the Son alone. The world clamors for food that does not satisfy, while they give little credence to the Son who gives eternal food. He must give everlasting life because the Father approved Him for that task. Only God can give eternal life. Therefore, Jesus of Nazareth is able to offer eternal life since He was God. Reach for it.

The Multitude Thought They Understood Jesus

Even after Jesus challenged the people to work for everlasting food, they still asked for mere bread (vv. 28-34). Is it fair to criticize them when it appears that they were convinced that they were interested in doing the works of God (vv. 28-29)? They asked Jesus, "What shall we do that we may work the works of God?" Jesus challenged them to work for eternal satisfaction. They responded by asking a question about God's work (v. 28). It really appeared like they were ready to do God's work. There response is so typical of human nature. Many people honestly ask, "What can I do to earn eternal life?" The Bible records many examples of this kind of question. The crowd at Pentecost heard Peter preach and, "when they heard this, they were cut to the heart, and said to Peter and the rest of the apostles, 'Men and brethren, what shall we do?'" (Acts 2:37). The Philippian jailer witnessed the power of God when He freed Paul and Silas. "And he brought them out and said, 'Sirs, what must I do to be saved?'" (Acts 16:30). One day a brilliant young man asked Jesus, "Good Teacher, what shall I do to inherit eternal life?'" (Luke 18:18). Many people sincerely want to know what they must do in order to gain eternal life.

Jesus explained the work of God (v. 29). He said that in order for the people to do God's work, they needed to believe in Jesus, the man from Nazareth. They had already admitted that they believed in Christ hadn't they? These same people had already confessed that Jesus was the Prophet sent from God (v. 14). True, but when it came time to make the tough decisions about this man from Nazareth, these same people really could not accept this Prophet as the Messiah. When He challenged them and their friends about full dedication and service, many left Him. When He talked about suffering and death, even His closest followers rebuked Him. The problem was that Jesus of Nazareth was not their kind of Messiah. They were much like people today who readily accept their own view of Christ, but the Christ of the Bible is too restrictive or too unbelievable.

Ultimately, these people revealed their failure to believe Christ when they exalted Moses above Jesus (vv. 30-34). The people told Jesus that they would not believe that the Father sent Him unless He showed them a sign validating that claim (vv. 30-31). Wasn't the sign of feeding 5,000 sufficient? It appears that the people argued, "You fed 5,000 people once, but our forefathers had bread from Moses for forty years." The implication is that they believed Moses gave the bread to their ancient relatives through his own power. They were still unable to get their eyes off of humanity and fixed on God who alone is the true source of blessing.

Therefore, Jesus explained the real source of Moses' miracle (vv. 32-34). The Father provided the literal bread from heaven in the same way that the Heavenly Father still provides the true, everlasting, satisfying bread from heaven. Jesus tried to get the people to see that the real bread from heaven is "HE." He who came to earth from the Father. He who alone gives life to the world. Oh, that the world wanted life! But they do want life don't they? That would appear to be the case since these people said, "Give us this bread all the time." Notice that even their request for bread uncovers their ignorance. The words "all the time" indicate that they were still thinking about physical bread. They could not get their minds off of the mundane, material, temporal satisfaction of physical hunger. They were like the Samaritan woman Jesus met at that well who said, "Sir, give me this water, that I may not thirst, nor come here to draw" (John 4:15). She did not understand the truth about spiritual thirst and spiritual water.

Jesus explained to the multitude that He is the bread of life (vv. 35-40). He tried to help them understand why some people continued to have spiritual hunger (vv. 35-36). He wanted them to realize that everyone who truly comes to Him will have spiritual hunger satisfied forever. He promised that everyone who truly believes Him will never thirst. In spite of the Lord's promise, a problem persisted in the minds of the people (v. 36). Those people, just like people in every age, saw the truth but could not really believe it. Multitudes in this age cannot believe that they are so spiritually deficient that they cannot satisfy the offended God with their personal works of righteousness. They cannot believe that Christ's blood alone is sufficient to cover their sins. They cannot believe that the only way they can please God is to believe what He said. They see all of the facts and all of the truth that the Bible reveals about Christ, but they cannot thrust themselves on Him in faith. That is the story of the majority of people in the world.

The good news is that some people do believe. Jesus explained the Father's will to the multitude (vv. 37-40). He affirmed that He came to earth only to do the Father's will (vv. 37-38). He explained that it was the Father's will to give people to Him as they expressed faith in Him. He knew that everyone the Father gave will come to Him. Jesus Christ will never refuse to give eternal life to anyone who comes to Him in faith, accepting Him as the Savior from sin. Therefore, Jesus could reveal the Father's will (vv. 39-40). He promised that He will raise up from death every single person whom the Father gives to Him. Those who will be raised from the dead in the last day are the ones who see the Son, which means that they have observed Him, investigated Him, and perceived that He is the only Christ, the only Savior. Those who will be raised from the dead are the ones who believe.

Jesus' explanation of the Father's will is eternally relevant. Nearly everyone has an opinion about Jesus. Most people believe that He was a special person. Most people are willing to admit that He is the Messiah, that He is the Savior; and yet, even while they make this claim, they do not understand the eternal ramifications of the claim. How can a person admit that Jesus Christ alone is the Savior from sins and then attempt to gain salvation from sin by doing good works? It is good and proper for God's people to challenge their peers to abandon their attempts to be saved through righteous works and accept Christ as the payment for their sins. It is fitting to challenge people who are sunk in sin to work vigorously to believe in Christ. It is appropriate to rejoice when they do believe, knowing that God has drawn them to His Son and given them eternal life. It is proper for Christians to rejoice in God's work of salvation knowing that Christ will raise us up from the dead to the glory of God the Father.

CHAPTER 13

HIS OWN PEOPLE REJECTED JESUS

JOHN 6:41-59

Some years ago, I was in a social setting where an acquaintance introduced me to some of his friends. The group engaged in small talk for several minutes before word leaked out that I was a pastor. Sometimes that little bit of information tends to put a damper on conversation. As soon as the group became aware of my life's calling, one of the fellows apologized profusely because he had repeatedly called me by my first name and had not shown respect that he thought a minister deserved. Frankly, it didn't make any difference at all to me. It's actually refreshing to be treated like a normal person on occasion. This man's response revealed that somewhere in his upbringing someone taught him to regard ministers with high esteem. He was embarrassed suddenly to realize that he had been ignorant of my station in life.

One day millions of people are going to be more than just embarrassed when they discover that Jesus, the man from Nazareth, is actually the King of kings and Lord of lords. Probably there are many people who believe they are kind and complimentary to acknowledge that Jesus of Nazareth was a good man who went about doing good deeds. They are convinced that they are condescending to admit that Jesus was a great teacher who influenced world religion in an unusual way. In fact, it is possible that many people take pride in their toleration and gracious acceptance of One who has been so controversial over the centuries. Surely they believe that Jesus, Mohammed and Confucius all share the same high level of respect.

People are going to be shocked one day when they discover who Jesus really is. They will be without excuse just like the eye witnesses of Jesus' ministry are without excuse. Many of Jesus' peers believed that He was special—maybe even as special as Moses. They mistakenly thought that Moses gave their ancestors manna through his own power for forty years, and they knew that Jesus gave them bread on a couple of occasions. They were convinced that Moses was a prophet, and it also seemed to them that Jesus was a prophet. Did they really understand Jesus' teaching about Himself?

In this text, Jesus plainly instructed the religious leaders in Capernaum about His deity, God's plan for eternal life, and their personal responsibility to God. They didn't get it. Most people don't. However, rejection of truth or denial of truth never changes the reality of truth. The few verses of this text provide a brief explanation of three of the most important Bible doctrines about salvation through Jesus of Nazareth.

Jesus Is Divine

Jesus declared that He came from heaven. People who heard Him did not doubt the intent of His words. They struggled with the idea that Jesus was the bread that came down from heaven. Actually, Jesus had not yet stated exactly that He was, "the bread which came down from heaven." However, the Jews were able to draw this conclusion by putting together the various truths Jesus had stated up to this point. He had told them that His "Father gives the true bread from heaven" (v. 32). He had said that, "The bread of God is He who comes down from heaven and gives life" (v. 33). Jesus also said, "I am the bread of life" (v. 34). Within the same conversation He told the people, "I have come down from heaven" (v. 38). Therefore, the Jews' conclusion was exactly right. Jesus did say that He was the bread that came down from heaven.

This was a very important conversation because the Jews found it difficult to accept the possibility that anyone was more powerful or more significant than Moses who had delivered their ancestors from bondage. Therefore, Jesus of Nazareth presented Himself as the heaven-sent bread in contrast to the manna that the Jews vaunted. They looked back to the miracle bread that God provided hundreds of years earlier while their forefathers wandered in the wilderness (v. 31). According to their arguments, the Jews gloried in Moses' provision of bread for a period of forty years while they wandered in the wilderness. However, these people failed to acknowledge that the bread came from God through the hand of Moses (v. 32). They believed that Moses' provision of manna was a wonderful miracle. However, if the provision of manna was such a miracle one wonders why their forefathers belittled the provision. Their forefathers complained to Moses that their, "whole being is dried up; there is nothing at all except this manna before our eyes!" (Numbers 11:6). Their forefathers did not esteem the miracle bread very highly. Therefore, Jesus sought to get the people's attention away from the past and focused on the present work of God. They needed to realize that Jesus of Nazareth was the real, life-giving bread that came from heaven.

Jesus' teaching at this point is critical because He laid claim to deity. He told the people that He came from heaven. He told them that the Father sent Him (v. 38). If Jesus' claim was true, this ordinary looking man who addressed the multitude was the Son of God sent to earth from heaven by the Heavenly Father. He was God! If He was God He could not be a mere human! Furthermore, if He can impart eternal life, which He affirmed He does (vv. 35-36), He must be God. But if He is really God, He could not be born through natural processes. If He was not born through natural processes, only birth through a virgin would explain His existence. That controversy has raged from the day Jesus was born until the present day.

It all seemed so fantastic to human ears. But Jesus did not waver in this claim. He knew that He was God in the flesh. He understood that He was fully divine and at the same time fully human. The religious leaders complained because Jesus made such a radical claim. When Jesus said that He was "the bread which came down from heaven," they understood exactly what Jesus claimed. The people who were engaged in this conversation were not ordinary Jews. These were some of the spiritual leaders of Israel. In the beginning of this discourse, Jesus conversed with the multitude of people who had gathered by the seashore in the morning. They were the ones who looked at the boats and wondered how Jesus had arrived in Capernaum (vv. 22-40). Ordinary folks wonder about such ordinary things. At this point in the story, Jesus had walked into town and was now speaking in the synagogue (v. 59). Therefore, it seems most reasonable to conclude that, in this conversation, Jesus was arguing with Jewish leaders who had gathered around Him in the synagogue.

John recorded that the leaders complained about Jesus' statements regarding the bread from heaven. The verb tense indicates that they kept on complaining. The religious leaders in Israel opposed Jesus for many different reasons, but now Jesus had given them a new reason to complain. Why? What was the real issue? The leaders complained because they could not see beyond temporal bounds. The idea that this ordinary looking man who was standing in their presence was the bread of life sent from heaven transcended all human reason. It did not fit the common interpretations and understandings of the day. In their thinking, this man could not be Messiah who was to be sent from God. Why not? They were convinced that the Messiah would be a mighty, powerful, warrior who came to set the nation free. They looked for a national Savior, not for a Savior who saves from sin. This man from Nazareth named Jesus was born in obscurity under questionable circumstances. He was not a mighty warrior nor did He appear to have any potential to become a great general. In fact, it appeared that this man did not even like war!

Furthermore, Jesus from Nazareth had been scoffed by "men in the know" almost since the beginning of His public ministry. He continually suffered humiliation because the wise religious leaders did not accept Him. Therefore, since religious leaders, as a whole, rejected Him, Jesus from Nazareth could not be divine. Surely the religious leaders would recognize a divine being. But Jesus? How could He be Messiah? The people in Capernaum knew quite a bit about His family over in Nazareth. The village where He grew up was not far away and news traveled quickly. They knew Joseph the carpenter and assumed that he was Jesus' biological father. They knew Mary and were convinced that she could not have been a virgin and, at the same time, given birth to Jesus. Virgins don't have babies! Everyone knows that. Surely she and Joseph concocted that story in an attempt to cover the shame of premarital sex. That old story was well known in Capernaum.

Human wisdom prevented the men in the synagogue from accepting Jesus as the Christ whom God sent to provide eternal life. Human wisdom still rejects the idea that God came to earth in the flesh. Human wisdom rejects the possibility that God would die for His people's sins. Human wisdom rejects the idea that no one is able to do works that are sufficient to gain salvation, the forgiveness of sins. Human wisdom still preaches the "good works equals salvation," equation. Evidence of such wisdom abounds. Nearly all false religions require adherents to work diligently in order to win their own salvation. Agnostics are multiplying at an astonishing rate. Atheists abound even in the very religious culture of America. Human wisdom ultimately leaves sinners with no hope and no help. But what choice does the sinner have? If human wisdom rejects Christ's divinity there is no other means for salvation from sin.

The Father Draws Sinners To Jesus

Jesus explained to the religious leaders that human limitations preclude everyone from accepting Him as Savior through their own strength (vv. 43-44). Sinners come to Christ only when they are drawn by God the Father. God Himself draws sinners to Jesus who is the Christ. Jesus told them that, "No one can come to Me unless the Father draws him." The word draw means to pull along against resistance. It is the kind of resistance a fisherman felt when he dragged a net full of fishes to the shore (John 21:6, 11). It is the kind of resistance the Philippian merchants fought against when they dragged Paul and Silas to the authorities (Acts 16:19). It is what the Jewish leaders sensed when they dragged Paul out of the temple (Acts 21:30). Natural resistance is obvious in each of these cases. Fallen human nature requires that God drag sinners to Christ. Sin causes a natural resistance to that drawing.

But the word drag does not always require stiff resistance. Peter drew his sword from its scabbard (John 18:10). Surely the sword did not resist. But neither did it come out of the scabbard of its own accord. One of the most instructive uses of the word is when Jesus said, "And I, if I am lifted up from the earth, will draw all peoples to Myself" (John 12:32). When God the Father draws sinners to Jesus Christ, it is a supernatural work in the hearts of people. One means that God uses to draw sinners to Christ is through the witness of Himself in nature. He also draws sinners through conviction in their consciences. God draws sinners to Christ primarily through the revelation in His Word.

Every person whom God draws will come to Christ. Jesus established this truth in a couple of statements in the context of this conversation. In verse thirty-seven Jesus promised, "All that the Father gives Me will come to Me, and the one who comes to Me I will by no means cast out" (John 6:37). Two verses later Jesus said, "This is the will of the Father who sent Me, that of all He has given Me I should lose nothing, but should raise it up at the last day" (John 6:39). When God draws a sinner to Christ, that person will confess sin, will express faith in Christ, will be forgiven, and will become a redeemed saint.

God must draw us sinners to the Savior because the natural human will is inclined against Christ. It is not that people are physically incapable of coming to Christ, rather the sin nature causes each sinner's will to be predisposed against yielding to Christ. People do not bow in humble submission to Christ because they do not want to submit. It is a matter of desire, or lack thereof. There is no natural desire in the sinner that makes him or her want to go to Christ. The natural will is so opposed to God that it is rightly considered dead to God. Because that is true, people who have come to Christ and received Him as Savior from sin should be most thankful for God's intervening work. Paul expressed the gravity of the problem by saying, "you He made alive, who were dead in trespasses and sins" (Ephesians 2:1). To be dead in trespasses is not the same as being literally, physically dead. To be dead in sins is simply a description of each person's natural condition. Everyone is born predisposed toward sinning against God. In that condition, no one has any desire to please God, to delight in Him, or to be right in his or her relationship with Him.

Even in that natural condition of predisposition against God, people have a conscience that tells them what is acceptable and what is not. That is the law of God written on the conscience (Romans 2). It is also true that sinners normally have enough intellectual capacity to collect data that indicates that there is a God to whom they must answer. However, the desire to empty ourselves of self-sufficiency and trust God alone for our eternal state escapes us. God must do that for us. God does that for sinners. He draws the sinner to Christ, and Jesus promised that sinners who are drawn to Christ will be resurrected. This is the end result of the promise of eternal life. It is such a significant truth that Jesus repeated it three times in this conversation (vv. 40, 44, 54).

God draws sinners to Christ in various ways, and those who learn from the Father come to Christ (vv. 45-46). This fact requires that God teaches sinners (v. 45). Here Jesus quoted an Old Testament principle that is found in several places in the Scriptures. He said, "And they shall all be taught by God." This is a general statement from Isaiah 54:13 that promises that God Himself will teach all people in the Millennial kingdom. Jesus employed the statement to teach the people that, while God is drawing sinners to Christ, He is also teaching sinners. Therefore, every sinner who listens and learns from God will come to Christ. Genuine faith in Christ is rooted in hearing and responding to God's Word. Paul told the Christians in Rome that, "faith comes by hearing, and hearing by the word of God." (Romans 10:17). God teaches sinners through His completed Word, the Bible.

God takes the responsibility to draw sinners and teach them, and yet it is impossible to comprehend God apart from Christ (v. 46). God draws us to Christ, and Christ reveals God. The writer to the Hebrews explained this truth by saying that, "God, who at various times and in various ways spoke in time past to the fathers by the prophets, has in these last days spoken to us by His Son, whom He has appointed heir of all things, through whom also He made the worlds" (Hebrews 1:1-2). Because the Father speaks to the world through His Son, He must draw all sinners to Christ. That being true, Pilate's dilemma is still the eternal question that everyone must answer: "What shall I do with Jesus who is called the Christ?" Many people still reject Jesus Christ, just like Pilate and the Jewish leaders did, because they cannot accept the fact that the Savior of the world could come from such humble beginnings and live such a humble life. That is why God must draw sinners to Christ by teaching them. We have no natural will to accept Him. Human wisdom will never allow for Jesus of Nazareth to be God.

Sinners Gain Eternal Life Through Faith

Having explained His divinity and the Father's work of drawing sinners, Christ offered Himself to the Jews as the bread of life (vv. 48-51). He reminded them that their forefathers ate the miraculous manna, but they also died (v. 49). Jesus pointed out this grim fact because the Jews tried to make their forefathers' experience the perfect example of God's care. They failed to acknowledge that the miraculous manna did not give eternal life. Maybe they didn't care about manna's limitations since their entire focus was on temporal life. Life, as they saw it and lived it, mattered more than eternity to them.

Jesus Christ presented Himself to the temporally minded Jews as a contrast to what they held at the center of their attention. He told them that He was the living bread (vv. 48, 50-51). He is still the living bread that came down from heaven. That statement reiterated His argument in which He affirmed His divinity (v. 50). Since Jesus is the living bread, and since He came from heaven, Jesus is also the bread that imparts life. Only the Divine Savior can impart eternal life. Jesus must be God. And because He is God, anyone who partakes of Him will live forever (vv. 50-51). Indeed, Jesus, the man from Nazareth, taught the Jewish leaders that He came from heaven so that others may eat or partake of Him (v. 50). Everyone who eats of this living bread will never die (v. 51a). Of course, at this point Jesus was speaking about eternal death or eternal separation from God the Father. Those who partake of Jesus Christ, the living bread, may very well experience physical death. But at the point of physical death, the living souls who partake of Christ will ascend directly to God in heaven (2 Corinthians 5:8). At the rapture of the saints, the bodies of those believers, whose souls already entered heaven, will be resurrected and changed into everlasting bodies.

But how could the Jews partake of this bread? How can sinners in any age partake of Christ? Jesus taught that His flesh is the bread He offers. How can that be? When Jesus spoke of His flesh it was a reference to the actual sacrifice of His physical body on the cross. Jesus did not recommend that anyone should literally eat His body. That would be impossible. Rather, He used the picture of eating to describe how believers are intimately identified with Him and His sacrifice.

Here Jesus taught one of the most amazing truths in the Bible. Jesus offered the living bread, His sacrifice, to the world. That does not mean that He offered eternal life just to the elect, but that He offered it to the entire world. Christ's sacrifice was sufficient to cover all of the sins of the entire world. Therefore, He is able to offer salvation to the whole world. However, while Christ's sacrifice was sufficient for all sins, it is not efficient for the whole world. Many people respond to Christ's offer like His own kinsman did and choose to have no part of it. They limit the effectiveness of Christ's sacrifice. Nevertheless, Jesus of Nazareth promised eternal life to all who believe (v. 47). The individual who believes is granted eternal life. Then, what does it mean to believe? To believe is to have faith. Faith is more than mental assent. Many people acknowledge certain facts about Christ, but there is never a noticeable change in their lives because they do not have faith. To truly believe requires that the sinner exercises full confidence that God is in Christ reconciling sinners to Himself. It means that I must have full confidence that I am a sinner and have nothing at all to offer God in order to be reconciled to Him. It demands full confidence that God has accomplished all that is necessary for me to be saved according to His plan.

Christ promised that He will give everlasting life to every person who has that confidence. Eternal life is a matter of a God-like quality of life now in this world, and the promise of a God-like quality of life forever in God's presence. It is available for every person who will believe. Jesus Christ, who identified Himself as the bread of life, who offers Himself for eternal satisfaction, offers eternal life freely. Why do people insist on trying to find satisfaction in the experiences of their ancient forefathers when Christ offers eternal satisfaction through Himself alone? How foolish to reject the truth that Jesus of Nazareth was God offering only what God can offer.

CHAPTER 14

JESUS' FOLLOWERS REJECTED HIM

JOHN 6:60-71

Sincere Christians desire that other people would share their faith. A person who has discovered new life in Christ, naturally longs for other people to accept the teaching of the Bible that has become so dear to them. Believers might even hope that, one day, true Christianity will be popular. We expect a person to feel that way if he is convinced that the Word of God is true. Since the Bible is true, there is no doubt that the world would be a better place if everyone would just believe and do what the Bible says. Serious Christians have read about or heard about God-sent revivals in various places at various times in the past and we long for God to do it again.

That is why news about revivals piques our interest—at first. A generation ago even Hollywood seemed to experience some kind of revival, or at least some of the stars were talking about religion. More recently, news came from Texas and Florida that God's power had inundated hundreds of people. That is exciting news—at first. When evangelists report massive responses to their sermons and invitations for salvation, the news is exciting—at first.

Why do some Christians respond to news about revivals with guarded optimism? Why is it that some very sincere Christians don't get excited and jump on the proverbial bandwagon when they hear about sinners making decisions for Christ? It seems like this trend to greet such good news with an unmoved spirit is most obvious in the older generation of Christians. Have they lost the joy of the Lord? Has life been so unkind to them that they can no longer rejoice that God has sent revival?

Maybe the older generation of Christians has lived long enough to learn that all that glitters is not gold. Maybe they have discovered through years of experience that not every decision made in a spat of emotionalism is the true evidence of God changing a sinner's heart. Maybe they learned what Dietrich Bonhoeffer expressed when he wrote:

> Cheap grace is the preaching of forgiveness without requiring repentance, baptism without church discipline, Communion without confession, absolution without personal confession. Cheap grace is grace without discipleship, grace without the cross, grace without Jesus Christ, living and incarnate. Costly grace is the treasure hidden in the field; for the sake of it a man will gladly go and sell all that he has. It is the pearl of great price to buy [for] which the merchant will sell all his goods. It is the kingly rule of Christ, for whose sake a man will pluck out the eye which causes him to stumble, it is the call of Jesus Christ at which the disciple leaves his nets and follows him. . . . Such grace is costly because it calls us to follow, and it is grace because it calls us to follow Jesus Christ.[3]

Jesus of Nazareth never misidentified revival when the multitudes flocked around Him during His ministry. He, being God, knew the hearts of the people. He knew that the time was coming when the multitudes would forsake Him. Therefore, when He taught the "Bread of Life principle" (John 6:22-40), He was not surprised to see many of His followers turn back and stop walking with Him. Jesus experienced the result of people following Him briefly without understanding who He was and what He came to do. When the multitudes finally discovered the actual cost of following Christ, they went back to their old ways. That principle is lived out frequently among our peers and friends. Knowing why followers stop following or how this conclusion is reached tempers the true disciples' discouragement. Jesus, God in the flesh, explained in this conversation why disciples go back to the old ways.

Jesus' Followers Had To Deal With A Hard Saying

Jesus' teaching about the Bread of Life was a hard saying for many would-be disciples. They could not accept the amazing truths Jesus' taught about Himself (John 6:60-61). What did Jesus say that was so difficult to accept? In a previous part of this conversation (John 6:53-58), Jesus required His followers to participate intimately in His sacrifice. In other words He asked them to identify intimately with His sacrifice for sins by putting complete faith in Him, His deity, and His finished work for salvation.

Many of Jesus' disciples struggled with His words. If they were true disciples, shouldn't they have already come to grips with this faith? The answer to that question lies in the fact that the word translated disciple can refer to more than a committed follower. In classical Greek literature the word speaks of someone who forsakes all else in order to follow a teacher with the hope of becoming just like the teacher. This is the most exact definition of a disciple. Sometimes that Greek word is used in the New Testament to refer to the twelve followers, those famous men who left all to follow Jesus, in order to become just like Him. They exemplified the classical definition. But in this text (also in Matthew 10:24, 42; 27:57 and Luke 14:26), the word refers to people who followed Jesus, but who were not fully dedicated to Him. They were curious. They had high hopes. However, it might be more accurate to call them "would-be" disciples. They were like the multitudes today who are satisfied to follow Christ at a distance, but who are unwilling to make any kind of sacrifice that fully identifies them with this controversial Jesus.

The would-be disciples who heard Jesus teach about the Bread of Life struggled with His words. He taught, "I am the living bread which came down from heaven. If anyone eats of this bread, he will live forever; and the bread that I shall give is My flesh, which I shall give for the life of the world" (John 6:51). Furthermore, "Jesus said to them, 'Most assuredly, I say to you, unless you eat the flesh of the Son of Man and drink His blood, you have no life in you'" (John 6:53). Jesus also taught regarding Himself, "This is the bread which came down from heaven not as your fathers ate the manna, and are dead. He who eats this bread will live forever" (John 6:58). It is not surprising that His followers struggled with those words. Human wisdom is aghast at the suggestion of eating another person's literal body. But it is unlikely that the would-be disciples stumbled on a cannibalistic interpretation. Those disciples almost certainly understood what Jesus meant.

The wannabe followers were, for the most part, devout Jews who had been trained in the details of the Passover lamb and the feast. No doubt they had participated in the blood sacrifices of lambs and bulls on many occasions. They understood the concepts of expiation and vicarious suffering (the covering of sins by identification with the sacrificial lamb). Therefore, it's likely that they plainly understood that Jesus spoke about the sacrifice of His body and His blood, and that they must be identified with the sacrifice. They knew, based on their past training in the Jewish sacrificial system, that Jesus had just established the need for them to be intimately associated with Christ's sacrifice. They also understood that Jesus made this identification the ultimatum. There was no other way for them to achieve forgiveness of sin. "Jesus said to them, 'Most assuredly, I say to you, unless you eat the flesh of the Son of Man and drink His blood, you have no life in you'" (John 6:53). The requirement was crystal clear.

Intimate identification with Christ's sacrifice is still the ultimatum for those who would have eternal life. In the New Testament there are 290 references to God's love. Two hundred and ninety times God has declared His love for humanity. But in the same chapters and the same verses, there are more than 1,300 references to the atonement (Christ's bloody sacrifice to cover sins), and more than 1,300 assurances that salvation can be gained only through the blood of Christ. The would-be disciples doubted this truth.

Jesus knew that the followers found the saying impossible to accept (vv. 60-61). The Jewish leaders complained (v. 41) and argued among themselves (v. 52), refusing to believe that Jesus came from God. They rejected Jesus' teaching about how He came from heaven because it breached their traditions. In similar fashion, the would-be disciples could not accept Jesus' teaching. They found it to be a "hard saying." They concluded that Jesus' words were hard to accept. The disciples understood what Jesus taught, but they could not accept it. They heard what Jesus taught, but they "could not listen to" it (the literal meaning of the verb). They understood Jesus' words perfectly well, but they could not give intellectual assent to what He taught.

Ultimately the disciples' problem was that they could not accept a suffering Messiah nor could they agree to be intimately identified with His death. Jesus asked them if His words offended them (v. 61). To offend means to trap or ensnare. It's precisely what Jesus' teaching did to them. The words they heard from Jesus of Nazareth trapped them in eternal failure because they rejected the work of Christ. The work of Christ did not fit with their concept of Messiah's work. The would-be disciples demonstrated that human wisdom cannot fully accept divine teaching. That was the essence of Paul's argument in 1 Corinthians 1:18-25 where he showed the superiority of God's wisdom and the limitations of human wisdom. Human wisdom abhors the necessity of Christ's cross.

Furthermore, Jesus fleshed out the certainty that the would-be disciples also could not believe the possibility of His ascension (v. 62). This failure is rooted in the idea that the Jewish leaders, who argued with Jesus in the synagogue at Capernaum, rejected the truth of His incarnation (v. 41). They essentially complained, "How could Jesus, the man from Nazareth, be from God?" They were not alone in their disbelief. The vast majority of the human race has rejected this truth. Very few people actually believe that Jesus of Nazareth was God, and therefore, Jesus' ascension into heaven is a mute issue.

In light of their refusal to believe Jesus' incarnation and suffering for their sins, there was not much chance that these followers would believe His subsequent return to heaven. Christ's ascension was the validation of His vicarious atonement (v. 62). If the leaders convinced the followers to doubt Jesus' coming from heaven, how would the disciples accept His returning to heaven? There is one more important matter that must be inserted between Christ's sacrifice and ascension. Before He returned to heaven, Jesus must rise from the dead after being killed. Asking the followers to believe that their Messiah was going to die, then rise from the dead, was asking entirely too much. Human wisdom concludes that divine incarnation, perfect life, death, resurrection, and ascension to the throne of God is impossible, it is fodder for fairy tales not relevant teaching. However, Jesus Christ's ascension was the ultimate validation that God the Father accepted His sacrifice for sin. God stamped with approval the work of Christ. That stamp was His miraculous ascension to heaven where He is glorified and intercedes for sinners.

The would-be disciples refused to believe the possibility of such astonishing works by Jesus of Nazareth. He had taught them many times that He came from heaven to earth in order to die in the place of guilty sinners. He taught that He would submit to death in order to offer the sacrifice that covers all sins. He taught that this covering was available for everyone who would believe Him. He taught that sinners only needed to trust His finished work, confess their sins and repent, and they would receive eternal life. The whole idea is too fantastic. Therefore, Jesus also rose from the dead in order to prove His victory over death and sin. He ascended to heaven where He intercedes for sinners who confess their sins and, by faith, accept His payment for their sins. These are the fundamental truths of salvation. People who appeared to follow Jesus Christ could not accept them. They still don't. The story is too impossible for a mere man from Nazareth. Indeed, that is true. But the story is a fact for God who came to live on earth in human form.

Jesus Explained Why The Disciples Struggled

The root problem for the disciples was that the Spirit gives life, but they didn't receive it (v. 63). They erred to assume that they could gain eternal life through human efforts or human wisdom. Jesus taught that human strength could not win spiritual salvation. He sacrificed His literal body and blood in order to cover over sins. If the followers thought that they could gain salvation by going to the extreme of eating Jesus' literal flesh and blood, they were mistaken. Even Christ's flesh was of no profit for gaining salvation. Jesus tried to help the disciples understand that they needed to move the whole question of eternal life out of the literal, physical, and mundane realm, and into the spiritual sphere. He taught that no person can do enough good works through the power of their flesh to gain eternal life. There is nothing in this human life that can win God's favor. "NO PROFIT" is the grand total at the end of life's ledger. Do what you will in your own strength—sacrifice what you will—but when you stand before the eternal judge He will say, "NO PROFIT!" Everyone who depends on the accomplishments of the flesh will lose for eternity.

However, Jesus promised that anyone who seeks can find life eternal in His words. Jesus told the disciples that it is the Holy Spirit who gives life. Does this reveal an inconsistency in teaching? Earlier Jesus had taught, "Whoever eats My flesh and drinks My blood has eternal life" (v. 54). Now He taught, "The Holy Spirit gives life" (v. 63). Which is true. By connecting these two truths, it becomes clear that in order for a person to participate in Christ's bodily sacrifice, he must have the intervening ministry of the Holy Spirit. Participating in Christ's sacrifice is a spiritual matter. No one can achieve this goal through personal strength and wisdom. The Holy Spirit's ministry must be active if a sinner would gain eternal life through Christ. But who can demand that the Holy Spirit obey him or serve him? Who commands the Holy Spirit of God? Only God! The work of the Holy Spirit is completely removed from the demands of human flesh. Sinners must depend on God to bring them into a right participation with Christ's sacrifice.

How does the Holy Spirit give eternal life? Jesus of Nazareth taught that the Holy Spirit gives eternal life through His words of instruction. No wonder the Jews recoiled at these demands. They still believed that Jesus was the carpenter's son. This is the same truth Paul taught the Roman Christians when he wrote to tell them that, "faith comes by hearing, and hearing by the word of God" (Romans 10:17). Salvation comes only when the Holy Spirit awakens the sinner's heart with the word of God.

It is important for Christians to convey a calm and confident spirit to a world that is dying in the grips of sin. That kind of confidence displays an attitude that is so different than anything the world can offer. That kind of confidence attracts attention. People who are enslaved to sin should be compelled to ask Christians why, or how, they can have hope in a dismal world. All of that is important, but not because it opens conversations about happiness. The primary goal of a cheerful attitude must be to open an entrance for the Word of God. Often it is a question about the observable differences in Christians (positive or negative) that opens an opportunity to talk to sinners about the promises of God's Word. A smile shared, a warm heart manifested, is encouraging to the needy world. That is a good start, but we must press on to the reason for a Christ-like countenance—the words of Christ.

When a sinner hears the words of the Bible, the Holy Spirit shoots those words like an arrow into the sinner's mind. Sometimes folks hear the Word of God and sense the convicting power of the Holy Spirit, but no change occurs. Why not? People do not accept spiritual words if God does not draw them (vv. 64-65). Jesus of Nazareth knew that some of the would-be followers were unbelievers (v. 64). He was never impressed with big crowds. Wise Christians realize that not all who seem to follow Christ are actually born again.

Jesus explained how apparent followers can actually be unbelievers (v. 65). It appeared that many had come to Christ. But Jesus reiterated that true repentance, confession, and conversion unto eternal life is the Father's prerogative not the sinner's choice. In other words, Jesus said that no person comes to Christ apart from the Father drawing that person (v. 44). This truth points out how dangerous it is for sinners to put off trusting Christ until a more convenient time. There may not be a more convenient time.

Not everyone in the crowd was elated to hear Jesus' words. In fact, His teaching caused a division (vv. 66-71). The religious leaders argued among themselves and ultimately rejected Jesus' teaching. The would-be disciples struggled to understand and finally decided that they could not accept Christ's teaching. Peter articulated the true believer's position when he said, "Lord, to whom shall we go?" There is no one else to whom sinners can go in order to find eternal life (vv. 66-69). Jesus' explanation of these critical truths regarding eternal life caused many wannabe disciples to turn back (vv. 66-67). They could not accept Jesus' teaching because their human nature drove them to believe that they were responsible to win salvation from God through their own works. They heeded the desires of their flesh. Jewish teaching, which they had heard all their lives, had entrenched the error of human works in them. To depend wholly on God's kindness alone apart from fleshly works was asking too much. When many disciples turned away, Jesus also questioned the dedication of those twelve special disciples (v. 67). It is interesting that He asked the question expecting a negative answer: "You also want to go away, don't you?" Of course the disciples didn't want to go away!

Peter explained why he and the other true disciples could not turn back (vv. 68-69). He spoke for the other ten real disciples when he said that they realized that Jesus had the words that opened the door to eternal life (v. 68). They (with the exception of Judas) understood this truth because God drew them to Christ (v. 69). Peter confessed that they had come to believe Jesus' teaching, and it had continuing results in their lives. He confessed that they had been convinced and their knowledge had continuing results. What caused Peter and the other ten authentic disciples to have such confidence? Shortly after this event, Jesus would ask who the disciples thought He was. Peter responded to Jesus' question by confessing that Jesus of Nazareth is the Christ, the Son of the living God. Jesus explained that Peter understood the deep truth of the incarnation because God revealed it to him. (Matthew 16:17). Peter's response to Jesus' critical question proved exactly what Jesus taught in this conversation. When God draws a sinner to Christ through the Holy Spirit's application of His Word, that person gains eternal life. It's guaranteed.

There are some people who appear to have been drawn to Christ by God, but in the end, they remain unbelievers. Judas illustrated that kind of unbeliever's plight (vv. 70-71). In an amazing display of God's grace, Jesus chose to expose Judas to truth (v. 70). Judas heard Jesus teach volumes of God's truth and saw Him demonstrate God's mighty power through many miracles. Judas was privileged to experience many opportunities to know God. Most Americans also have multiplied opportunities to know God. But all of that privilege did not change Judas. In his heart he was an accuser, a slanderer, an unsaved child of the devil (v. 71). For a long time he appeared to be one of the twelve, but eventually he proved that he was an unregenerate sinner. He took a horrible downward slide to suicide from a position among the most privileged men in history. So is the plight of all sinners who reject God's truth.

When Leonardo da Vinci was painting his masterpiece "The Last Supper," he sought long for a model for his Christ. At last he located a chorister in one of the churches of Rome who was lovely in life and features, a young man named Pietro Bandinelli. Years passed, and the painting was still unfinished. Leonardo had portrayed all of the disciples except Judas Iscariot. Now da Vinci started to look for a man whose face was hardened and distorted by sin. At last he found a beggar on the streets of Rome with a face so villainous he shuddered when he looked at him. He hired the man to sit for him as he painted the face of Judas on his canvas. When he was about to dismiss the man, he said, "I have not yet found out your name." "I am Pietro Bandinelli," he replied, "I also sat for you as your model of Christ." The downward path that begins with rejecting Christ never has a good ending.

Peter said, "God drew us, we have believed, we have become convinced, we cannot possibly turn away." Judas would say, "I had manifold opportunities, but I did not believe, I was not convinced." Judas died as a religious, knowledgeable, sinner destined for hell. When God draws a sinner to Jesus Christ through the Holy Spirit's convicting power, the sinner must humbly confess God's truth about himself and receive eternal life. God's hand of conviction is not a bothersome nuisance. It is a kind expression of grace. The multitude of followers turned away. Wise men do not.

CHAPTER 15

PETER UNDERSTOOD WHO JESUS WAS

MATTHEW 16:13-20

There is a story about a young woman who was engaged to Mozart before he rose to fame. However, when more handsome men caught her eye, she became disenchanted with Mozart because he was so short. Responding in immature, girlish fashion, she gave up Mozart for a tall and attractive man. Today no one knows who that man was because neither the young woman or the tall handsome man became famous. When the world began to praise Mozart for his outstanding musical accomplishments, the woman confessed that she regretted her decision. "I knew nothing of the greatness of his genius," she said. "I only saw him as a little man."

The world generally sees Jesus of Nazareth as a "little man." It is true that some people speak great swelling words about the good teacher who went about healing sick people and handing out free food. Nevertheless, most people see Christ through the lens of human wisdom. They draw the same conclusions about Him that some of His early followers drew. According to John 6:22-71 many of the early disciples turned away because identification with Jesus of Nazareth was too costly. True, Jesus did some amazing things. He taught on a level that far exceeded the teaching His contemporaneous authorities.

Sometimes it seemed obvious to the crowds that Jesus must be the promised Prophet who would be like Moses. Some of the people were quite sure that the man from Nazareth was the promised Messiah. Other people were not as easily convinced. "If this was really the Messiah, where was His army?" they wondered. According to the way some people thought, Messiah had to have an army because He was supposed to deliver the nation of Israel from the rule of pagans. The authorized teachers of Judaism had taught that Messiah would come to reign over the restored nation of Israel that would never end. Where did they get that kind of information? They found that God promised things like that through the prophets in the Old Testament.

But Jesus of Nazareth did not have an army that He could lead to defeat the enemy and set up the new kingdom. He did not even have a horse that He could ride as He led the army into battle. He had no house, no land, no palace, no throne, and no scepter. How could He be the Christ, the anointed One, the Messiah?

Then who was Jesus? His works and teaching were so powerful that they still cause people to marvel two thousand years after the fact. Very few people of this modern generation dismiss Jesus out of hand.

It's hard to ignore Him. Various surveys taken over the years prove that there is a wide range of opinion about Jesus. Not everyone agrees with Peter. One day Peter looked Jesus, the man from Nazareth, in the eye and confessed, "You are the Christ!" What did Peter know that has escaped the majority of people since that day? Peter must have seen something in Jesus that convinced him that this man was the promised Messiah. Or maybe Peter had special insight about Jesus that cannot be explained within the context of human wisdom. Maybe Peter became convinced about the truth of Jesus the same way everyone else becomes convinced about the same truth. Peter concluded that Jesus was the Christ, not because common evidence demanded it, but because God Himself convinced Him. Peter demonstrated the truth that a right view of Jesus Christ comes through supernatural means. In other words, if God does not enlighten a person's mind, no amount of evidence will convince him or her that Jesus of Nazareth was God in the flesh.

The Setting Of The Great Confession

In the days leading up to this great confession, Jesus and the disciples had been in the Gentile region near the cities of Tyre and Sidon. They had returned to minister to people for a few days near the Sea of Galilee. Then, on this particular day, Jesus led the disciples to the town of Caesarea Philippi, which lay several miles east (v. 13). The disciples must have sensed that this was a "time out" of sorts. Such time outs away from the crowds in Galilee and Judea were becoming more necessary since Jesus' ministry had gained much attention. The multitudes realized that Jesus of Nazareth was a unique man (at the very least) from the moment He changed the water into wine at the wedding feast in Cana. Furthermore, people traveled for miles to hear His teaching. They concluded that He taught with authority, which was something they never experienced when the official teachers, the scribes, rambled on about meaningless traditions. The masses gathered frequently hoping to see, or to personally experience, one of His miracles. They sought healing from physical and spiritual ailments, and they wanted the free food. Just days before this trip to Caesarea Philippi, Jesus had confronted the crowds about this very issue. They besieged Him for days after He miraculously fed the 5,000 men plus women and children, hoping to get some more free food.

With a nearly unanimous voice, the people wanted this Jesus from Nazareth to be the Messiah. Many of them had longed for the promised Messiah, not so much because they longed for closer fellowship with God, but because—in their thinking—Messiah would free them from the Roman government.

Now it was the late spring of 29, the time when Jesus' ministry was reaching the apex. He had taught amazing truth and worked many miracles for almost three years by this time. During those months Jesus occasionally revealed bits of information about the final days of His ministry warning that it would end in persecution, crucifixion and resurrection. The disciples never quite understood what Jesus meant by those words. Apparently their gaze was so fixed on the throng that was begging Jesus to be their king that they could not see how Jesus had also stirred the wrath of the religious leaders in Israel. The rulers' ire made it expedient for Jesus to leave the crowds in order to spend time alone with the disciples. He needed to get the disciples away from the pressures that mounted in the hot spots of Judaism. They accomplished their goal by visiting regions that were predominantly Gentile.

Surely the disciples understood that Jesus took them to this Gentile region twenty-five miles northeast of the Sea of Galilee because of the escalating attacks the religious leaders launched against Jesus. By going to Caesarea Philippi, they moved outside the jurisdiction of Herod Antipas into a sector ruled by Philip the tetrarch. However, while the disciples might have understood the need for respite, it is unlikely that they anticipated the full significance of Christ's teaching at this point.

Jesus had led the disciples to a town that was notorious for idolatry. It was not an accident. Caesarea Philippi was a significant town in many other respects apart from being famous for idols. It was located in a beautiful region at the foot of Mt. Hermon near the headwaters of the Jordan River. Caesar Augustus had given that whole region to Herod the Great. Upon his death, Herod willed the area to his son Philip the tetrarch. Philip enhanced the city and named it after Caesar. He gained glory for himself when he attached his own name to the city, which distinguished it from Caesarea on the Mediterranean coast. Thus it was called Caesarea, honoring the Caesar, and Philippi honoring Philip the Tetrarch.

The city of Caesarea Philippi expressed the human penchant for religion. Originally the city was named Panias (or Paneas) because it was thought to be the birthplace of the Greek God, Pan. The modern town located in the same place is called Banias. Legend said that Pan was born in the imposing cave located north of the town. This belief motivated the idolaters to erect a large temple at the mouth of the cave where Pan's followers could worship him. In addition to that temple, Herod the Great built a magnificent temple of white marble where the citizens could worship Caesar. Also, various temples dedicated to the ancient worship of the Syrian Baal gods were scattered throughout the area. About two miles to the west was the ancient town of Dan. This was the home of Jeroboam's golden calf, which proved to be a gateway through which idolatry entered ancient Israel.

The whole area smacked of man-made religion. It pictured the same kind of dead religion that is at home in many cities in the world today. As Solomon said, "There is nothing new under the sun." The proliferation of man-made religion, whether it is protestant in name, or pagan, or traditional is evident throughout the world. Today, approximately 750,000 Hindu people live in Britain, which was the home of the Sunday School movement and the modern missionary movement. Carey Hall, the large Baptist church named after William Carey, who left his pastorate in Leicester in 1783 to reach Hindus in Burma and India, now houses Leicester's largest Hindu temple. The Islamic religion is the fastest growing religion in the United States. The citizens of the Unite States, a nation that was founded on Christian ideals, face burgeoning man-made religion and idolatry. What hope is there that anyone will come to believe that Jesus is the Christ? There is as much hope for people living in the wake of idolatry here as there was for a humble disciple standing in the midst of rampant idolatry to be enlightened. Jesus asked His closets followers who they thought He was while they stood surrounded by monuments to false gods. The mass of evidence all around them praised human wisdom and efforts for searching for meaning, but it did not keep Peter from drawing the right conclusion to Jesus' question.

The Great Question

Surrounded by pagan idolatry, the evidence of mankind's religious quest, Jesus asked the disciples, "Who do men say that I am?" He wanted them to admit what the people were saying about the Son of man. To many Jews, the title Son of man applied to the promised Messiah. Jesus frequently used the term, according to the record in the Gospels, in order to emphasize His association with humanity. According to Jewish tradition, Son of man carried Messianic overtones. Jesus used it to identify Himself with people He came to save. Therefore, the term was ambiguous enough to generate questions like, "Is He Messiah or just a special man?"

There was no consensus of opinion about Jesus, who came from Nazareth. Nearly everyone concluded that He was unique, but there was much disagreement about the nature or scope of that uniqueness. Jesus asked the disciples who people said He was. The disciples answered that some of the people thought he was John the Baptist. Herod was one of those people. The tetrarch had killed John the Baptist in order to please his wife, whom he had stolen from his brother Philip. Now he feared that Jesus was John, risen from the dead to haunt him (Matthew 14:1-2). Other people thought that Jesus was John risen from the dead in order to continue the ministry as Messiah's forerunner. Some of the people believed that if Jesus was really John risen from the dead it would fit well with His supernatural ministry. A dead man who comes to life ought to be able to do miracles!

The disciples offered that other people thought that Jesus was the prophet Elijah reincarnated. Elijah was the most significant of the Old Testament prophets, in the opinion of many Jews. Again that opinion might have hinged on the fact that God also used him to perform many miracles. They expected an actual appearance of Elijah on earth to serve as the forerunner of Messiah. They based their expectation on the prophecy of Malachi 4:5, "Behold, I will send you Elijah the prophet Before the coming of the great and dreadful day of the LORD."

Still others said that Jesus was a reincarnation of Jeremiah. Why? Legend held that just before Nebuchadnezzar attacked and destroyed Jerusalem in 586 BC, Jeremiah took the ark and the altar of incense out of the temple and hid them somewhere in Mount Nebo. The legend claimed that just before Messiah arrived, Jeremiah would appear and retrieve the temple articles in order to use them in sacrifice and worship again. All of these conclusions had something to do with Messiah, but none of them recognized Jesus as the anointed one of God.

The people held many different views regarding Jesus of Nazareth. But what did the disciples, Jesus' closest friends, think? Jesus uncovered their opinions when He asked, "Who do you say that I am?" They had been with the Master for almost three years. If anyone knew Jesus, it should have been these fellows. They watched His miracles, they received the benefits of His miracles, they heard His teaching, and they received specific explanation of His teaching. They must have known Jesus quite intimately.

In fact, the disciples had pondered whether Jesus was the Messiah from the time they met Him. They had to wrestle with the question because John the Baptist introduced Him as the Lamb that takes away the sins of the world (John 1:36). How could the disciples ignore that statement? They couldn't. That is why Andrew described Jesus to Peter by saying, "We have found the Messiah" (John 1:41). Philip told Nathanael, "We have found Him of whom Moses in the law, and also the prophets, wrote—Jesus of Nazareth, the son of Joseph" (John 1:45).

Those words of confidence do not imply that the disciples immediately concluded that Jesus was the Messiah and never doubted it for a moment thereafter. In fact they wavered in their conclusion as much as some other people did. Many of the people confessed at some point that Jesus of Nazareth was the Christ, but because they misunderstood Messiah's purpose, they wavered. Ultimately it appears that almost everyone in Israel gave up hope that Messiah had come in the person of Jesus. They were unable to accept the suffering Messiah. Even John Baptist wavered. He sent "two of his disciples to . . . Jesus, saying, 'Are You the Coming One, or do we look for another?'" (Luke 7:19).

The answer to the question "Who do you say that I am?" is critical. The correct answer is the difference between eternal life and eternal condemnation. The promised Christ is the Lamb slain before the foundation of the world (Revelation 13:8). The Christ is the anointed one from God who would be slain to complete the work of redemption. The Christ is the promised seed of the woman (Genesis 3:15). He came to redeem sinful humanity from the penalty and power of sin. The Christ is the only one who could live perfectly under the law (1 Peter 1:19). He is the only acceptable substitute for sin's penalty. His shed blood is the only acceptable sacrifice to cover sins (1 Peter 1:18-19). He is the only means for salvation (Acts 4:12). Christ's perfect life and precious sacrifice is the only door to eternal life (John 14:6).

Everyone must answer the same question. Who is Jesus? Is He the Christ? Is He the only means for sinners to be reconciled to God?

The Great Confession

Peter confessed that Jesus was the Christ (v. 16). His confession was not mere words strung together without meaning. Rather, Peter declared that Jesus of Nazareth fulfilled everything that Messiah entails. When he said, "You are the Christ," Peter admitted that every prophecy, every promise, about the Christ would be fulfilled in this man named Jesus. There were going to be times when Peter wavered in his understanding or waffled about his association, but he truly believed that Jesus was the promised Christ.

Peter was fully convinced that Jesus was the Christ, the Son of the living God. He was sure that Jesus of Nazareth, who often called

Himself the Son of man, was actually the Son of God. This title pointed out a unique relationship with the true and living God that no one else could ever experience. Therefore, Peter's confession flew in the face of every religion represented in Caesarea Philippi that day. Peter's confession flies in the face of every man-made religion or church in every age.

It was an astonishing confession. Try to picture this Jewish man looking into the face of another man who was very similar to him in many respects. Jesus was probably about the same height and build, had the same Middle-eastern complexion, the same dark eyes, wore the same kind of clothes, and spoke the same language with the same accent. Peter spoke to the man he had accompanied for nearly three years. To this man he said, "You are the One anointed by God to take away the penalty and power of sin." That is shocking! Only a fool would draw such a conclusion. Or only a man whose heart had been changed by divine power could utter such a confession.

Jesus revealed that the source of Peter's understanding was beyond humanity (v. 17). Human ability cannot comprehend the marvelous truth of the God-Man. Human ability measured against divine enabling reveals human inability. Therefore, salvation cannot be derived through human wisdom. In the most elementary spiritual matters human wisdom utterly fails to ascertain divine truth. Natural human depravity prevents spiritual comprehension. Paul warned that "the natural man does not receive the things of the Spirit of God, for they are foolishness to him; nor can he know them, because they are spiritually discerned" (1 Corinthians 2:14). Therefore, the redeemed Christian rejoices to read:

> *You He made alive, who were dead in trespasses and sins, in which you once walked according to the course of this world, according to the prince of the power of the air, the spirit who now works in the sons of disobedience, among whom also we all once conducted ourselves in the lusts of our flesh, fulfilling the desires of the flesh and of the mind, and were by nature children of wrath, just as the others. But God, who is rich in mercy, because of His great love with which He loved us." (Ephesians 2:1-4)*

Jesus told the would-be followers that, "'It is the Spirit who gives life; the flesh profits nothing. The words that I speak to you are spirit, and they are life. But there are some of you who do not believe.' For Jesus knew from the beginning who they were who did not believe, and who would betray Him" (John 6:63-64) . He also upbraided His critics telling them that they did not understand His teaching because they were virtually incapable of listening to His words with discernment (John 8:43).

God grants fallen sinners the ability to comprehend the amazing miracle that Jesus is the Christ. Apart from God's gracious enlightenment, no one is able to comprehend the important truths about the person of Christ. Such a dearth of understanding leads people to establish their own religion or to build their own organizations. The resulting doctrines or churches are nothing more than the products of human wisdom and human effort. As a result those concoctions often have little or no resemblance to God's true work. Salvation is built on the confession that Jesus of Nazareth is the Anointed Messiah who takes away sin through the shedding of His own blood. The whole idea is ridiculous to those who are spiritually blind, but it is a marvelous revelation for those whom God enlightens.

CHAPTER 16

Jesus Rebuked His Friend

Matthew 16:20-23

A few weeks ago the Duke University basketball team entered the "Dean Dome" in Chapel Hill to play the University of North Carolina for the game of the year. Tickets to that game are seldom available, so it was surprising to see an elderly lady sitting near court side with an empty seat beside her. Someone asked her why the seat was empty. She replied, "We have been season ticket holders for twenty-five years and that seat belonged to my late husband." "Couldn't you find a friend or a relative to come with you to the game?" "Why no," the woman replied, "They're all at my husband's funeral." It's just a story, but if it were true, no one would doubt what was important to that woman.

At some point, a person's priorities become obvious. Jesus taught that a person's words reveal what is in the secret places of his heart. Words uncover the hidden part for everyone to see. When we speak, we tell the whole world what is important to us and what is not important. What does the average Christian reveal is the most important thing to him or her? Surely Christians should be intently interested in the things that bring glory to God. Christians ought to hold God's glory as the most important thing. "Therefore, whether you eat or drink, or whatever you do, do all to the glory of God," (1 Corinthians 10:31) are words that should determine priorities. One wonders how many people who quote that verse or comment on it really intend to do what it says. If God's glory is the chief interest, actions and habits will back up the person's words.

No doubt most Christians are sincere when they claim they want to do all things for God's glory. But how do God's people determine what brings Him glory? The answer to that question is often considered to be a matter of personal opinion or preference. One Christian is convinced that a particular kind of lifestyle is the best way to glorify God, while another sincere Christian is just as convinced that a different lifestyle is the best way to bring God glory. Which one is right? Which of the Christians drew his conclusion from the truths of God's Word? The best way to determine a lifestyle that glorifies God is to flesh out what God has already taught in His Word about living for His glory. Building huge church buildings or creating well-known religious organizations may not glorify God at all. Those goals seem to be the preferred standard of the day, but they are not necessarily God's priorities. If a religious organization's programs attract a crowd of excited people who freely invite others to join the excitement, the world concludes that it glorifies God. Where does God's Word teach that attracting curiosity seekers to an exciting event guarantees that God will receive the glory and honor? The conclusions of human wisdom do not always jibe with God's standard.

Peter struggled with this kind of conflict. He sincerely wanted to do things that would advance Christ's program. He truly had Christ's exaltation in view, but at the same time, he was confused about how to exalt Christ. Jesus Christ is exalted when His people take up their crosses and follow after Him. He is glorified when His strength is made perfect in their weakness. Peter's failure in this story reveals how easy it is for our help, plans, and desires for God's work to actually become a distraction from His glory.

Jesus Drew An Unacceptable Picture Of Messiah

Peter had just confessed that Jesus, the man from Nazareth, was, in reality, the promised Christ (vv. 13-19). It was an astonishing confession. Peter bared his deepest feelings about the Christ against a backdrop of outright paganism. Jesus had taken the disciples to Caesarea Philippi, a city given over to idolatry and paganism. For several weeks before this trip, Jesus had been working among the people of Galilee where He taught in their synagogues or in the open air. He had healed the sick and had repeatedly rebuked the Pharisees and scribes for their unwise adherence to man-made rules. After many days of this high pressure ministry, Jesus and the disciples needed a break. Jesus led the little band out of Galilee into the Gentile region of Phoenicia. While they were in that region near the cities of Tyre and Sidon, a Canaanite woman came to Christ and expressed great faith.

After the sabbatical in Phoenicia, Jesus and the disciples came back to Galilee, skirted the sea of Galilee, fed 4,000 hungry people, and argued with the Pharisees and Sadducees (Matthew 15:29-16:4). Within a few days, Jesus led the disciples out of Galilee again traveling north to Caesarea Philippi. This town, also known as Panias, was near the ancient city of Dan. Dan, the northern most city of ancient Israel, was the place where Jeroboam established idolatry and false worship. That idolatry eventually led to Israel's defeat and exportation at the hands of the Assyrians. During those years of rebellion, the false religion of Baal was firmly established in Dan. In Jesus' day, Baal worship was not the problem in and around Caesarea Philippi. During the third century BC, the Greeks made this town the center for worshiping Pan, a false god connected with pagan idolatry. That explains the name Panias for the town also known as Caesarea Philippi. Today one can still see the carvings in the face of the rock where the old temple of Pan once stood.

Also in Caesarea Philippi was an impressive temple that Herod the Great built for Caesar worship. There was so much pagan mythology and idolatry in that area that it was almost as if Jesus and the disciples were standing in the center of New York City or Los Angles or any other major city of the world.

The setting for Peter's confession about Jesus heightens the incredibleness of his words. He confessed to a man who looked very much like himself, that he was convinced that his peer was the Christ. That is astonishing! He told this man, "You are the promised Messiah. You are the One ordained by God to take away the sins of His people. You are the Lamb of God who takes away the sins of the world" (John 1:29). In light of the circumstances of that day, Peter's confession was remarkable; and yet it is the same conclusion every sinner must reach if he or she would be saved from sin. Every person must come to the point where he or she says sincerely, "I am a sinner who has offended God. I have nothing to offer to atone for my sins. I need a Savior to save me, and Jesus, the man from Nazareth, is that Savior."

Peter's confession that Jesus is the Christ is so marvelous because natural depravity precludes such a conclusion. Jesus pointed out that human depravity does not lead anyone to acknowledge Him as Savior. He revealed that Peter was able to make the astonishing confession only because God gave him the ability to understand this truth (v. 17). Peter drew his conclusion through supernatural revelation. God opened the eyes of his understanding—he could not reject the truth. The fact that Peter's conclusion was supernaturally conveyed to him is obvious from the further fact that the vast majority of his fellow-Jews disagreed with his conclusion.

Many professional academicians study the life and words of Jesus, but are never able to admit with a clear conscience that He is the Christ, the Savior from sin. Many average people spend a lifetime going to church services on Sunday where they hear preachers say interesting things from the Bible. But those same people never gain the confidence that Jesus of Nazareth was God in the flesh. It seems too impossible. Therefore, they never confess sin against God and never ask God to cover their sins with the blood of Jesus. Instead they continue to seek reconciliation with God by doing good works through human strength. Confessions like Peter made are the result of divine enlightenment. If God does not quicken the heart of spiritually dead people, they will remain forever hopeless. It is a great tragedy when God stirs the sinner's heart, but the sinner chooses to ignore God's prompting.

On the heels of Peter's marvelous confession, Jesus told the disciples things that were hard to understand (vv. 20-21). First, Jesus said that the disciples must not tell anyone that He was the Christ. Since the truth of Peter's confession was revealed to Him by God Himself, why shouldn't he and the disciples be free to spread the good news? If the disciples were really convinced that Jesus was the Christ, they would certainly want to tell others. Why shouldn't they.

Jesus knew that even the disciples had a jaded understanding of the Christ concept. The Old Testament prophets promised that the Christ would save His people from their sins (Zechariah 9:9). The disciples understood that. Probably almost everyone in that age who had studied the Old Testament Scriptures was convinced of this truth. It was also clear that John the Baptist had introduced Jesus as the Savior from sins. As a result, many people believed that Jesus of Nazareth was the Messiah. But the popular opinion believed that Messiah would be the savior from human government and the tyranny of Rome. Jesus' peers looked for the king who would sit on David's throne not for a savior from sin. They longed for the king who would throw off Rome's bondage. They wanted the earthly king who they anticipated would finally bring peace to their beleaguered nation.

Much to the multitudes' disappointment, establishing political peace was not the reason God came to earth as baby Jesus. At the end of the age, this same Messiah will return to the earth and set up the literal, earthly kingdom, which will be the fulfillment of God's promise to David. After God's amazing judgment against sin in the Great Tribulation, Jesus of Nazareth will establish political peace on earth. That is yet to come. The people in Jesus' day were disappointed with Jesus because they looked for the physical kingdom instead of the spiritual kingdom.

The disciples were not exempt from this confused opinion about Messiah. Therefore, Jesus told them not to spread the news about who He was. Also, because the disciples held a jaded view of Messiah, they must have been quite shocked to hear Jesus say that He must go to Jerusalem in order to suffer, die, and rise from the dead. That didn't make any sense at all. Jerusalem was supposed to be the city of peace, which is a literal interpretation of the name. It has existed since about 2000 BC. Sometime around 1050 BC, David made Jerusalem the capital of his kingdom, and it became known as David's city (2 Samuel 5:9). God called Jerusalem His city (Psalm 46:4). He said that it was the place of His dwelling (Zechariah 2:10).

How could a city with such a name, such a history, and such favor of God, be the place where God's Messiah must go to suffer? The idea must have seemed ridiculous to the disciples. Nevertheless, Jesus told the disciples that He must go to Jerusalem. He had to go to Jerusalem because God had chosen it to be the city where His people must make sacrifices that were pleasing to Him. Through Moses, God had promised Israel that, "there will be the place where the Lord your God chooses to make His name abide. There you shall bring all that

I command you: your burnt offerings, your sacrifices, your tithes, the heave offerings of your hand, and all your choice offerings which you vow to the Lord" (Deuteronomy 12:11). In keeping with the Father's instruction, Jesus had to go to Jerusalem to offer Himself as the sacrifice for the sins of humanity.

For Jesus to go to Jerusalem also meant that Jesus would suffer many things at the hands of the elders, chief priests, and scribes. David foresaw the coming suffering of Messiah and prophesied that, "the mouth of the wicked and the mouth of the deceitful have opened against me; they have spoken against me with a lying tongue" (Psalm 109:2). The Psalmist Asaph promised Messiah would give His "back to those who struck [Him], and [His] cheeks to those who plucked out the beard; [He] did not hide [His] face from shame and spitting" (Isaiah 50:6). Because Jesus of Nazareth was the Messiah, He had to go to Jerusalem where He would face such suffering.

Jesus also told the disciples that when He went to Jerusalem He would be killed. The Greek word translated killed referred specifically to the act of murder, intentional killing. Isaiah pointed ahead to this murder when he prophesied God's plan for Messiah: "Therefore I will divide Him a portion with the great, and He shall divide the spoil with the strong, because He poured out His soul unto death" (Isaiah 53:12a). God gave Daniel the same prophesy when He revealed that "after the sixty-two weeks Messiah shall be cut off, but not for Himself" (Daniel 9:26a). The authorities had to murder Messiah in order to fulfill the Father's plan. God the Father promised it.

The great news was that this same Jesus must also rise again. Messiah said confidently through the prophet David that "You [God] will not leave my soul in Sheol, nor will You allow Your Holy One to see corruption" (Psalm 16:10). The Father's plan is obvious from the Scriptures. Jesus of Nazareth had to go to Jerusalem and endure suffering, death, then be raised from the dead, because He was the Messiah. The plan sounded radical to the disciples, but it was God's plan.

Jesus Rebuked Peter Because He Tried To Help

As soon as Jesus told the disciples what He must do because of the Father's plan, Peter offered conflicting advice from the human perspective (v. 22). Peter, who had just confessed that Jesus of Nazareth was the Christ the Son of the living God, could not accept the plan this same Jesus had just unfolded to him. According to Peter's understanding, since Jesus was the Christ, He could not die. Therefore, Peter took Christ aside to rebuke Him. See Peter, the mere man, boldly pulling Jesus, the Christ, aside from the path where he brashly exercised presumptuous authority. Apparently Peter felt quite comfortable to rebuke the Master. He presumptuously claimed that God's mercy would deliver the Christ from such tragedy. Peter said, "Far be it from You." Simply put he meant, "Mercy on You," or "God will not allow such a thing in His scope of mercy." His rebuke was sincere and well-intentioned. Nevertheless, Peter foolishly contradicted what Jesus had just said.

When Peter rebuked the Christ, he virtually rejected the Father's will. He failed to apply the Scriptures that he had learned as a child. Did Peter forget that Isaiah 53 had promised suffering and death for Messiah? Maybe Peter fell into the same kind of interpretational trap God's people often fall into in this age. It is not that Christians are unaware of what the Bible says, nor are they always guilty of bad memories. The problem is that Christians tend to interpret Scripture in light of their personal preferences. Peter's preference was that Messiah would not suffer and die. His personal opinion superseded the Father's plan. Peter wanted Messiah to be the mighty king of an actual, earthly kingdom. One day He will be. But Peter's timing was off by a few thousand years.

One cannot help but wonder if Peter's rebuke was motivated by personal concern. Was it possible that he feared that Messiah's death meant, no kingdom, and therefore, no chief position for him in Messiah's cabinet? Maybe Peter feared personal loss. Thoughts like that entered the disciples' minds on other occasions. On the night of the Last Supper, "there was also a dispute among them, as to which of them should be considered the greatest" (Luke 22:24).

The disciples lived in ancient days but they were very much like people in these days. Many professing Christians are satisfied to follow Jesus as long as it's convenient. Doing God's will isn't too bad as long as it coincides with our plans. However, if God's will involves loss of position, esteem, or even possessions, that is a different story. If the matter involves inconvenience or loss, then it must not be God's will. That is the reasoning of many modern disciples. Too many of Christ's followers are quick to rebuke Christ, just like Peter did, when divine plans do not appear to fit their predetermined desires.

Peter stated his opinion in clear terms and might have been satisfied that he had just saved the Messiah from a tragic mistake. Maybe he was feeling quite confident about his role when suddenly he was shocked beyond belief at Jesus' response. When Jesus identified the source of Peter's advice He revealed how ugly sin really is (v. 23). Jesus bluntly said that Satan himself influenced Peter's advice. Satan? Jesus told Peter, "Get behind Me Satan." Peter must have felt like Jesus had just hit him in the head with a brick.

It is instructive to compare Jesus' response to Peter with His response to Satan at the temptation early in His ministry. After Jesus successfully blocked all three of Satan's temptations to sin, Jesus said to him, "Away with you, Satan! For it is written, 'You shall worship the Lord your God, and Him only you shall serve'" (Matthew 4:10). According to Luke, the second temptation ended when Jesus answered Satan, "Get behind Me, Satan! For it is written, 'You shall worship the Lord your God, and Him only you shall serve'" (Luke 4:8). That rebuke sounded like the same thing Jesus said to Peter.

Luke also wrote that after Satan's temptations failed, "when the devil had ended every temptation, he departed from Him [Jesus] until an opportune time" (Luke 4:13). It seems rather clear that Peter's attempt to deter Jesus from doing the Father's will was one of those opportune times. Jesus recognized Satan's influence in Peter's rebuke. Surely Peter did not willingly become an instrument for Satan. Surely he did not intend to be in league with Satan. Rather, Peter erred when he yielded to the normal, fleshly desires, and Satan capitalized on his weakness. Christians often follow Peter's example. Christians can become careless and allow Satan to use their natural sinful desires to oppose God's will.

Peter became a distraction to Christ's ministry because he misunderstood the Father's will. Jesus would not tolerate anything that might have sidetracked Him from the divine purpose. No one would have blamed Jesus for attempting to avoid the suffering and crucifixion. After all, Jesus was fully human. He experienced every weakness known to the human race. The difference between Jesus Christ and the rest of humanity is that Jesus never failed when He was tested in the flesh. The agony He experienced in the Garden of Gethsemane was very real. It could have deterred Him from following the Father's will. Matthew recorded the intense emotional pain Jesus endured when, "He went a little farther and fell on His face, and prayed, saying, 'O My Father, if it is possible, let this cup pass from Me; nevertheless, not as I will, but as You will'" (Matthew 26:39). Peter did not understand how dangerous it was for him to tempt the Christ to circumvent the Father's will.

How much damage is done to God's work because careless Christians mind the things of this world like Peter did? The world is opposed to God's work and will. Therefore, God's people must fix their sights on God's things. The unsaved citizens of earth naturally care for, think about, and pursue the goals equated with this ungodly system. Christians must fix their minds on God's things. What are God's things? They are the matters defined in the Bible. Peter learned this truth well. He learned that God's "divine power has given to us all things that pertain to life and godliness, through the knowledge of Him who called us by glory and virtue, by which have been given to us exceedingly great and precious promises, that through these you may be partakers of the divine nature, having escaped the corruption that is in the world through lust" (2 Peter 1:3-4). Ask typical Christians whether these things that pertain to life and godliness, these principles of God's Word, are more important to them than a new house or a better job. To focus on the things of this world instead of God's things generally interrupts God's will.

Jesus Taught The Underlying Principle About God's Things

Peter wanted things to work out according to his plan. Jesus' death did not fit his plan. He needed to learn that whole-hearted dedication to Christ must often be accompanied by sacrifice. Jesus taught that successful following after Him is preceded by a strong desire to follow Him. God is kind enough to prompt His people to follow Christ, but the one who is prompted must respond. Multitudes of people, most people throughout history, have rejected God's prompting through the Holy Spirit because they prefer to do their own religious thing. They press on with their own desires and purposes and hope that, in the end,

God will approve of their choices. They fail to understand that each person is accountable to God for his or her desires. Wise men and women mark their desires well and seek to have desires that fit God's plan first. Genuine followers of Christ must determine to do His plan even if it means trashing their own personal desires.

Since God's will generally requires the sacrifice of personal desires, pictured in the taking up of a cross, it is important to count the cost of following Christ. How much does it cost? It costs everything that people normally hold dear. Quinton Hogg, founder of the London Polytechnic Institute, devoted a great fortune to the enterprise. Asked how much it had cost to build up such a great institution, Hogg replied, "Not very much, simply one man's life blood." That is the cost of every great achievement, and it's not paid in a lump sum. It is bought on the time-payment plan, a further installment each new day. Fresh drafts are constantly being made. Can the pursuit of Christ be less costly? Following Christ should never be confused with making a religious decision. Many decisions cost nothing. Following Christ costs everything. Count it carefully.

Bearing a cross does not sound very rewarding. However, Jesus promised that the rewards for bearing His cross in this life and the next are innumerable. One time Peter asked the Lord, "See, we have left all and followed You." He wondered, "What's in it for us?" Jesus responded, "Assuredly, I say to you, there is no one who has left house or parents or brothers or wife or children, for the sake of the kingdom of God, who shall not receive many times more in this present time, and in the age to come eternal life" (Luke 18:28-30).

Sacrifice alone does not guarantee eternal reward. Following Christ alone does. That is a difficult challenge because it is more natural to follow our own interpretation of Christ's path. It is natural to want to do your own desires and, at the same time, have God stamp them with His approval. Most people naturally want to do religious traditions that fit with personal desires and believe that those traditions will be sufficient to please God. Conversely, Christ established a path that glorifies the Father. He did earthly ministry for God's glory. Such a path results in great joy. Wise men and women follow that path. Peter's response was natural, but Christ's response to trouble was God-honoring.

CHAPTER 17

JESUS EXPLAINED WHY
THE WORLD HATES HIM

JOHN 7:1-13

When someone claims that the world hates him, most people immediately conclude that the poor fellow has extremely low self-esteem, that he is probably in a serious state of depression, and that he is not being realistic. The world really doesn't hate anyone. Even men like Hitler or Saddam Hussein could find someone who claimed to be on their side.

So how does one interpret Jesus' words to his brothers when He told them that the world hated Him? Was He just having a bad day? Was He depressed? If we really understand the truth about Jesus Christ, those seem like foolish questions. Of course He didn't have a bad day or become depressed. The Christ was tempted in every way known to humans, but He never succumbed to the testing. So what did He mean when He affirmed that the world hates Him?

About nine months before this event, Jesus told the disciples, "Do not think that I came to bring peace on earth. I did not come to bring peace but a sword" (Matthew 10:34). That was not an admission of a pessimistic world view. Rather His statement uncovered the central truth about the relationship between God and His fallen creation. From the time that Adam and Eve introduced sin into the world, the world's way of thinking has been opposed to God and His standard of righteousness. When Jesus said that the world hated Him, He referred to the system of thought that is represented in the minds of most people. Every person who does not yield to God and receive Christ as the Savior from sin is opposed to Jesus Christ. Furthermore, every person who identifies with Christ will face the world's hatred just like He did. Why?

The world hates the Son of God, and those who are related to the Son of God, because He reveals the vast difference between God's righteousness and the world's unrighteousness. In essence, Jesus' life was a ministry of telling sinners they were sinners, and no person enjoys being so exposed. Because sinners do not favor having their sins exposed, Christians discover that the world tolerates them to a point. The sinful citizens of earth generally tolerate Christ's followers until those people have the audacity to say something that indicates that the world's way is wrong. The world's system of thought tolerates Christians until they imply that God's truth is the only truth. To believe such a thing is bigoted and intolerable, according to popular opinion. The world believes that only uneducated or intellectually backward people could be so naive.

Jesus understood His purpose on earth well. He also understood how His world would respond to Him and to His teaching. Nevertheless, He did all things in perfect timing in order to bring glory to His Father. He came to earth to do the Heavenly Father's will. The outworking of that will caused some people to turn against Him. It still does.

Jesus Remained In Galilee For A Time

Jesus of Nazareth purposely stayed at home in Galilee until the time for the Feast of Tabernacles (vv. 1-2). The specific statement in the first verse of this text is that "He did not want to walk in Judea." It was expedient for Jesus to stay out of the political "hot spot," of Jerusalem for a season. The opening words, "After these things," point back to the feeding of the 5,000 and the Bread of Life discourse which occurred in the Spring of AD 29 (John 6). By stretching the context one more chapter in John's Gospel, we discover that "After these things" also includes Jesus' healing of the lame man at the pool of Bethesda in Jerusalem (John 5). This means that, with the exception of the events recorded in chapter six, John skipped the whole Galilean ministry. That was the major time period of Christ's ministry.

John said that Jesus stayed out of Judea because things were beginning to heat up with the religious authorities. The Pharisees and the scribes (most of whom were Sadducees) had already determined to kill Jesus. In retrospect it is clear that this was ultimately the Heavenly Father's chosen path that would lead to the eternal sacrifice of His unique Son. The sovereign, omnipotent God would allow the religious and political leaders to slay the Perfect Lamb through the outpouring of their wickedness. However, it was not time yet for this grand, culminating event to take place. The Father's timing is always perfect, and in this case, the Father's time was not yet fulfilled. All events were winding down to the eternal sacrifice. Jesus needed to stay away from the rulers in Jerusalem lest they attempt to put Him on the cross before the Father's appointed time.

The downward spiral of people's reactions to Jesus is obvious in the Gospel records. Two and one-half years before this time, the fine citizens of Jesus' hometown Nazareth attempted to throw Him over the cliff (Luke 4:16-30). That happened in the summer of AD 27, in the early days of Christ's ministry. Their anger with Jesus was unusual because in the early days of ministry most of the people were in favor of Jesus. His own towns people were some of the first people to become hostile toward Him. One and one-half years before the events recorded in John chapter seven (in the spring of AD 28), the Jewish leaders plotted to kill Jesus because He healed on the Sabbath (John 5:16). Then, only four months before this event (in the summer of AD 29), Jesus began to teach the disciples plainly about His inevitable suffering and death. From the time that Peter confessed that Jesus of Nazareth was the Christ "Jesus began to show to His disciples that He must go to Jerusalem, and suffer many things from the elders and chief priests and scribes, and be killed, and be raised the third day" (Matthew 16:21). Jesus had taught the disciples that this day was coming, but they were still taken by surprise.

Against the backdrop of deteriorating relations with the religious leaders, Jesus' brothers reminded Him that the celebration of the Feast of Tabernacles was at hand (v. 2). This was a very special time of the year. God required His people to observe the Feast of Tabernacles in order to remember how He provided for their forefathers in the wilderness. Leviticus 23:33-44 and Numbers 29:12-40 establish the regulations for this feast. God required every adult male who lived within fifteen miles of Jerusalem to go to the city and celebrate the Feast of Tabernacles.

The celebration of Tabernacles actually fell within a greater context of celebration. Tishri (the last part of our September and first part of October) was the busiest month in the year for celebrations. On the first and second days of the month, Israel celebrated the Feast of Trumpets. This was a time of public thanksgiving to God for the harvest. Then on Tishri 10, the whole nation celebrated the Day of Atonement. The celebration is now called Yom Kippur. This was the day of national repentance when the high priest offered an offering for all of Israel's sins. It was the most important day of the year for Israelites. Five days after the Day of Atonement the people celebrated the Feast of Tabernacles for seven days (Tishri 15-21).

The feast was a time of great rejoicing. Many Jews who lived in foreign nations returned to Jerusalem during this month of celebration. Many of the people set up booths they made from branches. These booths reminded the people of their forefathers' temporary conditions in the wilderness. During this week of celebration, the priests offered more sacrifices in a seven-day period than during any other feast of the year. The Feast of Tabernacles was really big! Josephus called it "The holiest and greatest feast of the Jews." A common saying of the Rabbis exclaimed that "The man who has not seen these festivities does not know what a jubilee is."

Jesus' brothers challenged Him to attend the feast (vv. 3-5). They argued their point on the basis of human wisdom (vv. 3-4). They concluded that the Feast of Tabernacles was the best time for Him to try to regroup His followers (v. 3). When they encouraged Jesus to rally His disciples, they used the word disciples in the generic sense to speak of the many would-be disciples who followed Jesus when it was convenient. Jesus discouraged many of those kind of disciples from following Him (6:60). Notice that Jesus' brothers did not deny that He did mighty works. That would have been foolish and dishonest. They agreed that the excitement and gathering of the feast was the best time for Jesus to do more mighty works in order to gather a strong following.

What was their point? Why did Jesus' brothers try to argue Him into re-gathering the troops? Did they see Jesus' popularity dropping? Was the news reporting unfavorable dips in the polls? Were they honestly concerned for their half-brother's success?

Whatever their reason for challenging Jesus, the brothers limited their argument to the popular world view (v. 4). They were convinced that Jesus' primary goal was to be well-known by the masses. They believed that spectacular works would gather a huge following. They mistakenly believed that the people who followed Jesus would be just like all the other people in the world.

Jesus' statements, according to the sixth chapter in John's record, are extremely important to explain His response to His brothers' arguments. Jesus taught that the true body of Christ is not a loose gathering of worldlings who happen to be assimilated into a local assembly. Rather, He declared that real believers are drawn to faith in Him by the Father (6:44), as opposed to being drawn by supernatural events alone. Jesus taught that no one believes in Him unless the Father teaches that person (6:45). Jesus taught that real believers must identify with His sacrificial death (6:54). Jesus' teaching was so clear that the would-be disciples (non-genuine ones) abandoned Him immediately (6:66).

Jesus taught that His genuine followers are drawn to Him through God's supernatural working in their hearts. Then why would the brothers argue that Jesus needed to go to Jerusalem during the big feast and do mighty works in order to attract a large crowd of followers? The root problem was that Jesus' brothers didn't believe Him (v. 5). His own brothers who grew up with Him didn't believe Him. Their names were James, Joses (Joseph), Simon, and Judas (Jude) according to Matthew 13:55. They were real people who lived with Jesus every day while they were growing up. They too watched Jesus grow in spirit and in wisdom. But they were not convinced that He was the Messiah. It is good news indeed to learn that, after Christ's resurrection, the brothers also believed in Him. It is encouraging to discover in the history of the early Church that Jesus' brothers were in the mix. Luke wrote that "These all continued with one accord in prayer and supplication, with the women and Mary the mother of Jesus, and with

His brothers" (Acts 1:14). But while Jesus was still with them, the brothers stumbled at His ministry.

Failure, like Jesus' brothers' failure, is still obvious among religious people. Many religious leaders and their followers believe that the chief goal in church things is to make Christ popular. They seek to attract and enlist people who are firmly and gladly rooted in the world's way of thinking. They attempt to build large, noticeable organizations with people whom God has not drawn. They are satisfied with external confessions and shallow commitments because big is always better. Size of the organization is the most important standard of measurement to many people. Popular seminars do not encourage pastors to investigate the supernatural calling of God in individual's lives, but teach them how to manipulate sinful people so that they appear to be righteous, so that the organization appears to have God's blessing. That is how Jesus' brothers thought. They were unbelievers. Is it possible that much modern teaching about church growth is actually rooted in unbelief?

Jesus refused to yield to peer pressure (vv. 6-9). He explained to His brothers that He must do His work in the right time (vv. 6, 8). He told them that He needed to do His work within a particular time frame. This was not a reference to the predetermined events that would close out Christ's ministry. Here the word time simply speaks of the most appropriate time to do something. It would have been unwise for Jesus to go to Jerusalem with the caravan that traveled from Capernaum. It would not have been proper for Him to burst on the celebration and present Himself as a popular leader. The brothers could do whatever they wanted when they wanted because they were unbelievers. They could march into Jerusalem with the rest of the crowd, and not be concerned, because no one wanted to force one of them to be King. No one wanted to kill the brothers. As unbelievers, they fit with the majority which did not call attention to themselves.

Jesus explained to His half-brothers that the time was not right for Him to present Himself for kingship. He also explained His relationship with the world so that the brothers would understand His real purpose (v. 7). Jesus said that the world hated the Christ, but it did not hate the unbelieving brothers. The people who were conformed to the world system of thinking did not detest the brothers because they all held the same views, opinions, and mind set. The world agreed to detest Christ. How could this possibly be the result of all of His good works over the past three years? What went wrong? Actually, when Jesus said that the world hated Him, He did not mean that everyone in the world hated Him. More specifically, Jesus pointed out that the people who espoused the system governed by Satan hated the Christ. Of course that would be the majority of the earth's citizens at any given time. People who live under the influence of Satan, in concert with Satan's unrighteousness, still hate Christ. They are still the majority.

Why does the world hate Jesus of Nazareth so much? Jesus explained that the world hated Him because He is Christ. He is the anointed One. He is God in the flesh, and therefore, He represented perfect truth and goodness. The fact that He, the incarnate truth and righteousness, lived in the world required that He expose the falsehood and evil of the world. His teaching drew back the curtain and exposed the religious leaders' sins. Everyone who is exposed by Christ either hates Him or they confess their sins, repent, and accept Him as Savior.

Jesus Attended The Feast Of Tabernacles

According to verse ten, after the brothers left with the caravan to attend the feast in Jerusalem, Jesus also went. However, He went to the feast secretly. Jesus went to the feast according to His plan, not according to His brothers' plan. The previous verses seemed to indicate that He was not going to the feast at all, but that would be an inaccurate conclusion. Jesus planned all along to attend the feast, but He planned to go in a particular way and at a particular time. Jesus was determined to do the Father's will, which did not coincide with His brothers' will. The Father's will required Jesus to show up at the feast inconspicuously. Maybe He and the disciples walked along the back roads to the city instead of joining up with the caravan. They needed to arrive at the feast without calling attention to themselves.

The activity of the people at the feast proves how well Jesus understood the hearts of men. Verse eleven states that before He arrived at the feast, the Jews were busy searching for Him (v. 11). That is precisely what Jesus planned to avoid. The general term Jews almost certainly refers to the religious leaders. John used this term consistently throughout his record to speak of the leaders. In 6:41

He wrote that the Jews argued among themselves about what Jesus said. In the same context, (verse fifty-nine) he wrote that the Jews he referred to were the leaders who argued with Jesus in the synagogue. Often in this Gospel John contrasted the Jews with the people.

The Jewish leaders anticipated Jesus' attendance at the feast. They must have thought along the same worldly-wise lines as Jesus' unrepentant brothers did. They fully expected Jesus to be in the crowd, and they were perplexed when it appeared that He was not going to attend the event. Why were they so interested in finding Jesus? Did they plan to expose Him as a fraud? Did they want to kill Him? Their repeated question, "Where is He?," might have sounded like a favorable question to the average person in attendance. The leaders had other plans.

The people who were at the feast were divided in their opinions about the man from Nazareth (vv. 12-13). Generally the multitudes held two opposing views about Jesus (v. 12). Some people thought that Jesus was good. Surely those people whom Jesus had healed held Him in highest esteem, and those who marveled at His teaching must have believed that He was good. The four Gospel accounts often draw a picture of the outcasts and those who did not fit into popular society following Jesus most fervently. That picture is consistent with the list of people who were Jesus' company in the end as He hung on the cross and as those few friends buried Him in the borrowed tomb. In that little group of followers were people like Mary, Mary Magdalene, Salome, Joseph of Arimathea, John, and John's mother. Not many mighty; not many noble. They loved Him and were convinced that Jesus of Nazareth was good.

That picture is also in keeping with Paul's lesson to the Corinthian believers about God's useful servants. The Corinthian Christians tended to get hung up on the value of human wisdom. They needed to learn that God often chooses the people whom the world calls weak to be His servants. Paul said that he and his friends rejected human wisdom in favor of God's choice:

> *But we preach Christ crucified, to the Jews a stumbling block and to the Greeks foolishness, but to those who are called, both Jews and Greeks, Christ the power of God and the wisdom of God. Because the foolish-*

*ness of God is wiser than men, and the weakness of
God is stronger than men. For you see your calling,
brethren, that not many wise according to the flesh, not
many mighty, not many noble, are called. But God has
chosen the foolish things of the world to put to shame
the wise, and God has chosen the weak things of the
world to put to shame the things which are mighty;
and the base things of the world and the things which
are despised God has chosen, and the things which are
not, to bring to nothing the things that are, that no flesh
should glory in His presence (1 Corinthians 1:23-29).*

The people whom God chooses believe that Jesus of Nazareth
was not just good, but divine. In contrast, there were some people in
the crowd at the Feast of Tabernacles who believed that Jesus was
a deceiver. Many of those people, no doubt, were led astray by the
religious leaders.

John observed that everyone in the crowd that day was afraid
to speak openly about Jesus (v. 13). Obviously, the religious leaders
wielded great power. Unbelieving leaders still attempt to silence conversation about Jesus. A quick review of current news proves that there
is an obvious increase in litigation to attempt to remove every vestige
of God, the Bible, and Jesus Christ from modern culture. Unbelievers
are shameless in their attacks. Nothing is too absurd. Nothing is out
of bounds for them as they seek to silence references to this ancient
Christ. Why?

The world still hates Christ. The world still hates Christ because
He still uncovers the exceeding wickedness of the world. They know
what His word does and they do not appreciate it. Sinners are often
like rodents that hate the light of day and scurry to escape it when it
shines on them. The unbelievers in society tolerate talk about Christ
for awhile but at some point they turn in vengeance against it and seek
to eliminate all light of the truth.

Sincere believers should be thankful that God has enlightened
their spiritual eyes. Sinners whose spiritual eyes are blinded by sin
do not understand the joy of spiritual enlightenment. They assume
that all religion is the same, that it is nothing more than an opiate
for the people. They errantly believe that they have the power within

themselves to accomplish all that matters in life. Therefore, God's people are foolish to expect unenlightened, unregenerated sinners to share their joy in Jesus Christ. Christians should not be surprised to learn that their sinful relatives, neighbors and co-workers actually hate Christ. They conceal their hatred well until someone confronts them with Christ's words. At some point they clearly expose their dislike of Jesus of Nazareth. Since the world hates Jesus they will, to some extent, hate everyone who is related to Jesus.

Christians act in a Christlike way when they pity sinners whose spiritual eyes are darkened and who live in bondage to sin continually. Christians should be concerned enough for such people to tell them the good news that Jesus of Nazareth is the Christ who offers them eternal life through faith in Him. Jesus explained the problem to His half-brothers and the matter escaped their understanding. Christ's followers must realize that the principle of Satan's system hating Christ will never change. Therefore, we live in hope looking for the return of Christ to reign in a world without sin

CHAPTER 18

JESUS JUDGED WITH RIGHTEOUS JUDGMENT

JOHN 7:14-24

Who has not been amused or offended by the ludicrous headlines splashed across the front page of tabloids in the supermarket checkout line? It is amazing that such nonsense sells. Do people buy those rags because they think that the stories behind the headlines are true, or do they buy them because the foolishness is entertaining. Hopefully the tabloids sell to provide entertainment because otherwise their popularity indicates that there are people in our neighborhoods who believe things like:

Dinosaurs Honked Like Buicks.

Cow Mattresses Help Cows Produce More Milk.

Mother-To-Be On Diet Of Only Chicken, Lays Huge Egg

WWII Bomber Found On The Moon.

Woman Gives Birth To 2 Year Old Baby: Child Walks & Talks In 3 Days.

Adam & Eve's Bones Found In Asia: Eve Was A Space Alien

Maybe some folks read this diatribe in order to be amused by the absurd. However, there is a natural tendency for some people to believe strange things without thinking through the rumors carefully. That problem is broader than it appears to be on the surface. Because of their tendency to take things at face value, many people believe whatever they read or hear. That is a frightening thought! Does anyone ever try to look behind the curtain to see if the Wizard of Oz is a hoax?

Human nature is so prone to believe the first bad news or incredible news, that some folks accept as truth things that are not true at all. If a religious spokesperson were to say, "As a devout Christian I have learned that the best way to serve God is to ignore sin and just love everyone," naive Christians welcome him with open arms. They conclude that if this fellow Christian has learned a new principle for Christian living it must be true. In fact they may even copy the fellow's error in their own lives. The results are disastrous. Another religious leader might declare, "The Bible is full of mistakes, but we can still trust God and go to heaven." Masses of people embrace teaching like that and count speakers like him as a brother.

Recently, a religious leader claimed that people do not need to believe the creation story in order to enjoy fellowship with Christ. Religious people were delighted to learn that they could be acceptable to pagan scientists and God at the same time. Recently, some thinkers concluded that it is no longer politically correct to refer to the Judeo-Christian moorings of the United States. Instead, the proper reference now is to the Judeo-Christian-Islamic foundations of the nation. That is an impossible conclusion in light of this nation's history. Christian and Jewish teachings are rooted in the Bible. Most Islamic teachings are rooted in the Koran which, in many areas, is opposed to the Bible. How can conflicting doctrines be shared in the foundation of a nation?

Jesus of Nazareth taught that it is critically important for His followers to judge righteous judgment. That instruction cuts across the grain of human nature. If Jesus was simply another human, it is unlikely that He would have advanced such a notion. However, because Jesus is divine, He understood that everyone will pass judgment on some things or on some people at some time. When that time comes, Jesus taught, the one who passes judgment must be fair, honest, and accurate. Accuracy in judgment requires knowledge of the real issues. Accuracy desires to know what the underlying motivation is that drives the issue or the person. In a conversation with the religious leaders at the Feast of Tabernacles, Jesus, the God-man, illustrated the divine principle for ferreting out underlying motivations.

Jesus Illustrated Righteousness

At some point during the Feast of Tabernacles in the year 29, Jesus went up to the temple to teach (7:14-15). According to verses two through ten, Jesus had lingered at home for awhile before going to the feast. His brothers argued that He should go to the feast, do some mighty works, and gather a following. After Jesus explained that they were ignorant of God's plan, the brothers left for Jerusalem. The text seems to imply that the brothers were part of the caravan that went up to the capital city from Capernaum. Jesus did not go with the multitude. He chose to go into Jerusalem secretly during the feast in order to keep from attracting a raucous crowd.

It is possible that Jesus did not arrive in Jerusalem until the third or fourth day of the seven day feast. At that time Jesus quietly entered Jerusalem and went to the temple area where He planned to teach everyone who gathered to listen. Jesus always managed to gather a crowd of people who desired to hear His words. His world considered Him to be an unusually gifted teacher. He practiced the same methods of teaching the Rabbis used. In fact, some of the people were so sure that He was a Rabbi that they used the title to address Him. Many other people concluded that He was better than the Rabbi's because His teaching was almost supernatural. Therefore, when Jesus went to the temple to teach, His action was not odd. It was the kind of thing Rabbis did with regularity. They would go to the outer court and sit on one of the porches while the people gathered around them to listen to their teaching. This is where Jesus' parents found Him when, as a boy, He was debating with the scholars at the temple (Luke 2:46).

On this day of the Feast of Tabernacles, as Jesus taught, the religious leaders "marveled" at His teaching (7:15). Why? Obviously, they recognized, along with many other people, that Jesus' teaching was authoritative. The crowds had concluded long before that Jesus' teaching was quite unlike the scribes' and Pharisees' teaching. What did Jesus teach that impressed even the religious leaders that day? The Scriptures do not say. Jesus often taught the simple principles of Scripture like those found in the parables or the Sermon on the Mount. Whatever He taught, it always caused the people to marvel at the authority He exhibited while He taught. "For He taught them as one having authority, and not as the scribes" (Matthew 7:29). The people "were astonished at His teaching, for He taught them as one having authority, and not as the scribes" (Mark 1:22).

It is unlikely that the religious leaders were supportive or excited about Jesus' teaching. They did not marvel because they thought that Jesus from Nazareth was a wonderful teacher. They were amazed because Jesus did not have the advantage of their approved education. Jesus was not an accredited teacher, but He spoke with more authority than the most accredited teachers in Israel. In this case, as in other places throughout John's Gospel, the term the Jews referred to the religious leaders (i.e., the scribes, Pharisees, and priests). They all knew that the recognized teachers of the day, the Rabbis, had graduated from the Jewish seminaries. Luke probably referred to one such seminary a couple of times in the Acts. During the early history of the Church the religious leaders debated about what they should do with the apostles who turned Jerusalem on its ear with their teaching about Jesus. During the meeting "one in the council stood up, a Pharisee named Gamaliel, a teacher of the law held in respect by all the people, and commanded them to put the apostles outside for a little while" (Acts 5:34). It appears that this authoritative member of the Sanhedrin named Gamaliel conducted a seminary that produced approved Jewish teachers.

The apostle Paul acknowledged that he had attended Gamaliel's seminary. One day, many years after Jesus had ascended to heaven, a mob in Jerusalem attempted to tear Paul limb from limb. After authorities quelled the rebellion, Paul asked permission to speak to the crowd. In his speech he defended himself saying, "I am indeed a Jew, born in Tarsus of Cilicia, but brought up in this city at the feet of Gamaliel, taught according to the strictness of our fathers' law, and was zealous toward God as you all are today" (Acts 22:3). Paul was one of the shining examples of the scholars who came from that school. He was one of their prized graduates until he was born again. When Paul embraced the teaching of Jesus, the fine seminary of Gamaliel rejected him.

The Jewish schools had good reputations in Jerusalem. But Jesus never attended any of those schools. That is why the Jewish leaders were astonished that Jesus taught with such authority. They trained seminarians, they could identify quality teachers. Jesus was certainly a quality teacher but He was not one of theirs. He never graduated with their approval. "How could He be so effective?" they wondered.

Attitudes about theological credentials have not changed much over the centuries. Technology changes rapidly, but the people who use technology are essentially the same century after century. Therefore, men still seek credentials from other mere men as their authority for doing God's work. When God sends His true spokesmen, they are not required to have man's credentials. God's people recognize God-sent teachers. A piece of paper signed by a religious authority is not a requirement. No amount of human credentials will make a speaker authoritative if God has not equipped and sent him. When God's servants preach God's message it should be obvious that the message is authoritative. Jesus's teaching proved that He was God in the flesh, the divine teacher, and the religious leaders refused to believe Him.

Jesus hammered on the question of His divine authority in this conversation with the religious leaders. They were amazed that He taught with authority—authority they had not approved. Therefore, He explained the issue they struggled to understand. He told them that there was a connection between His teaching and righteousness (7:16-18). He laid down the critically important principle that obedience to truth results in more truth.

Jesus of Nazareth proved to the religious leaders that His teaching emanated from a higher authority than they could offer to their students. Indeed, His teaching came from the divine authority. Jesus, the man from Nazareth, did not contrive the content of His teaching, nor did the scholars of His day originate it. Jesus' teaching was the word of the Everlasting God. This was no new revelation. The man from Nazareth tried to tell the leaders on other occasions that His teaching came directly from God, but they refused to believe Him. A short time after this event Jesus told the leaders, "When you lift up the Son of Man, then you will know that I am He, and that I do nothing of Myself; but as My Father taught Me, I speak these things" (John 8:28). In the context of His suffering and crucifixion Jesus reiterated, "I have not spoken on My own authority; but the Father who sent Me gave Me a command, what I should say and what I should speak" (John 12:49). Devout Jewish leaders would not accept that kind of claim!

In every age since the ministry of Christ it is common for most devout religious people to refuse to accept the claim that Jesus, the man from Nazareth, taught the truths of the one true God in Heaven. They recoil at the idea that anyone has a "corner" on truth—including Jesus the carpenter's son (which He was not). The popular conclusion is to view all religious teaching as equal. The prevailing attitude of toleration requires that all teachers of religion must be accepted on equal basis. One is as good as the other. No one is allowed to have exclusive rights to truth. Modern thinkers conclude that only extreme bias or stupidity would hold that one teaching alone expresses the truth. They say that truth is relative. They teach that every person is free to accept the doctrine that he or she chooses. Personal desire or choice is the only criterion that counts.

It is certainly true that each individual should be free to choose to submit himself to any teaching he prefers. But the progressive thinkers fail to acknowledge that this freedom means that it is possible for a person to choose error over truth to his eternal detriment. Modern thinkers cringe when Christians claim that there is only one God and that the Bible is the only teaching that comes from the one God. Such a position is intolerable to human wisdom. Many people also cringe to hear that Jesus was God in the flesh and the premier teacher of that one exclusive truth. People in Jesus' day believed much the same way and that is why the religious and political authorities of the day hung Him on the cross.

Some people don't fit into the world's system very well. Genuine Christians really believe that Jesus is the Christ, God's Messiah, who came from heaven. The person who is wholly given to that truth desires to do God's will. Jesus promised the religious leaders that anyone who desires to do God's will is able to grasp this great truth (7:17). But a common argument says that it is impossible for a sinner who is dead in his sins to know what God wills. How can a person know God's will, even to the slightest extent, before he is regenerated or enlightened? The Bible states that God reveals His righteousness in various ways even apart from the Bible. According to the first chapter in Romans, God reveals much about His nature and character in creation. The second chapter of the same letter, teaches that God has written his law on the conscience of every person. Therefore, unregenerate sinners already know much about God's will. The person who desires to do what God has already revealed, the person who pursues the truth God has already given, will receive greater knowledge. God put that promise in His law and commanded Moses to write, "from there you will seek the LORD your God, and you will find Him if you seek Him with all your heart and with all your soul" (Deuteronomy 4:29). People in Jesus' day could have pursued the truth they already had, but most of them chose to hide it behind man-made religious rules.

This modern generation does not need more truth. This generation needs to act according to the truth it already has. The leaders who marveled at Jesus's teaching already knew much about God. They had studied His law and knew the prophecies about Christ very well. They were not deficient in truth about God. The problem was that they refused to do what they already knew God required them to do. They wanted to do their traditions instead of God's truth. They wanted a Messiah who would fit in their scheme. They were always concerned that Roman officials would come and take away their "position." If the hard-charging Messiah of their dreams would come and destroy Rome, they would be sitting in a good position for the rest of their lives. The religious leaders held a very temporary, earthy, view of things. That view did not allow for the suffering Messiah. Jesus of Nazareth claimed that He was the Messiah. But He was definitely not the hard-charging warrior they wanted, so they refused to accept any of His teaching as truth.

This is precisely where many people still get sidetracked in religion. God the Holy Spirit stirs their hearts to respond to Christ's teaching. They know that they need to be reconciled to God through the forgiveness of sins. But they want God on their own terms. Therefore, instead of accepting the truth, they invent their own religion or adopt one that fits their desires. Unfortunately, their desires are opposed to God's desires for them. They will not accept Christ as the Bible presents Him because the Christ of the Bible requires the death of self for sinners. That is asking too much. Conversely, people who really want to please God easily discover the amazing reality that Jesus is the truth! Anyone who really desires to know God's will also knows that Jesus of Nazareth is God incarnate.

Furthermore, Jesus taught, according to verse eighteen of this text, that righteousness is achieved only when the teacher seeks to glorify the authority who sent him to teach. Teachers who speak on the basis of their own authority glorify themselves. That is a logical conclusion. The world is replete with such examples. When crowds of people gather to hear a teacher and respond to his teaching favorably, it is natural for the teacher to become impressed with his own authority. Human wisdom logically concludes that the speaker creates the ideas he conveys, and ought to receive glory for his creative acts. This danger comes to bear in many modern ministries. Radio preachers and television evangelists often attract great followings. But how many of their sermons are actually the communication of God's Word? Is their teaching rooted in the Bible or do they invent ideas that attract a large following. Too often their sermonic meanderings are far removed from the authority of God's Word and are comprised of their own faulty conclusions which are based on their limited experiences in life. Some religious public speakers seem to get hung up on the idea that people in their invisible audience owe them money. Is it possible that these religious leaders speak solely for the purpose of gaining wealth and notoriety? If so it would be difficult for those preachers to be any further removed from the authority of God's Word. Surely they fulfill Peter's warning and "twist the scriptures to their own destruction" (2 Peter 3:16).

Conversely, people who speak God's words seek His glory alone. God's Word (the Bible) is the word of Him who sends His servant with authority. Christians must seek His glory alone in all they say or do. It is good for God's people to always ask, "How will God receive glory from this?" before they take up the tasks of ministry and religion. Yea, God's people must "do all to the glory of God" (1 Corinthians 10:31). This is pure righteousness. This is the description of Jesus of Nazareth, and the religious leaders refused to accept it.

Jesus Illustrated Unrighteous Judgment

Because the religious leaders were astonished that Jesus would teach not having their authority, Jesus leveled a serious accusation against them. Unfortunately, as verses nineteen and twenty indicate, the people who were standing in the multitude did not understand the import of Jesus' statement. Jesus exposed the truth about the religious leaders through an argument that combined their response to Moses' law with their desire to kill Him. He asked the religious leaders two questions. "Did not Moses give you the law, yet none of you keeps the law?" and "Why do you seek to kill Me?" (John 7:19) Surely anyone who heard Jesus' words thought that His argument was completely disconnected with the conversation that had preceded it. Where did this come from? A careful consideration of Jesus' argument answers the question.

Jesus had been talking to the leaders about His teaching. Suddenly He said that Moses gave the law, they refused to keep the law, and they wanted to kill Him. Maybe one can draw the connection between the prohibition in the law, "Don't kill," and the accusation that the leaders wanted to kill Jesus. Actually, the Lord's reasoning follows this line:

1) "You leaders won't accept my teaching."
2) "You leaders glorify yourself with your teaching."
3) "My teaching glorifies the Father Who sent Me."
4) "You want to kill Me because of My teaching, and therefore, break God's law."

The people were incredulous at Jesus' accusation. They said that Jesus was out of His mind! They said, "You have a demon. Who is seeking to kill you?" (7:20). It is important to realize that at this point Jesus shifted the focus of His conversation from the religious leaders to the people in the crowd. He had been addressing the Jews but it was the people who answered His accusation. Why didn't they believe Jesus' accusation? Obviously they did not realize that their leaders were plotting Jesus' death. This is not surprising in light of the fact that the religious leaders generally duped the masses which caused the people to live in spiritual darkness. The record is clear that within six months of this accusation and the peoples' negative reaction, a multitude of the people cried out, "Crucify Him." Surely some of the people who cried for His crucifixion were in this crowd who accused Jesus of having a demon! It is also important to notice that while the crowd went to the leaders' defense, the leaders did not deny Jesus' accusation. This is why righteous judgment is so important!

Jesus explained the principle of righteous judgment in verses twenty-one through twenty-four. First, He made the connection between Moses' law and the threat of murder. He told the people that they marveled because He "did one work" (v. 21). Which one was it? It appears that the people agreed among themselves that the work to which Jesus referred was the healing of the lame man at the pool of Bethesda. Jesus performed that miracle near the beginning of His ministry, about two years before this conversation at the temple. Everyone seemed to know about it. Why? It was a signal miracle because Jesus healed the lame man on the Sabbath in downtown Jerusalem. There was probably no more effective way to raise the ire of the religious leaders. They were so angry at Jesus that they immediately began plotting how to kill Him.

Using the miracle that all the people remembered (or had heard about) as a springboard, Jesus required the people to look deeper into the circumstances and learn the truth. The religious leaders claimed to protect God's law. The law they claimed to protect required all Jewish parents to have their sons circumcised on the eighth day after his birth. Invariably that circumcision day would fall on a Sabbath for someone's son. When it did, the religious leaders did not hesitate to do the work of circumcision because the law required it. Jesus drew this conclusion for the people so that they could understand the underlying issues of Jesus' work and the leaders' accusations. Essentially He said, "You do not mind mutilating one part of a man's body on the Sabbath" (the Jews identified 248 parts to a man's body). "But you plan to kill Me because I healed an entire body on the Sabbath." Therefore, He concluded, "You are inconsistent because the Sabbath was not broken in either case!"

Having exposed the leaders' inconsistency and their illegal charge as a reason for seeking His death, Jesus admonished the people to judge according to the truth. He warned them not to "judge according to appearance, but judge with righteous judgment" (7:24). He informed the people that their leaders planned to kill Him, and He told them why they planned to kill Him. He told them that they needed to know His teaching which would help them to know the Father who sent Him. When a person concludes that God the Son, Jesus Christ, came from God the Father, to reveal Him on earth, he is aghast that mere men would kill God's unique Son.

The principle Jesus established is critical in a day when people accept almost anything that comes along in the name of religion. On one hand, it is easy to judge some people too favorably simply because they do "approved" kinds of religious works. Since the person in question does works of which we approve, we conclude that they are godly people. But an honest assessment of his life might indicate that guy who is doing religious works also has serious spiritual problems and his heart is far from God. On the other hand, it is easy to err in judging other people unfavorably because they do not do the exact works that people in our circles approve. It is too easy to conclude that such people must not love God because they do something that our accepted traditions forbid. In reality, those same people might love God deeply and do the things they do with clear consciences.

True righteousness seeks to uncover the evidence in such circumstances. Jesus' teaching requires that we measure evidence against God's standard of righteousness before drawing conclusions. Righteous judgment is not personal judgment at all. It is always judgment rooted in God's words. Knowledge of God's words and fair application of God's words, always results in glory to Him. No one receives glory when judgment is rooted in and flows from God's Word. Righteous judgment always glorifies God. God the Son taught this divine truth and illustrated how it works.

CHAPTER 19

JESUS CAUSED PEOPLE TO WONDER

JOHN 7:25-36

Who was Jesus, the man from Nazareth? Anyone who grew up going to Sunday School and church can answer the question easily. At about the same time a child learns his alphabet and basic math facts, a dedicated Sunday school teacher also teaches her about the divinity of Jesus Christ. The negative side of that common scenario is that adults who learned Bible truth from childhood often take important Bible doctrines for granted. They never question the divinity of Jesus of Nazareth. They cannot prove it, but they never question it. It is an assumed truth.

First-century Israelites did not have the advantage of being taught about Jesus in Sunday School. All they knew is that this man from Nazareth suddenly burst on the scene with teaching like they had never heard before. Added to His amazing teaching was the fact that the Man performed miracles with regularity. He turned the nation of Israel upside down. Who was He?

Jesus had been born in relative obscurity. A few lowly shepherds arrived at the stable shortly after His birth and then went out to tell others what they had witnessed. A couple of years later, some scholars from the east aroused interest in Jerusalem when they came searching for the king of the Jews. Apart from these incidents, Jesus' childhood and young adulthood aroused little notice.

Then one day John the Baptist introduced Jesus of Nazareth to a crowd who had gathered near the Jordan River. John told the people that Jesus of Nazareth was "the Lamb of God who takes away the sin of the world" (John 1:29). Immediately after this introduction, Jesus went out to the desert where He stayed for over a month. Returning to the region called Galilee He called a few men to follow Him and learn from Him. It was a typical students/teacher relationship of that time. One day, Jesus and His followers were at a wedding feast in Cana. Jesus turned water into wine and suddenly everyone's attention was riveted on this carpenter from the village of Nazareth. Shortly thereafter, Jesus went to Jerusalem where all of the important religious leaders hung out. While He was in the city Jesus healed a lame man. Everyone would have been happy except for the fact that He healed the guy on the Sabbath. The religious leaders did not appreciate Jesus doing good works on the Sabbath, especially in Jerusalem. That was the beginning of conflicts with the religionists. Soon it became evident that Jesus taught with unusual authority. To compound the friction between Him and the religious leaders, when Jesus taught, He regularly uncovered their hypocrisy.

By the time the events recorded in the seventh chapter of John's gospel took place, Jesus had been going about Galilee doing wonderful works for about three years. Probably most of the people in Israel had heard something about this amazing teacher. However, there was not much agreement about who He really was. Some people were sure that Jesus was the promised Messiah. Other folks thought that He was a reincarnation of a great prophet from the past. Some people (especially the religious leaders), believed that Jesus was an imposter. Few really grasped the concept that Jesus of Nazareth was God the Son who had come to earth in the flesh. From the beginning of His public ministry, the multitudes were impressed with Jesus. But after three years of benefitting from His kindness, they rejected Him. Why? How could they? Jesus did not fit their concept of a Messiah, a Savior, or a Redeemer.

Any person who rejects Jesus because He does not measure up to his or her personal expectations consigns himself or herself to eternity separated from God. In blunt terms that means that each person who holds a wrong view of Christ will spend eternity in the hell which

God created for Satan and the fallen angels. That is what is at stake in the question about Jesus of Nazareth. Many people throughout history have held varying opinions about Jesus, who is called the Christ. Sadly, most of their opinions have never come any closer to the acceptable standard for eternal salvation than the views of the religious leaders of Jesus' day did. The religious leaders in Jesus' day should have been the first people to receive Him as Messiah and Savior. They understood much about God's Word because they had spend years in deep study of the Old Testament scriptures. But almost all of the religious leaders in that day chose to deny the truth they knew. They were like many religious people today who are very faithful to their religion, while at the same time, refusing Jesus Christ as their Lord. They want a Savior who will save them from their sins within their prescribed parameters. They want a Messiah who is different than the one the Bible presents. Therefore, they are forced to be dishonest about their relationship with Jesus Christ. They know many facts about Jesus of Nazareth. They know much about what the Bible says about Jesus. In the end, they are unwilling to submit to the truth they know. Jesus' conversation with the people during the Feast of Tabernacles illustrates how dangerous that position is.

The People Were Confused About Christ

A multitude of people were gathered around Jesus while He taught on the porch of the temple area. Many of them were curious and wondered, "Is this not He whom they seek to kill?" (7:25). It appears that some of the people were confident in their conclusions about Messiah. Some of the people were sure that no one would know the Messiah's lineage when He came, and that disqualified Jesus the son of Joseph and Mary.

It is possible that the subtle distinctions between the varying opinions of the people in this multitude reveal the different groups of people who were in the city for the festival. Many of the people were pilgrims from outlying regions who were just visiting Jerusalem for the feast. Other people in the multitude were the residents of Jerusalem. If that is true, probably the visiting pilgrims were unaware that the leaders' had been plotting to kill Jesus. That conclusion explains why some people in the crowd were incredulous when Jesus asked why they sought to kill him. The residents, on the other hand, would be more aware of the religious leaders' animosity toward the man from Nazareth. According to verses twenty-one through twenty-four, Jesus had directly exposed the religious leaders' inconsistent handling of God's Law. That accusation stirred their ire, which reminded some of the people that the leaders were already planning to kill Jesus.

The events of the recent days at the feast added to the cacophony of opinions about Jesus. Many people concluded that if the religious leaders wanted to kill Jesus, He could not be the Christ. What gave them the right to draw such a conclusion? Popular opinion. Popular opinion has been the sole determiner of truth for many people in many different ages. However, using popular opinion as the sounding board for truth almost always leads to error, and often leads to tragic results.

Some of the people wondered if the leaders had changed their minds and now agreed that Jesus was the Messiah. They asked, "Do the rulers know that this is truly the Christ?" (7:26). They knew that Jesus spoke boldly while He taught on the temple grounds. If the leaders were really so opposed to Him why didn't they stop Him? If they really wanted to kill Him, they should have stepped up and prevented Him from teaching. Since they did not attempt to silence the teacher from Nazareth, it was reasonable for the people to conclude that the leaders had also decided that Jesus was indeed the Messiah.

The picture laid out in these verses is not altogether unusual. People still draw conclusions about Christ based on how others respond to Him. How many children believe that Jesus is the Christ simply because that was their parents' opinion? How many adults have never thought through the lessons they heard in Sunday School when they were children? It is wise for every Christian to determine at some point in life that he is not just parroting what a teacher, preacher, or parent has said for the past twenty years. Religious people would be wise to stop and consider what they really believe about the man from Nazareth. Maybe popular opinion has shaped their beliefs about the Christ. Maybe the reason they do not live life differently than their unbelieving neighbors live is because they simply adopted another person's opinion about Jesus. They chose to believe what their leaders in the past believed, not what they have discovered for themselves from the Bible record.

Some people in the crowd that was gathered around Jesus that day chose to believe what the religious leaders believed. Other people in the crowd were not so sure. Some of them were firmly convinced that Jesus was not the Messiah. How could they be so sure? They knew that Jesus was from Nazareth. No doubt many of those people assumed that Jesus was merely the carpenter's son. That was the common consensus. They knew His mother, and they knew His brothers (Matthew 13:55). They supposed, as did many of their peers, that Joseph of Nazareth was His father (Luke 3:23). Maybe there were people in the crowd who had been offended because Jesus presented Himself as Messiah (Mark 6:3). They knew better—or so they thought.

Some of the people were sure that the authentic Christ would appear suddenly and that no one would know his background. They concluded that, "when the Christ comes, no one knows where He is from" (7:27). Since they knew Jesus' background, He could not be Messiah. Where did the people get the idea that Messiah's lineage would be unknown? It was a popular opinion of the day, but it had no basis. Did any of these people consider what the Old Testament scriptures said? What does the Scripture say? Experience teaches that the opinions of authoritative people generally overrule the truth of Scripture. It is shocking to realize that the people in Jesus' day drew eternal conclusions about the eternal Christ based on a popular story.

The great problem was that the people forgot, or chose not to consult the Scriptures. They concluded that Christ would suddenly come out of nowhere. The Bible promised, "But you, Bethlehem, though you are little among the thousands of Judah, yet out of you shall come forth to Me the One to be Ruler in Israel, Whose goings forth are from of old, from everlasting" (Micah 5:2). The Bible said, "When Israel was a child, I loved him, and out of Egypt I called My son" (Hosea 11:1). God promised these truths about the Christ years before He came to earth. Jesus of Nazareth fulfilled these promises, as well as many other prophecies in the Old Testament. An honest evaluation of Jesus proves that He fulfilled promises God had recorded in the Bible centuries earlier. He was born in Bethlehem even though He grew up in Nazareth. He was called out of Egypt to which Mary and Joseph had fled to escape the wrath of Herod. Why didn't the people consult the scriptures? It seems obvious that many of them did not want to believe that Jesus was the Christ.

This problem did not disappear with the advent of modern technology. It is also a modern issue. It is still true that people choose to draw conclusions about Jesus Christ apart from scriptural authority. They refuse to consider what the Scripture says. Or worse, they add spurious writings to the Scripture and prefer to believe confusion. They do not want to have their minds changed by Bible teaching. They are content to feel good about their chosen position. They do not realize that there is great danger in being willingly ignorant. Peter admonished people in his day who were determined to ignore the Bible. He warned that "they willfully forget: that by the word of God the heavens were of old, and the earth standing out of water and in the water" (2 Peter 3:5). Most of the modern generation has willfully forgotten that God created the world. The Bible clearly states the truth about God's creative acts in the first two chapters of Genesis. The problem for sinners is that, if God created the world and its inhabitants, then all of the inhabitants are responsible to Him. If earth's citizens are responsible to Him, each of them is in deep trouble because of personal sins and offenses against that creator-God. Many people conclude that it is best to deny that God created the world, and therefore, dismiss all responsibility toward Him.

The good news is in verse thirty-one. While many of the people rejected Jesus as Messiah, many other people chose to believe that Jesus was the Christ. What convinced them? They believed because of the miracles He did. They connected miracles with the Christ. They were sure that anyone who could do the mighty works that Jesus did must be the Messiah. The fact that at least some people in the crowd chose to believe that Jesus was who He said He was, is cause for rejoicing. But notice that even these people drew eternal conclusions based on experience instead of applying the truths of Scripture. They chose to believe because human wisdom connected their experience with the supernatural to the Christ.

Were these people converted—born again? One naturally prefers to think so, but the text does not indicate that such was the case. To say that some of the people believed in Jesus does not necessarily require that they believed unto salvation. They believed that Jesus was the Messiah, but their ideas about the Messiah might not have measured up with Scripture. Often their concepts of Messiah were not at all what the Old Testament promised. The popular ideas about Messiah generally had nothing to do with faith that Jesus of Nazareth was the Lamb of God who came to atone for sins. In light of the fact that only a few people were present at the cross, just a few months after this event, it is fair to assume that most of the people were disappointed with Jesus. He did not turn out to be the kind of Messiah they wanted. Did they believe that He was the Messiah? Yes, but their opinion of Messiah was unscriptural. They believed in the mighty king who would deliver them from Rome. When it became clear that Jesus of Nazareth had no interest in being a mighty earthly king, they changed their minds and shouted with the rest of the crowd, "Crucify Him, crucify Him."

Jesus, who knew the peoples' hearts, emphatically confronted them about their errant opinions about Him. The text says in verse twenty-eight that He cried out. The word translated "cried out" means that Jesus got quite emphatic at this point. He lifted up His voice. In light of the entire Gospel record, it must have been unusual for Jesus to do this. It was unusual, but on occasion, Jesus purposely became demonstrative. The norm for Jesus is expressed in Isaiah's promise that "He will not cry out, nor raise His voice, nor cause His voice to be heard in the street" (Isaiah 42:2). However, including this event, the Gospel record reveals that on four occasions Jesus raised His voice to make a point. Later in this book John wrote that "Jesus cried out and said, 'He who believes in Me, believes not in Me but in Him who sent Me'" (John 12:44). Similar statements appear in Matthew 27:50, Mark 15:37, and John 7:37.

Jesus raised His voice and told the crowd that they did indeed know Him. He spoke with irony. The phrase can be punctuated as a statement or as a question. Probably He posed a question that struck with irony: "So you know Me and know where I am from?" You think you know Me do you? The question confronted the people's arrogance. They we quite sure that they knew all about Jesus of Nazareth. However, Jesus quickly pointed out their ignorance. He told those opinionated people that they didn't know nearly as much as they thought they knew. He told them that they erred when they harkened to their religious leaders. He confronted them because they thought they knew all about Messiah and the way to salvation. He proved to them that in reality they did not know the truth at all.

Jesus explained to the multitude that the Heavenly Father who sent Him is true. This statement recorded in verse twenty-nine affirmed that Jesus of Nazareth was on the Heavenly Father's mission. If He was on the Heavenly Father's mission, He had to know Him. Indeed, Jesus affirmed that He knew the Father intimately because He was from Him. He told the people in the crowd that He knew God because He was from God. Then Jesus quickly informed the people that they did not know God! This is still the issue with religious people. They have a lot of opinions about Christ, but their opinions are baseless. They are just opinions. People believe what they believe because of popular teaching, not because the Word of God reveals what they should believe. People who know God through His Word, believe that Jesus of Nazareth is the Christ.

The Religious Authorities Attempted To Silence Christ

The religious rulers did not appreciate what Jesus taught. Therefore, they intended to arrest Him. Because they were the religious authorities they had the right and power to do so. Rome gave the religious rulers limited authority to govern internal religious matters in Israel. These leaders could have banned Jesus from the synagogue. Teachers who were banned from the synagogue were humiliated, and as a result the people ignored them. The leaders could have arrested Jesus for teaching heresy, at least heresy according to their standards. However, they did not attempt to silence Jesus on any of those points. The real motivation for their attempt to silence Jesus was a fear that the people were beginning to believe Him. The leaders knew that if there was a popular uprising among the citizens, Rome would get involved. If the Roman government got involved, the religious leaders would lose their authority. Caiaphas, the High Priest, articulated the problem well when he told the other members of the counsel, "If we let Him alone like this, everyone will believe in Him, and the Romans will come and take away both our place and nation" (John 11:48). The leaders' position in life was the real issue here.

Therefore, the leaders were determined to arrest Jesus and silence His teaching. God the Father foiled the authorities. According to verse thirty, no one laid a hand on Christ. They wanted to take Him into custody, but they could not. The Greek text points out that the leaders were anxious to arrest Him. What happened? Maybe circumstances changed so that the authorities could not find an opportune time. Maybe the leaders were afraid that the crowd would interfere. Maybe Jesus just walked away or something supernatural happened. Whatever the reason, the authorities could not apprehend Jesus. They could not because it was not yet the hour of trial and sacrifice for Christ. "His hour had not yet come" (7:30). Jesus was inviolable until His hour came. The triune Godhead controlled every detail of the Son's sacrificial ministry. Christ's sacrifice for sin was accomplished exactly as the Trinity ordained it! Therefore, it is of utmost importance for sinners to receive it as it is.

Christ Declared A Frightening Ultimatum

Jesus informed the religious leaders that He would leave them (7:33, 35). He promised that He would soon return to the Father. This statement should not have surprised the leaders because Jesus continually reminded them that He had come from God the Father. Now He promised that in a little while He would return to Heaven. They misunderstood His promise and wondered, "Where does He intend to go that we shall not find Him?" (7:35). They errantly concluded that Jesus implied that He would go to the Diaspora. The Diaspora is a term that describes the Jews who were scattered among the Gentile nations. This meant that Jesus would go outside of Palestine to teach His gospel to the Jews. It might even mean that He would teach His gospel to the Gentiles. What a prophetic utterance! And the rulers didn't even know what they said.

The religious leaders came to this wrong conclusion because they misunderstood the basic truth about Jesus. They refused to acknowledge that He was Divine, God in the flesh. They refused to acknowledge that He was their Savior from sin, the Lamb of God. They would have fit well in this modern culture where there is a plethora of opinions about Jesus. However, one thing is still certain: only the Bible truth about Jesus explains who He is and what He did.

Jesus informed the religious leaders that they would not be able to go to heaven. He told them that they would seek for Him but not find Him. He promised that the time would come when their hearts would yearn for the Christ, but they would not be satisfied. The leaders did not realize it, but they were seeking the Christ even as He talked to them. People like them continue to seek Christ. They spend their lives running after satisfaction not knowing that they are seeking Christ. But they cannot find Him! Why not? Because God must draw them. A few days earlier Jesus had taught, "No one can come to Me unless the Father who sent Me draws him; and I will raise him up at the last day" (John 6:44). God had drawn these people and they refused to submit to His truth. The prophet Zechariah said that this would happen. "'Therefore it happened, that just as He proclaimed and they would not hear, so they called out and I would not listen,' says the Lord of hosts" (Zechariah 7:13). Jeremiah reiterated the problem when he pointed out that God had "set watchmen over you, saying, 'Listen to the sound of the trumpet!' But they said, 'We will not listen'" (Jeremiah 6:17). Just before the religious rulers finally had their way and killed Jesus, He wept, "O Jerusalem, Jerusalem, the one who kills the prophets and stones those who are sent to her! How often I wanted to gather your children together, as a hen gathers her brood under her wings, but you were not willing!" (Luke 13:34). They had so many opportunities to receive Jesus as the Messiah and Savior, but they would not. God drew the people. They rejected God's calling.

Now they could not go to where Jesus is. Jesus used present tense verbs here to teach that even at that moment He, being part of the Godhead, was in heaven. What a sad reality that the most religious people of His day could not go to heaven! What words of finality! No doubt the Lake of Fire will be full of people who are convinced too late that Jesus is who He said He is. Too late they will repent. True repentance is never too late—in this life. Once this life is over true repentance is pointless. Where are all of those people who doubted that Jesus was the Messiah? Where will the multitudes of people be in this culture when they breath their last breath. "Who is Jesus the Christ" is the most important question in eternity.

CHAPTER 20

JESUS DEFENDED HIS SELF-WITNESS

JOHN 8:13-20

Occasionally I go to the doctor. When I am finally called from the waiting room, I go into an examination room and sit on a table. I look at the equipment for testing blood pressure and the gadgets the doctor uses for examining eyes and noses and throats. Sometimes on the way into the examination room I pass an x-ray machine and some other basic laboratory equipment. After awhile the doctor comes in and asks me a battery of questions and shakes his head knowingly when I answer. He listens to my lungs and heart and then scribbles something illegible on a piece of paper and tells me to take those pills for ten days. I walk to the front of the office, pay my bill, and leave.

Now let's say that one day as I exit the doctor's office a fellow approaches me in the parking lot and begins to ask questions about my doctor. He claims that he is thinking about visiting the doctor himself, and he would like to know all about the physician before he makes a commitment. So I tell the guy everything I know. I talk about how nice my doctor is, how thorough he is, about all the diplomas hanging on the walls. And I tell him about the neat equipment my doctor uses. At that point the fellow knows all he needs to know about my doctor, right?

That is about all a patient generally knows about his physician, which means that most patients really don't know their physicians very well. Only another physician can really appreciate what a physician has endured to reach the level of a private practice. The average laymen doesn't have an inkling about the rigors of medical school or the inhumane hours of an internship. The patient cannot begin to tell the real story about what it takes to be a doctor. Only another doctor knows those details. A close family member, such as a spouse or a parent, also has a good idea about what it takes to be a doctor. But lay-people do not know. Because that is true, it is not wise to seek medical advice from a person who has no medical training, or whose experience with medicine amounts to looking at the interesting gadgets in his doctor's office.

Unfortunately, the average patient knows as much about medicine as the religious leaders knew about God the Father and God the Son. They boasted that they were the possessors of the knowledge of God. They were sure that they knew all about God-ness, and therefore, they rejected Jesus the man from Nazareth out of hand. They thought that they had studied all the right stuff so that they could know God, but they were wrong. The problem was that they did not have a personal relationship with God. Being part of the family goes a long way in affirming the truth about God.

Jesus taught the Pharisees that the only way for them to know the truth about Him was to know God. And the only way to know God was through Him. Therefore, since they rejected Jesus Christ, they proved they were ignorant about God. Thus, they spent their entire lives stumbling around in the darkness of sin and ignorance all the while claiming that they had the light.

Jesus Declared That He Is The Light Of The World.

This was an astonishing claim. The setting of the statement, the event when Jesus made it, energized the words. Jesus declared that He is the Light of the world in the context of the Feast of Tabernacles. In fact, the feast had just ended the day before. The feast began on the fifteenth of the month and lasted until the twenty-second. Jesus made the statement on the next day when many of the visitors had, no doubt, started for home. Nevertheless, a crowd still gathered to hear Jesus teach. He was teaching in the area near the treasury, according to verse twenty. This would have been the inner courtyard or the court of the women as it was called. On the previous days, Jesus had been teaching on the porches of the outer court where everyone, even the Gentiles, could gather. Now He had moved to the more restrictive area of the women's court. Only Jewish men could enter here, or Jewish women who were going to give an offering or sacrifice.

On the first day of the feast, right in this area of the temple, the priests lit four giant candelabra. This ritual was called the Illumination of the Temple, and it must have been quite a spectacle. It is said that the light from those candelabra was so bright that every courtyard in Jerusalem was illumined by them. Then, after the lighting of the candelabra, the wisest, most holy men of Israel sang psalms, rejoiced, and praised God all night. The whole feast harkened back to when God had led His people through the wilderness, and the lighting of the candelabra reminded the people that their forefathers had lived in the light of the fiery pillar. Against that backdrop, which was still fresh in the people's minds, Jesus declared, "I am the light of the world."

Furthermore, the context states that Jesus made this claim while it was early in the morning. The light of the sun was just rising in the sky and illuminating the dark shadows around the temple area. Maybe Jesus motioned toward the rising sun when He declared that He is the light that lights the whole world.

When He made that declaration, Jesus claimed a title that was reserved for the Messiah. He said that He was the light of the world! Scripture connected such light with the true God. For example, David wrote, "The LORD is my light and my salvation; Whom shall I fear?" (Psalm 27:1a). Isaiah promised, "But the LORD will be to you an everlasting light, and your God your glory" (Isaiah 60:19b). Job spoke of the time, "When His lamp shone upon my head, and when by His light I walked through darkness" (Job 29:3). And Micah declared, "Do not rejoice over me, my enemy; when I fall, I will arise; when I sit in darkness, the LORD will be a light to me" (Micah 7:8). The connection between God and light was irrefutable, and therefore, the Rabbis had taught that God's Messiah would be the Light.

This was a wonderful promise. Jesus promised that whoever follows Him, the Christ, the true light, does not walk in darkness. The world is steeped in the darkness of sin. Indeed, the term darkness is used often in Scripture to speak of sin and ignorance. Jesus promised that those who follow Him will not be trapped in sin or ignorance. It seems easy enough to follow Christ and stay out of sin until one considers the full meaning of the word follow. That term was often used to describe soldiers who followed their commanders. It speaks of slaves who submit to their master's orders, of students who understand their teacher's line of reasoning, and of citizens who are committed to the laws of their city.

The word follow also pointed back to the picture of the nation Israel following the pillar of fire throughout the forty years of wilderness wandering. In order to be obedient to God, they had to move when it moved. For them not to move indicated rebellion. Their obedience kept Israel's forefather's in the light of the pillar, and conversely, disobedience meant darkness for them.

Likewise, if a person would follow Christ, it will require submission of his entire person—body, soul, and spirit. People who try to follow the Light at a distance are really not following at all. Such people are often intrigued by the Light. Something in their conscience tells them to follow the Light. But their flesh does not appreciate the revealing nature of the Light. So they seek to follow along at a good distance from the Light. In reality, that is not a possibility at all. Either a person follows the Light in close fellowship and direct obedience, or he does not follow the Light.

Jesus promised on that day that anyone who chooses to follow Him "will not walk in darkness." That is a certain conclusion, not a possibility, or not even a probability. It means that the person who is really following Christ will not be ignorant about Him, or about the Father, or about spiritual truth. Such a person will not be characterized by the sins of darkness as was the woman who had just left Jesus' presence.

This is a wonderful promise from Christ. But the vast majority of people live daily in sin and ignorance. They prefer the darkness of sin over a life that is enlightened by the True Light, Jesus Christ. They are quite sure that this kind of lifestyle is normal, and that people who have submitted themselves to follow Christ are out of the mainstream.

Furthermore, Jesus promised that whoever follows the Christ has the light of life. John expressed this same amazing conclusion about Jesus when he introduced his Gospel account. He wrote:

*In Him was life, and the life was the light of men. And
the light shines in the darkness, and the darkness did
not comprehend it. There was a man sent from God,
whose name was John. This man came for a witness,
to bear witness of the Light, that all through him might
believe. He was not that Light, but was sent to bear witness of that Light. That was the true Light which gives
light to every man coming into the world. (John 1:4-9)*

With these introductory words John taught that Jesus offers the
light of eternal life which is tantamount to saying that Jesus, the man
from Nazareth, offers salvation (v. 4). He taught that the darkness of
sin, though it be intense, cannot extinguish the light (v. 5). He promised that Jesus Christ offers this light to all people, but not all people
receive it (v. 9). The religious leaders in Jesus' day certainly did not
accept the light. In fact, most of the people in Jesus' day did not accept
it. Most people still do not accept Christ's offer to follow after Him
and walk in the light. They are much like the Pharisees.

Religious People Took Issue With Jesus' Declaration.

The Pharisees rejected Jesus' testimony that He is the light of the
world. According to verse thirteen, they accused Jesus of testifying
about Himself. That was unacceptable protocol in that culture. People
demanded proof that was more dependable than a personal opinion
about self. The Pharisees were already predisposed against Christ.
In their opinion, He was already guilty until proven innocent. This
meant that they would not accept His testimony about Himself at all.
They concluded that self-witness was not true and they needed more
proof about who Jesus was. They expressed the same reservations and
doubts that many people throughout the ages have expressed when
God shines the light of Jesus Christ on them. Often, when people are
introduced to the truth about Christ, they deflect making a commitment by declaring that they will think about the matter. They say that
they will not accept Christ as their Savior from sins until they have all
of the facts and until they fully understand all of the facts. However,

the person who must have all the facts before he accepts Christ as Savior will never be saved.

The religious people refused to accept Jesus' testimony about Himself because one's own opinion about himself is not sufficient proof. In response to their rejection, Jesus authenticated His testimony. He pointed out that a big part of the problem was that the religious people could not draw conclusions on His level. They thought that they had enough evidence to conclude that Jesus, the carpenter's son from Nazareth, was not the Christ. However, Jesus pointed out, according to verse fourteen, that they really did not even know some of the most basic truth about Jesus. They did not know where Jesus was from and where He was going. Contrary to common opinion, God the Son did not originate from Nazareth! The people thought they understood God and heaven, but they could not explain God in the flesh. They could not begin to comprehend the fact that God was dwelling among men as Jesus from Nazareth.

Most people cannot come to grips with this astonishing truth. Most Christians, like the ancient Jews, can recite creeds about the incarnation of God. But who can honestly describe the details of God? Who really understands God? Who can tell the details of heaven? Who can explain God's ways? Obviously, even Christians are limited by human finiteness. God reminded those who aspire to put Him in their theological box that, "as the heavens are higher than the earth, so are My ways higher than your ways, and My thoughts than your thoughts" (Isaiah 55:9). It is impossible for God's people to draw all of the right conclusions about God and His eternal Son because even we are limited by human wisdom.

Jesus pointed out that the Pharisees could only "judge according to the flesh" (8:15). They drew conclusions that were limited by the carnal nature. The flesh fights against faith. The flesh demands that all things be explained within the scope of human life and experience. This means that the flesh will always refuse to submit to the Holy Spirit. The child of God grows to know and understand the Savior only through the work of the Holy Spirit as He opens the spiritual eyes to the truth about Jesus Christ.

Jesus reaffirmed that He was not on earth to condemn. That trait stands in vivid contrast to the typical work and attitude of the Pharisees. John used the same word for judge two different ways at this point. He revealed that the Pharisees condemned everyone who did not measure up to their standards or rules. Jesus did not condemn people who did not measure up. He will do that at the Great White Throne. While He was on earth He showed compassion to the failing sheep. Because the Pharisees condemned everyone who did not measure up to their standards they condemned Jesus Christ. He did not measure up to their rules, and they condemned Him. His witness to the truth was not sufficient for them.

However, Jesus did not cease to be the Christ simply because the Pharisees refused His witness. He proved that His witness was validated in the Godhead. His witness about Himself was true because He knew Himself (v. 14a), and His judgment was true because He is one with the Father (v. 15b-16). Again Jesus informed the Pharisees of the same truth He revealed to the adulterous woman—He came to earth to save not to judge (v. 15b). But when He does pass judgment (which is not the same as condemnation), it is perfect (v. 16). Therefore, Jesus clearly taught that God the Father sent Him. That is why His judgment must be perfect.

Up to this point in the conversations Jesus had during the Feast of Tabernacles, He spoke of "Him who sent Me." Now He bluntly taught that He came directly from God the Heavenly Father. Therefore, His testimony really was validated by two. It was verified by Himself, God the Son, and it was verified by God the Father. This twofold validation fulfilled the requirements of the law about which the Pharisees were so paranoid. The religious people knew their law well. They knew that God had established through Moses that, "Whoever is deserving of death shall be put to death on the testimony of two or three witnesses; he shall not be put to death on the testimony of one witness" (Deuteronomy 17:6). God required that, "One witness shall not rise against a man concerning any iniquity or any sin that he commits; by the mouth of two or three witnesses the matter shall be established" (Deuteronomy 19:15). The Jews knew this fact. They also knew their own traditions and laws very well.

Therefore, since God's law required two witnesses, Jesus provided exactly what the Pharisees demanded. He told them that God the Father validates the witness of God the Son. He said, "I am One who bears witness of Myself, and the Father who sent Me bears witness of Me" (8:18). That makes two witnesses! But even that was not good enough for the religious people.

Jesus Explained Why The Religious People Could Not Understand.

Jesus explained that the Pharisees' problem was that they failed to see beyond the mundane. Their vision was limited to the earthly sphere. They could not grasp spiritual truth. Therefore, the religious leaders misunderstood Jesus' relationship to the Heavenly Father. They could not comprehend anything that was heavenly and eternal because they could not see beyond Jesus' earthly existence. Therefore, all they had to go on was human wisdom. Human wisdom is a limitation of every person. It is not sufficient to define the eternal God and Son.

Cultists argue that Jesus Christ cannot be coequal with the eternal Father because no son could possibly be as old as the one who begets him. However, in their argument they miss the fact that God can only be the eternal Father if He has an eternal Son. If Jesus Christ, God the Son is not eternal, He is not co-equal with the Father. But the Father is only eternally the Father if God the Son is eternally the Son. Apologetics is sufficient to present that kind of argument. But even apologetics has limitations. At some point, the argument of Jesus' origin or deity must be accepted by faith in God's Word alone.

The Jewish leaders were not easily convinced. When Jesus explained that God the Father was witness to Him, they sarcastically asked where Joseph was. They could not admit for a moment that Jesus was not of earthly origin. They did not like Jesus. They wanted to kill Jesus. But they could not even lay hands on Jesus. Wouldn't someone ask questions about this? Did it not seem strange to them that they were supernaturally prevented from harming the man from Nazareth? They failed to realize how God frustrated their plans.

Jesus revealed the tragic ignorance of religious people. The ultimate problem was that they really did not know God. They were sure they knew God better than any other people in that day knew God. But their rejection of Jesus as Christ proved their ignorance. They were trapped in spiritual darkness because they rejected the Light of Truth.

Multitudes of people are like the ancient Pharisees. Many modern people honor Jesus to a point. They call Him a great prophet, a miracle worker, a good man, an excellent teacher. But the person who refuses to accept Jesus of Nazareth as the only way, the only truth, the only life, will never be reconciled with the Father. Jesus promised, "I am the way, the truth, and the life. No one comes to the Father except through Me" (John 14:6). The person who accepts good works instead of Christ's atonement cannot see God. The person who depends on the "Church" instead of Christ's work will never see God. The person who relies on anything other than God's Christ, and all that He entails, will never go to heaven. The line is very clearly drawn now and will be painfully plain for eternity!

CHAPTER 21

JESUS ILLUSTRATED THAT HE IS THE LIGHT OF THE WORLD

JOHN 9:1-12

Most people resist change. Is it possible that as we grow older we resist change even more? Why is this response to change so natural? There is something comforting or assuring about knowing that things will be much the same tomorrow as they were today. There is something in human nature that enjoys the continuity of life. It is encouraging to know that the sun will rise in the east tomorrow, just like it has every day in past. There is no need to wonder if the sun might rise in the west, north, or south. That simple kind of assurance allows for advanced planning. Because certain things remain constant, plans can be projected far into the future. In the dead of winter people plan for vacations in the sunshine. In the heat of summer people plan for ski trips in the deep snow of the mountains. Occasionally plans like that are disrupted because of unseasonable weather. But, in this part of the world, no one expects snow in July and no one expects swimming weather in January. In fact if it turns out to be ninety degrees with ninety percent humidity in January, people would be deeply concerned.

Dealing with the unexpected might be why change is so difficult. Change might even frighten some folks because it brings uncertainty.

That might explain why so many people resist improvements or new methodology. The statement, "We've never done it that way before," might really mean, "We're afraid to try something new."

Is that also the reason why some people resist the new birth? If a person is comfortable in sin, why would he want to become like Christ? That possibility begs a question. Is anyone really ever comfortable in sin? Unfavorable consequences always accompany sin. Unfavorable consequences do not make for a comfortable life. Sin breaks fellowship with God and broken fellowship is not comfortable. However, it is possible that a person might be more confident in the misery of consequences and broken fellowship, than in leaping out into faith in Christ alone.

Jesus' conversation with His disciples and the blind man proves that when God makes the change it is always good, it is always beneficial, and it always gives confidence. Jesus' purpose was to effect change in a sinful world. A mere man cannot make a significant change in that realm. The best of leaders can only effect a small portion of the planet for a very short time. Jesus, God in the flesh, came to make an eternal difference for an innumerable host of people. Sinful people, whose sin has offended the holy God, need to change. Jesus came to earth to make that possible. When He healed the blind man, He did and said things that force careful thoughts about His wonderful work of changing sinners into saints. That is the work Christ does as He brings glory to the Father.

Jesus Came To Do The Father's Work.

As the story opens, a very important question about a blind man is posed in the first two verses. Whose sin caused the malady? It appears that this question came up as Jesus and the disciples passed a blind man in the everyday course of life. They were not out looking for someone to heal. The blind man did not have an appointment with mere men. He just happened to be at the spot at that moment (or so it would appear from the human perspective), and it prompted the disciples to ask a very expected question. This event probably occurred in the early winter (perhaps in December) of AD 29. Jesus had been in Jerusalem for the Feast of Tabernacles in our month of October, AD 29. The record of

John chapters seven and eight contains the conversations and arguments Jesus had with the people and leaders during that time. By this time the leaders were so enraged because Jesus kept exposing their hypocrisy that they tried to stone Him (John 8:59). But Jesus miraculously walked away from the people who desired to kill Him. He could do that because He was God. God is in control of all events, and the grand event of Christ's passion was not scheduled for a few months yet.

It is unlikely that the events in John chapter nine began immediately after Jesus walked away from the controversy with the rulers. The greater evidence seems to indicate that Jesus left Jerusalem for a few weeks and, at some point during that time, taught in a synagogue for the last time (Luke 13:10-17). In that situation, Jesus healed a woman, who had been an invalid for eighteen years. He healed the woman on the Sabbath, which stirred up the Synagogue Ruler's wrath.

Now, beginning with chapter nine, Jesus had returned to Jerusalem. While He and the disciples were walking near the temple, they saw a blind man. Probably the man was begging near the temple which was a common sight. In many countries it is common to see beggars seeking help in the vicinity of religious shrines and sacred buildings. No doubt needy people reason that religious folks are the most likely kind of people to have compassion and to show generosity. God required in His law that His people should take special care of needy folks who could not care for themselves (Leviticus 19:14; Deuteronomy 27:18). Devout people on their way to the temple would be likely to offer compassion through a donation to a needy blind man.

This particular man had been blind since birth. There are other records in the Gospels that describe incidents when Jesus dealt with blind people, but this is the only incident where the man was blind from birth. Possibly God included this story in the Bible because it is such a good picture of the natural condition of humanity. You and I are born in sin. We illustrate David's conclusion all too well: "Behold, I was brought forth in iniquity, and in sin my mother conceived me" (Psalm 51:5). David's statement teaches that each person is born in a condition of spiritual blindness. Everyone is born needing someone to lead them into spiritual truth. In spite of that great need, we needy people are naturally led by sin and Satan. Our great need is for someone to come beside us and compassionately lead us to Christ. You and I are born needing to have God open our eyes and shed light on the on the reality of our circumstances so that we can see our sinful condition. In many ways the blind man illustrates the sinner's natural condition.

The disciples asked a common question when they saw the blind man. They wondered whose sin caused this tragedy in life. They asked, "who sinned, this man or his parents, that he was born blind?" Was their question unkind, inconsiderate, or foolish? First, the disciples' question proves that they knew that this fellow had been blind since birth. The man was a well known personality around the temple area. Second, their question indicates that they connected sickness with sin. That is a fair connection. Sickness is certainly a possible consequence of sin. Why did the disciples attempt to apply it to this man? The conclusion that sin leads to sickness was based on common belief. The disciples could have drawn such a conclusion from the evidence of the Old Testament teachings. God's law warned, "For I, the LORD your God, am a jealous God, visiting the iniquity of the fathers on the children to the third and fourth generations of those who hate Me" (Exodus 20:5). The Psalmist prayed an invective against his enemy asking God to "Let the iniquity of his fathers be remembered before the LORD, and let not the sin of his mother be blotted out" (Psalm 109:14). Isaiah warned of God's judgment against sinners when he declared, "Behold, it is written before Me: I will not keep silence, but will repay—even repay into their bosom" (Isaiah 65:6).

Since the disciples knew the Old Testament teachings well, they could have naturally concluded that God might punish the man with blindness because of his parents' sin. Sometimes that principle is true. Sometimes divine judgment against sin appears to show up in the circumstances of life. It is possible to interpret the judgment as the natural consequences of sins, but there might be the deeper cause of divine retribution. For example, an irresponsible mother might drink much alcohol while she is pregnant. Her irresponsibility is a sin, but the result of her sin could be that her child will be born with Fetal Alcohol Syndrome. Or a father might be careless about his television viewing habits. While there appears to be no serious consequence to him for the sin of carelessness, the result could be that his son, taking the father's lead, gets hooked on pornography. This would not be considered a sickness but an addiction. How often does society label addictions as sicknesses? Consequences like these often come to bear on the children of the parents who sin. Therefore, the disciples' question is not too far fetched!

Furthermore, the disciples had probably heard much of the Rabbinical teaching that connected sickness in life with the individual's sin before birth. Some Rabbis taught that sin begins in the womb, while others taught that a soul had the capacity to sin while it was in a pre-existing state. They taught that the person who sinned as a soul before he inhabited a body could be punished with sickness in life. In that case, the disciples might have concluded that this person was responsible for his own sin, and that would explain his blindness.

The Bible teaches that there are times when God allows sickness as judgment against an individual's sin. That is not to say that all sickness should be interpreted as God's judgment against the sick individual. If that were true, Paul would need to explain his thorn in the flesh differently than the way he explained it in Second Corinthians.

There is the principle that sickness is a consequence of sin. When sin entered paradise in the Garden of Eden, it cast the whole creation into chaos. In response to the sin, God cursed the earth as well as mankind through Adam. Now people, along with the rest of creation, groan while waiting for redemption. Because of the consequences of the sin principle, humans spend life continually winding down, continually succumbing to more and more sickness, until they die. That is a universal principle. The disciples did not wonder if the blind man's blindness was the result of the sin principle. They wondered whether the man himself committed the sin that brought about blindness or whether it was his parent's sin.

Jesus used the question as an opportunity to explain that His work was to reveal God's glory. Sickness can be an opportunity for God to work a work of grace for His glory. He told the disciples that in this case neither the parents nor the individual had caused the blindness. Indeed, everyone in the picture (except Jesus of course) was guilty of sin. But blindness was not a consequent punishment for all of them. This was something God chose to use for His own glory. The affliction was present in this man's body because of the general law of sin. God chose to exalt His works through such a needy case.

Notice that the text says that God chose to reveal His mighty works in him—in that particular person. That particular individual was important to God. So is each person who receives God's grace unto salvation. The story is a wonderful reminder that every redeemed person is a trophy of God's grace. Every person whom God has cleansed from the defilement of sin will "in the ages to come . . . show the exceeding riches of His grace in His kindness toward us in Christ Jesus" (Ephesians 2:7). Real Christians should rejoice at the change God has brought about in our fellow-believers through the new birth. The blind man must have been amazed that Jesus chose to release the hold of blindness on him, even as we "stand amazed in the presence, of Jesus the Nazarene, and wonder how He could love me, a sinner condemned, unclean." (Charles Gabriel).

Jesus taught the importance of buying up opportunities to glorify the Father (vv. 4-5). He understood His purpose in this world. He understood that the Father sent Him to do His work for His glory. Jesus fulfilled the Father's will perfectly to the very end. He lived without breaking the Law, He died the substitutionary death, He rose again, and ascended to the Father's right hand when He had completed the work. In all things, Jesus manifested the desire to do exactly what the Father sent Him to do. That is why, in this case, He illustrated the Father's love and desire to counteract the effects of sin.

Jesus also made provision for the disciples to continue the works that bring glory to God the Father. He had called the disciples to Himself in order to make them like Him. He taught them and molded them so that they would continue His work after He ascended to heaven. They, in turn, gathered disciples, taught them the lessons they learned from Christ, and continued to pass on the work of God's glory to future generations of Christians. Jesus prayed to the Father, "I have manifested Your name to the men whom You have given Me out of the world. They were Yours, You gave them to Me, and they have kept Your word" (John 17:6). His ministry, was to provide the way for salvation from sin, but also to prepare the disciples to continue the work of glorifying God.

Jesus explained to the disciples that it was His time for doing the Father's works. He said that He needed to work while it was day, and it was day only while Christ was on the earth. The implication of this statement is that when Christ went back to heaven, His light on earth was diminished. This suggests that His followers have been continuing the work in comparative night. Paul expressed this truth when he challenged Christians to be busy about the Lord's work because,

"The night is far spent, the day is at hand. Therefore let us cast off the works of darkness, and let us put on the armor of light" (Romans 13:12). Soon the night will end. God's people must continue to work His work in this dark world until the night is over. Children of light should not be surprised that they must work in the darkness of a sin-infected world. Paul told the Thessalonian Christians that they, "are all sons of light and sons of the day. We are not of the night nor of darkness" (1 Thessalonians 5:5). That means that the work Christ left for His followers is to bring sinners out of the darkness, the blindness of sin, into the light of Christ. He is the light of the world. But blind men and women cannot see the light. They need God's work to cure their spiritual blindness.

The Father's Work Changes People.

Jesus glorified God the Father by healing the blind man (vv. 6-7). It was a miracle and the process was as unusual as the result. Jesus made a mud ball out of spittle and dirt and stuck the concoction on the blind man's eyes. This is the only record in the Bible of Jesus doing such a thing, even though Jesus healed more cases of blindness than any other particular physical affliction. There was one incident similar to this in which Jesus spit on a blind man's eyes (Mark 8:23). There was also the case where He put His fingers in the ears of a deaf and dumb man and then put spittle on his tongue (Mark 7:33). Those seem like gross thing to do. Why did Jesus heal in that manner? Some ancients believed that human spittle contained medicinal qualities. Is that why Jesus did it? No. He did what He did because that was His choice. Maybe there were times when He sought to set an example by His actions, but most of those matters escape common understanding.

Having mixed up the muddy poultice, Jesus put the mud on the blind fellow's eyes. Human nature concludes that such an action is foolish. Human nature concludes that putting mud on a blind man's eyes would, at best, make matters worse. The poor man was already unable to see. How could he expect to see better with mud plastered on his eyes? Human nature seldom understands the secrets of God's way. Therefore, in spiritual matters, human nature seeks to fix the problems of sin through human efforts. Human efforts make sense to the human mind. As a result, cults are man-made efforts to copy God's plan for salvation. Of necessity man-made efforts must always fall short of salvation. Human originators of unbiblical creeds eventually resort to teaching that human efforts are sufficient to gain reconciliation with God. They believe that it is possible for individuals to gain God's favor through good works. Nearly every religion invented by man draws the same conclusion.

God's rule states that the full effects of sin can be removed only by God's own mighty work. God's plan to grant rebirth through simple faith in the finished work of Jesus Christ on the cross makes no sense to many people. It is like putting mud in a blind man's eye! That is why, "the message of the cross is foolishness to those who are perishing, but to us who are being saved it is the power of God" (1 Corinthians 1:18). It is far better to trust God's plan, even though it is impossible to contain it within the boundaries of human reason.

Jesus put the mud on the blind man's eyes, and then instructed him about what he must do. He sent the man to wash in the pool of Siloam. The word Siloam means sent. There is a wonderful picture of the word in the reality of the pool. Hundreds of years before this event, King Hezekiah ordered his men to dig a tunnel from the Gihon Spring, which was outside the city walls, to this man-made pool inside the city. Ancient records state that when the two ends of the tunnel met in the middle, the water was sent rushing into the pool. In spiritual truth, God fulfills this picture when He sends the water of regeneration flooding into the repentant sinner's soul.

Jesus sent the blind man to the water of cleansing. Did he go? Obviously. Why? The man was compelled by faith to go to the Pool of Siloam. He would not have gone if he did not believe that his obedience would result in the ability to see. Faith is still the requirement of spiritual eyesight. It is still essential to believe Christ. Washing with water from the pool did not fix the man's eyes. Obedience in washing indicated his faith. Obedient faith brought sight to his blinded eyes.

Not surprisingly, people recognized the change in the blind man. However, at the same time, the change caused some debate. The change was undeniable. Everyone witnessed the difference. The change for the blind man was as undeniable as the change that takes place in a redeemed person's spirit. He who was once blind now could see. The person who could see only the darkness of sin, once cleansed by Christ, is able to see the light of spiritual truth.

Some of the people who witnessed the change in the blind man debated about what happened. Some of them even attempted to deny that anything happened. Why the debate? Was it not obvious that the blind man could see? They debated because the matter was so unexplainable. It was like trying to explain the change when a sinner becomes a Christian. The best explanation some people have is that the fellow "got religion." That conclusion does not begin to explain the complete rebirth that occurs at salvation. The penitent sinner didn't get religion—he or she was born again.

The blind man testified about what happened to him. He knew that something astonishing had taken place. Though he could not explain how it happened the blind man knew very well that he could see now. He knew that he was changed. The person who is not sure that anything happened, when Christ cleansed away his sin, never experienced Christ's cleansing. He or she is probably still lost in sins. Salvation bring an obvious change of spirit or heart!

The blind man tried to explain the change to the people who wondered what had happened to him. He knew that Jesus opened his eyes. He did not understand all of the details, but he knew that he was once unable to see and now he could see. That is a wonderful testimony. New believers might not be able to explain in detail what happened when they were born again, but they know that they know God through salvation.

To be able to give a blind man physical sight is an astonishing ability. No mere man could do that. That is why the religious leaders were so distraught at this miracle. They did not want Jesus to be the Messiah. They refused to accept that Jesus of Nazareth was God in the flesh. They, like many people of this age, preferred for Jesus to be a good teacher—but just a man none the less. More astonishing than giving physical eyesight to a blind man, is the gift of eternal life that Christ gives to repentant sinners. Only God can do that. Jesus is God. The testimony of every person who has received eternal life through faith in Jesus of Nazareth is a constant thorn in the flesh to men and women who attempt to deny His divinity.

CHAPTER 22

JESUS CAME TO HEAL SPIRITUAL BLINDNESS

JOHN 9:35-41

In the New Testament, God established a non-negotiable characteristic about people who are truly part of His family. Paul wrote to the Christians who lived in Corinth that, "if anyone is in Christ, he is a new creation; old things have passed away; behold, all things have become new" (2 Corinthians 5:17). At the very least, this principle requires change in a person's life when, by faith, he or she receives Christ as Savior.

That change frightens some folks. As a result they tend to accuse the person who trusts Christ of pride, arrogance, or conceit. The dramatic change that comes with salvation makes the new Christian so different that sinners often feel compelled to attack the change. Maybe the people who choose to remain in their sins criticize true Christians because it appears to them that the born again person thinks he or she is better than the sinner. He or she is! That is just the point. When Jesus Christ makes a new creation through the process of the new birth, the person with the newly created heart is in far better condition than he or she was before God's miracle of regeneration.

But that kind of distinction is not easily accepted by a society that wants everyone to be the same. It is strange, but true, that those who offer the most resistance to distinctions between people are often the ones who perceive that they themselves are more enlightened, more gifted, more intelligent, and, in general, more qualified to tell the rest of the culture how they should live in mediocre uniformity.

The religious leaders in Jesus' day were a lot like that. They perceived that they were the authorities in the field of godliness and true worship. They literally wrote the book on what it takes to please God—from the human perspective. When Jesus healed the blind man on the Sabbath, they were furious. The Pharisees were so angry because Jesus gave this poor man sight that they eventually disallowed the healed man to worship God in the synagogue. They exercised their supposed authority to excommunicate the recipient of God's favor.

This story is unique because it presents a beautiful picture of God's work of spiritual enlightenment when Jesus, God on earth, healed the blind man. More important is the fact that the story concludes by telling how Jesus gave the man true salvation when he expressed faith in Christ. John recorded the picture and the fulfillment of the picture in the same story. The lesson is plain in both. When God grants blinded sinners spiritual enlightenment, He draws a line of distinction that makes other sinners uncomfortable. When a sinner exercises faith, like the blind man, his new life of faith casts judgment on sinners who do not have faith.

Jesus Found The Healed Man.

Verse thirty-five in the text picks up the story following a long interlude in which the religious leaders barred the healed man from the synagogue. According to John's testimony Jesus heard that the religious leaders had excommunicated the healed man from the synagogue. That thought forces the reader to think back to the preceding section in order to understand why the leaders did such an unkind thing. The evidence proves that the Pharisees excommunicated the man because of the work Jesus did in his behalf. They were deeply troubled because Jesus had disregarded their laws (9:14). He healed this blind man on the Sabbath, and, as far as they were concerned, that was sufficient evidence to prove that Jesus of Nazareth was not sent from God. Surely a Divine being would keep the man-made laws of the Pharisees wouldn't he? They failed to see how ridiculous their arguments were. They demanded that God in the flesh obey them!

The Pharisees were so opposed to Jesus and His work that they actually refused to believe this healed man was the same man who had often begged near the temple or synagogue. They were not satisfied that it was actually the man until his parents affirmed that he was one and the same—the man who had been blind from birth (v. 18). The parents' response to the religious leaders' inquisition is informative. They chose not to say anything except the facts (vv. 19-20). That should be sufficient in any argument. They said, "We know this is our son." That was an obvious fact. They said, "We know that he was born blind." That was another plain fact. Then they said, "We know that he sees." That too was an indisputable fact. But the Pharisees were not interested in hearing facts. They had to admit that the blind man could now see. His sight was a reality. What bothered them is how or why he could now see. That the man could see was secondary to the fact that Someone disregarded their laws.

The real problem was that the Pharisees were agitated because Jesus, the man from Nazareth, had undermined their authority (vv. 24-34). This was the root issue for the "spiritual" leaders of Israel. Mustering all of their supposed authority, the Pharisees demanded that the man give God glory. Why should he glorify God when the leaders themselves did not glorify God? They glorified their traditions. They were convinced that Jesus, God in the flesh, was a sinner. That is hardly an attitude that glorifies God! The Pharisees could not glorify God because they were in total spiritual blindness.

Verses thirty through thirty-three reveal how the healed man pointed out the reality of the Pharisees' blindness. Ouch! That was not a good way to win the favor of the religious leaders. They were not happy at all with a former blind man accusing them of spiritual blindness. However, the healed man drew this conclusion through sound, logical, reasoning. His major premise was, "Jesus obviously did the miracle of healing" (v. 30). His minor premise was, "God worked the miracle through Jesus, which meant that Jesus must not be a sinner" (v. 31). Therefore, "Jesus is from God" (v. 33). That kind of reasoning flows from God-given faith.

The leaders, who presumed that they were more enlightened than this man, excommunicated him from synagogue attendance and worship. They were quite convinced that they were spiritual, and just as convinced that this man was born in sin. Was that to conclude that they were not born in sin?

After the religious leaders had cast the healed man from their graces, Jesus found him. That was a blessing for the man who had just endured the wrath of the hypocrites. When John said that Jesus found the man, he implied that Jesus had searched for him. It seems most reasonable to conclude that some time had passed since the healing. Maybe the foregoing events took place over a span of a few days. Jesus, being divine, already knew the things that had happened to the healed man, and He took the initiative to find the fellow in order to grant him a greater blessing.

The Lord's actions toward the healed man are similar to the actions of the good shepherd who went out to find the lost sheep (Luke 15:4-7). That is the picture of salvation. We are all lost sinners by nature. In this lost condition, a person tries to find answers to common grace. It is natural to ask, "Why are we here?" or "Where did the world come from?" It is common for spiritually blind people to wonder why they have a natural standard of right and wrong in their consciences. Or the sinner might ask, "Is this Bible true?" In response to the sinner's searching for truth, God sends His messenger with the good news that salvation is found in Christ.

The Bible is replete with evidence that God desires to communicate His message with everyone who seeks to hear it. He sent His messages of love and warning through the prophets to the rebelling Israelites in order to draw them back into fellowship with Him. Israel's historian remembered that, "the Lord God of their fathers sent warnings to them by His messengers, rising up early and sending them, because He had compassion on His people and on His dwelling place" (2 Chronicles 36:15). The Lord God sent Jesus His unique Son to the whole world as a revelation of Himself:

> *God, who at various times and in various ways spoke in time past to the fathers by the prophets, has in these last days spoken to us by His Son, whom He has appointed heir of all things, through whom also He made the worlds; who being the brightness of His glory and the express image of His person, and uphold-*

*ing all things by the word of His power, when He had
by Himself purged our sins, sat down at the right hand
of the Majesty on high. (Hebrews 1:1-3)*

He still sends His messengers with the good news. Thus Paul argued, "How then shall they call on Him in whom they have not believed? And how shall they believe in Him of whom they have not heard? And how shall they hear without a preacher? And how shall they preach unless they are sent? As it is written: 'How beautiful are the feet of those who preach the gospel of peace, Who bring glad tidings of good things!'" (Romans 10:14-15).

This principle is illustrated by a man who faced many difficulties in life. His many trials forced him to ask the hard questions, and he realized that he did not have the answers. He searched long enough to discover that his world did not have the answers to the hard questions either. Something in his soul kept pointing to God, but he was at a loss about how to proceed because he knew very little about religion. There was a Bible in his house that no one ever read. It had been a wedding gift. One Sunday afternoon, while he was watching a football game on television, he saw "The Sign." Every sports fan has seen the sign. It is usually held up by someone strategically located in the end zone so that when the television cameras focus on the "point after attempt," they also broadcast the Scripture reference John 3:16 to the entire world. On that day, this troubled, searching man saw the sign, recognized it as a Scripture reference, and decided to find it in the old, dusty Bible. He found the verse and then continued to read the wonderful news of the gospel until, by faith, he yielded his life to Christ that day. An amazing group of circumstances had to come together that day for him to be drawn to read the Good News of salvation. Who was in control of the circumstances? God still seeks sinners.

Because God seeks sinners, Jesus found the healed man who the Pharisees had cast out of the synagogue. He found him, taught him, and brought him into salvation (vv. 35b-38). It was a wonderful trade for the former blind man. He had eyesight in exchange for physical blindness, and he gained salvation in exchange for dead religious works. The Pharisees actually did the man a favor by excommunicating him from the demands of the synagogue.

As it is for all born-again sinners, this man's entrance into salvation hinged on faith (vv. 35b-36). Jesus asked the man if he believed in the Son of God. Some manuscripts recorded that Jesus used the title, "Son of man." Son of man was a title Jesus often used for Himself, but others seldom used it to refer to Him. Jesus used the term to identify Himself with humanity whom He came to save. It also identified Him with the promised Messiah whose coming Daniel's vision foretold. Hundreds of years before Christ was born, Daniel wrote that he "was watching in the night visions, and behold, One like the Son of Man, coming with the clouds of heaven! He came to the Ancient of Days, and they brought Him near before Him" (Daniel 7:13). That one like the Son of Man was Jesus Christ. He is the Son of man who "came to seek and to save those who are lost" (Luke 19:10). He is the same Son of Man who will come again on the clouds of glory to claim His rightful throne. He is God incarnate!

Other Greek manuscripts used the title "Son of God" to describe the man from Nazareth at this point. That title clearly identified Jesus as the promised Christ. He is the "one and only unique Son of God" (John 3:16). Whether Jesus was the Son of God was the difficult question for the religious and political leaders when they crucified Christ (Matthew 26:63). When He told them that He was indeed the Son of God, they concluded that His claim was tantamount to blasphemy. For a mere human to claim that he was God was sufficient reason to condemn the person to capital punishment. The religious leaders in Jesus' day did not debate whether Jesus of Nazareth declared that He was God in the flesh. That was their grounds for crucifying Him.

Eternal salvation hinges on complete faith in the Son of God. When Jesus asked the healed man if he believed in the Son of God, He was not trying to find out if the man had drawn an intellectual conclusion about the facts surrounding the man named Jesus. He pressed home the same requirement we press home to bring sinners into salvation. Jesus wanted to know if the man believed with all his heart that He was the Christ sent from God. That is still the critical question. Do you believe Jesus' own testimony that He is God come in the flesh? That is precisely the claim Jesus made when the authorities questioned Him. He had told them that their forefather Abraham had rejoiced to see His day. They countered that He was not even fifty years old and could not have possibly seen Abraham. Jesus responded, "Most assuredly, I say to you, before Abraham was, I AM" (John 8:58). Immediately, the religious authorities picked up stones to kill Jesus. Each one of those religious leaders understood that when Jesus uttered those words that He literally claimed to be God.

That is the kind of question Jesus asked the healed man. It is still the question that every sinner who seeks healing from the eternal disease of sin must answer. "Do you believe that His sacrifice covers your sin?" "Do you believe that He rose from the dead to affirm His finished work?" Those issues lie at the root of faith in Jesus Christ alone. Paul promised that if, "you confess with your mouth the Lord Jesus and believe in your heart that God has raised Him from the dead, you will be saved" (Romans 10:9). That is essentially the kind of question Jesus posed to this man.

The healed man honestly confessed that he did not know what to believe (v. 36). Who would criticize his honesty? He admitted that he did not know who Jesus was, but he also admitted that he wanted to believe. The desire of the heart is always the important matter. Where there is no desire in the heart to know God, there will be no new birth unto salvation.

Jesus identified Himself as the only acceptable object of the man's faith (vv. 37-38). The man said that he wanted to believe so Jesus gave him the ability to understand to that end. Jesus, who had earlier opened the man's blinded physical eyes, now opened his spiritual eyes so that He could see Jesus as the Son of God. That is the work that only God can do. God still satisfies each person who seeks Him by faith. Jesus promised that "those who hunger and thirst for righteousness" are blessed because "they shall be filled" (Matthew 5:6). Redeemed sinners, people who are satisfied with the righteousness God provides, worship the Savior. This man proved he was changed because he went from worshiping in the synagogue according to the Pharisees' rules to worshiping the Savior according to God's righteousness.

Jesus, the man from Nazareth, did not criticize the healed man for worshiping Him. Therefore, if Jesus was not God, He was a wicked and evil man to allow this former blind man to worship Him. However, because He was God in the flesh, it was altogether appropriate for the man to worship Him. The Pharisees hated Jesus because He proved that He was God. Religious people still hate Jesus, the man from Nazareth. They still refuse to accept the truth that He is God. But eternal salvation is still found by faith in Him alone.

Jesus Passed Judgment

Having granted salvation to the man who had been blind, Jesus taught, in the hearing of the Pharisees, that He came to establish distinctions (v. 39). He came into the world for judgment. Is this not the same Jesus who also said that He did not come to judge the world? Later in this Gospel John recorded Jesus' promise that, "if anyone hears My words and does not believe, I do not judge him; for I did not come to judge the world but to save the world" (John 12:47). Sometimes the word judge means to condemn or to carry out a sentence. In that sense, it is true that Jesus did not come to the earth to carry out the guilty sentences of sinners in the first century. He will judge sin and pass condemnation at the end of the age. In the final judgment He will condemn everyone who has rejected Him and His gospel to eternal punishment (1 Peter 4:5).

In this passage, the word judge means to mark out the difference. Jesus' presence in this world draws the line between truth and error. That is judgment. He taught on other occasions that His incarnation, His coming into the world causes divisions. That is what He meant when He said, "Do not think that I came to bring peace on earth. I did not come to bring peace but a sword" (Matthew 10:34). That is also what He meant by the words recorded in this text.

The perfectly righteous Son of God passes judgment, makes distinctions, by virtue of the fact that He came into this wholly sinful world. His judgment creates an eternal difference between two groups of people. Part of the difference that Jesus creates lies in the fact that He gives sight to the spiritually blind. He has the authority and ability to give spiritual sight because He is light (9:5). Those who turn to Him in faith have their understanding opened so that they are able to grasp spiritual truth. Paul said that it is a matter of "The eyes of your understanding being enlightened; that you may know what is the hope of His calling, and what are the riches of the glory of His inheritance in the saints" (Ephesians 1:18).

There is a noticeable difference between those who have had their understanding opened by the miracle of God's grace and those who are still blinded by sin. The same truth of Christ that opens a penitent sinner's understanding also causes the self-confident sinner to be blind to truth. Many people, like the Pharisees, are sure that they have discovered truth through their own efforts. They are satisfied to define truth for themselves. They do not believe that they need to consider any other standard of truth. They are satisfied that they are okay, and therefore, they reject the kind efforts of caring saints to give them light. They are willfully blind, "Having their understanding darkened, being alienated from the life of God, because of the ignorance that is in them, because of the blindness of their heart" (Ephesians 4:18). Jesus assessed the Pharisees to be suffering from that condition. It is the eternally damning condition of all self-satisfied sinners.

The leaders were offended by Jesus' teaching (vv. 40-41). They reacted negatively to Jesus' accusation that they were spiritually blind (v. 40). It was not that the meaning of Jesus' words escaped them. They understood perfectly well that Jesus had accused them of being spiritually blind. Therefore, they responded with sarcasm. The sinful person who rejects the help of spiritual truth consigns himself to condemnation. Last summer I conducted the funeral of my ninety-three-year-old aunt. Several years ago, when she was eighty-five-years-old, I sat on the edge of her bed as she was about to enter heart surgery. She said, "Dave, if I don't survive this operation, I am going to prove that you are wrong about hell." That kind of sarcasm in the face of eternal condemnation breaks the Christian's heart. In the intervening eight years of her life, Aunt Zelda's spiritual blindness remained unchanged.

The religious leaders of Israel were convinced that they were in great fellowship with God and that Jesus, the man from Nazareth, was an imposter. However, Jesus affirmed the leaders' blindness (v. 41). He taught that if they were truly ignorant of the truth, they would not be as guilty of transgressing God's truth. Because they were not ignorant, their sin remained. They knew the truth. They really knew that Jesus was the Christ, but they rejected that truth and reinterpreted the facts. That same sad story is repeated by the cults thousands of times over in every age. It is the story of sinners who are without excuse before God. Sin that is not dealt with through confession and repentance, having faith in God's truth, remains and brings eternal punishment.

God desires for all people to come to the understanding of the truth. He longs for every sinner to be like this man who came face to face with Jesus Christ and expressed the desire to believe. God opened his understanding, he was born again, and he worshiped Christ.

(FOOTNOTES)

[1] Rev. J. F. Cowan, D. D., as quoted by Rev. G.B.F. Hallock in, Five Thousand Best Modern Illustrations, 1927, p. 22.

[2] J. K. Van Baalen, The Chaos of Cults, (Grand Rapids: Eerdman's Publishing Co., 1979), 271.

[3] Dietrich Bonhoeffer, "The Cost of Discipleship," in Christianity Today, vol. 42, no. 8.